SACRED SCIENCE

R. A. Schwaller de Lubicz

SACRED SCIENCE

The King of Pharaonic Theocracy

Illustrated by Lucie Lamy
Translated by André and Goldian VandenBroeck

Inner Traditions International
Rochester, VT

Inner Traditions International
One Park Street
Rochester, Vermont 05767
www.InnerTraditions.com

Sacred Science: The King of Pharaonic Theocracy was first published in French
under the title *Le Roi de la théocratie Pharaonique* by Flammarion in 1961.

First Quality Paperback Edition 1988

Library of Congress Cataloging-in-Publication Data

Schwaller de Lubicz, R. A.
Sacred Science

Translation of Le roi de la théocratie pharasonique.
Bibliography: p.
Includes index.
1. Egypt—Religion—Miscellanea.   2. Theocracy—Miscellanea.
3. Kings and rulers (in religion, folk-lore, etc.)—Miscellanea.   I. Title.
BF1999.S361813   133'.0932   81-344
ISBN 978-089281222-6   AACR1
ISBN 0-89281-222-2

Topography Positive Type
Printed and bound in the United States

20 19 18

To my stepdaughter
Lucie Lamy
this work which owes so much to her conscientious efforts in the
gathering of texts as well as in the diagrams and illustrations.

To Georges Rémond
in memory of happy years spent in the radiance of Egyptian
temples.

Contents

Translators' Note

Each reader of this book will be in a sense a translator, translating the trend of the author's mind into his own. The rendering of the text into English, however, presented several technical problems which invite comment.

Wherever possible, to avoid translations of translations, standard English versions of Egyptian and Greek texts have been used or consulted. These sources are listed in the Bibliography.

Initial capitalization of nouns has been largely eliminated, in accordance with conventions of English orthography.

Central to Schwaller de Lubicz's theory is the notion conveyed by the noun *la symbolique,* a word which he employs in a distinctly personal way. Since his intention is to differentiate this concept from what is usually denoted by "symbolism" or "symbolics," the author would be ill-served by the use of either of these terms. "Symbolique" has therefore been retained on the model of such derivations as "mystique," "physique," and "technique." This Anglicizing eliminates the need to italicize the word as a foreign term. Furthermore, since much of the author's thrust is toward defining the very word "symbolique," no problem of meaning occurs.

Plate 1: Wood Panel from the Mastaba of Hesy
Sakkara, Third Dynasty

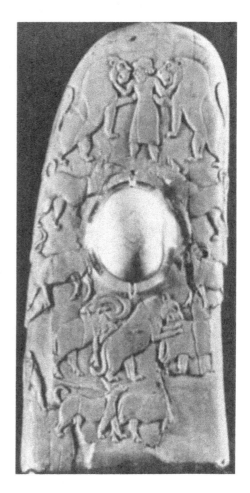

Plate 2: Ivory Handle of a Flint Knife
Gebel el-Arak

Plate 3: Isenheim Altarpiece (central panel)
Unterlinden Museum, Colmar, Alsace

Plate 4: Casing of fine linen covering the cranium of Tut-ankh-Amon's mummy, embroidered with gold beads and semiprecious stones depicting the double uraeus that marks the scissure between the two hemispheres of the brain.

SACRED SCIENCE

Introduction

Progress, by definition, signifies the expansion of accepted frame-works. But going beyond well-defined borders always provokes more or less sectarian objections, be they from science or religion, or merely routine. There are always two opposing camps: One is the domain of *belief;* the other is the faction of those who consider themselves "in the know." Whoever situates himself between these two extremes cannot be classified, and the effect of this position is to raise doubts as well as to incite the hostility of the two opposing camps.

Sometimes, however, there is an explosion that shatters the limits, breaking the quietude of a routine one likes to call "peace." Our century has experienced such an upheaval. I am referring, of course, to the atomic explosion; not to the bomb itself, but far more important, to the disturbance it brought which reversed the orientation of our mentality. With Lavoisier, the past century also experienced such an explosion of the framework of thinking. At that time, all the conjectures of a creation-mystique, considered as fanciful, were rejected, giving to those who presume to "know," a solid terrain for constructing a world according to their image. Nowadays, that terrain no longer seems as stable as had been expected.

Those who consider themselves "in the know" are already beginning to lose footing, but this does not suffice to give strength to those who believe. There is today a generalized sense of uncertainty causing disorder in the social domain as well as in moral conduct generally, but the majority of people endure this effect without understanding its origin.

Far more important to people's lives than economic or technical considerations is that state of mind, that mentality which can be inspired only by a higher authority, independent of the passion-ridden influence of the majority. But nowadays the world is governed by fictions—fictions of social doctrines, of scientific promises—and these fallacious promises are based on erudite arguments whose vicious circle is no longer noticed. Actually, the social order must bow to the techniques generated by science, and science in turn must constantly adapt to a social order whose stability is compromised by the uncoordinated passions of the human being.

The discovery and demonstration of energy as a kinetic phenomenon of mass does not explain the *mass,* which becomes an unknown. This formula amounts to saying that if I throw a stone, that stone (the mass) in motion represents energy. The extreme speed squared is then the stable element for all energy. The mass, the weight of the stone, stays variable. The speed of light squared is the great discovery in this Einsteinian formula. It is a practical tool that permits one to "make do," but yields no essential information; yet it opens the doors to all the discoveries in nuclear energy.

Now our little world thinks only in terms of atomic energy, referring to it all physical, chemical, and astrophysical phenomena.

Among those who have thus been led astray, the so-called alchemists of our time are of particular interest to us. They belong neither to the physicists nor to the dreaded "mystics" of pre-Lavoisier times, as they imagine they can identify atomic energy with *Spirit, the origin of matter.* May these few seekers understand that they must not allow themselves to be deluded by a rational science which is leading the world to disaster; as they willingly let themselves be called utopians, they might as well accept the principle of a sacred science that testifies to a divine science.

What proofs are there of this sacred science? Simple logic, no less, tells us that the material world, the world of the notorious "mass," cannot have been created with matter.

It is only after having studied most of the serious works on this strange subject, from Zosima to the latest writing (which dates back about a century), that I place sacred texts and myth in parallel to the development of what is called the Hermetic opus *(Oeuvre).* Whatever the images and terms of the sacred accounts—be they the Vedas, the Nordic sagas, the texts of ancient Egypt, the Old Testament, or the revelations of the Gospels—*there exists an undeniable parallelism between these two expressions of a knowledge concerning the origin, the becoming, and the aim of life.*

The question is: What object could be the aim of the Hermetic opus? It will necessarily be an undetermined substance and not a mineral, plant, or animal being. This substance can be none but the vital "fire," Life, capable of being transmitted to a specific being in order to lead that being *to its own perfection.* This indeed is what all good texts intimate. Because of its parallelism with the ultimate becoming of the human, this available "life-essence" is called the King, cosmic man; but it must be recognized that *attaining the aim of the Hermetic opus is not an end; it is the beginning of the light that illuminates reality.*

It would be a serious error, I am convinced, to fail to reverse the problem. Granted that the Hermetic opus elucidates and demonstrates the meaning of sacred texts and myths, it is evident that what is somehow of prime importance is the "hominization" of the Book of Genesis revelation. Man as a thinking, conscious being is the only important reality. It is he, the human being as bodily creature animated by the divine breath—absolute Being—who endures the entire passion of the Hermetic opus in order to attain, if possible, to the royal perfection represented by the renowned philosopher's stone.

Attempting to understand the significance of sacred science in its mere material representation distorts the intention of the sages. I am certain, moreover, that such comprehension is fated never to attain the aim proposed, be it in one sense or the other.

The *Neters* are the cosmic milieu, and it is the successive states of "conscious vision" of these principles that give true meaning to human life; the King, the true King, is the living being who has reached the stage of immortal and conscious return to the source of the soul that animates him. Such is the aim proposed.

Sacred science demonstrates and proves, but the spiritual ascent of man is the path to be realized.

1

Concerning Theocracy

Pharaonic theocracy is neither an institution worked out along logical lines nor a government imposed by a religious organization. It is difficult for our mentality to understand how and why royal power and religious guidance can be unified. The State and the government of the country are the essential concern of the administration with its hierarchy of power-representatives. Justice, economics, and military power are apparently incompatible with religion, whose aim is to govern personal conduct in life and the salvation of souls.

These are the terms by which we understand the organization of a civilized society. It is true that in the light of nineteenth-century science it is possible to eliminate the existence of a religious body as quite unnecessary to those who are "social beings," namely those who possess the herd instinct; from that point of view, man is but a living phenomenon without origin or continuity; a physicochemical accident. Accordingly, the problem posed by a theocratic order obviously does not exist: There is no "God"; there are only material needs that can be catered to through technocracy. Here it suffices that the individual submit to the life conditions laid down by the herd and follow its directives.

This submission can continue for a time, but it cannot continue forever.

The history of humanity has known similar crises several times before. But man, even when dazed by dialectic sophistry, is not a machine without a soul, and this soul which animates physical man necessarily transcends the corporeal.

Pharaonic theocracy is exceptional, a governmental and social order unique in all of Western history. Did a similar order exist during the great Celtic epoch of the Druids? The lack of documents does not permit us to so affirm. Assyria and Babylonia, on the other hand, never knew true theocracy, which is the domination of the entire life of a people by spiritual truths. We translate theological directive by the word "religion," but the meaning attached to this term nowadays is incompatible with the mentality of Pharaonic times.

According to the evidence inscribed during a period of over four thousand years, ancient Egypt did not have a "religion" as such; *it was religion in its entirety,* in the broadest and purest acceptation of the term.

We cannot understand this. Egyptologists have searched in vain to discover by what means a great people, visibly highly civilized, rich in the arts, powerful in organization, could have been led to accept such a unification of temporal and spiritual powers, always returning to this order despite grave crises and periodic interruptions in the long duration of the empire of the "Two Crowns."

In the conclusion of his convincing thesis on *the religious character of Pharaonic royalty,* Alexandre Moret admits his failure to understand how this conception of the king's divinity could have gained prominence:

> Egypt knew an original concept of religious royalty: The Pharaoh is distinguished from the other priest-kings in that he is connected to the gods by birth as much as by sacerdotal dignity. He is god because he is priest, but he is only priest inasmuch as he is the son of the gods.
>
> This concept of a royalty at once divine and sacerdotal existed from the first known times of Egypt's history; the political regime that stemmed from it endured for forty centuries and showed itself to be the most permanent element of the entire Egyptian civilization, the most immune to revolutions. The transitory accession of the priesthood to royalty did bring change to the reciprocal relationships between the king and the gods: The humble mortal, priest of Amon, promoted to king by a stroke of fortune, became subordinated to divine majesty. But if the person of the king occasionally underwent a diminution of authority during the course of several centuries, the principle of divine and priestly royalty survived until the Roman period and disappeared only with Egyptian religion itself under the influence of Christianity. New ideas concerning the character of the royal personage were doubtless introduced into Egypt with the Ptolemies and the Caesars: In the sovereign's entourage, a cult of the king was celebrated which was more in conformance with Hellenic civilization. But the Egyptian temples never knew and never acknowledged these modifications. Whether the king was Greek or Roman, whether or not he also claimed divine descent from his country's gods, this was of no importance: In the temples, where the foreign king was less and less frequently mentioned by name, the "son of Isis" or the "Pharaoh" continued to celebrate and to receive the unchanging Osirian rituals of ancient times. . . .

> One keeps wondering what elements were used by the theologians of Heliopolis to form the royal doctrine and how they progressively instilled into the minds of the people a belief that maintained a hold on Egypt for forty centuries.[1]

One element is missing from all the speculations attempting to clarify this enigma: the bond, the binder that joins cause to effect, as in the problem of magic raised by Dr. François Lexa.[2] But the effect, true theocracy, exists; hence the cause, the theology of the temple, necessarily commands a mean term as demanded by the law of causality.

As we shall see, this mean term indeed constitutes the entire thesis. It comprehends cause and effect as a single entity: *sacred science,* the preeminently *sacerdotal science,* which since the beginnings of the empire was the "science of Thoth," *Master of divine words and sacred writings.* This science, written on papyrus scrolls, included the myth as well as the religious rituals, medicine, geometry, astronomy, and the laws of everyday life and of justice.[3] These sacred books were kept in the sanctuaries of the Egyptian temples and were accessible only to the highest religious and royal authorities.

Yet it was quite natural for any scribe to call himself a "servant of Thoth"—the "patron of writing." The Greeks, therefore, in their contact with a declining Egypt, were prompted to speak of science in general as belonging to Thoth, or Hermes. The meaning of "sacred science" was thus vulgarized under the term "Hermetism."

In truth, the purpose of this modest offering is to convey a succinct understanding of the important reality of sacred science— which is not to be confused with the vernacular meaning conveyed by "Hermetism." This undertaking demands a look at the history of thought in the West and at the history of man in the light of that thought.

What is the general attitude in our day toward this Hermetic science usually referred to as alchemy? The word is of Islamic origin and signifies "the science of *al-Kemit*" encountered by the Arab invaders of Egypt, that ancient *Kemit* which gave so much light to an Islam setting out to conquer the world. For nearly everyone, alchemy is the science of "making gold" and nothing more. For some, it is a

---

[1] A. Moret, *Du caractère religieux de la royauté pharaonique* (Paris, 1902), pp. 320-321.
[2] See Chapter 6 "Magic, Sorcery, Medicine."
[3] See Appendix V, "Catalogue of Egyptian Books."

fantasy; for others, a mysterious science of fascinating discovery. There are also the "spiritually minded" who consider alchemy to be a psychospiritual science of transforming consciousness, and the acquisition of psychic if not spiritual powers.

Today, by means of violence perpetrated on the atom, nuclear science has managed to demonstrate the possibility of the transmutation of bodies previously considered to be simple and unalterable. It is claimed, therefore, that the dream of the old alchemists has been realized at last.

The fact of transmutation as demonstrated by contemporary science completely alters the conception of matter accepted in the nineteenth century, and every concept of evolution basic to materialistic science is thereby unsettled. These transmutations achieved by brute force have nothing in common, however, with what the Hermetic tradition understood transmutation to be. And yet there is something of sacred science that continues to radiate through a vulgarized alchemy; this aspect, however, has remained occulted.

The erroneous conception of transmutation given by our rationalistic and materialistic science causes the latter to be not only inhuman in its consequences, but evil as well in that it diverts us from the true endeavor.

The science of Thoth is the sacerdotal science of all times because it is founded on an irrational basis and would be totally absurd otherwise. Its foundations are identical to those of every other philosophy concerned with the beginning of things. No determinate body can serve as a point of departure for the alchemical opus, because what is involved is not a decomposition of matter (notwithstanding the beliefs of our atomists), but *a generation of the matter of the world in the image of creation.* Thus we are concerned here with *revealed* knowledge and not with a rational science.

Few are they who have been able to penetrate this secret of the beginning. As a spiritual commitment, those who have succeeded have left a token of the existence of this science. By means of riddles or allegories—and especially through theological reflections—they have described the process of work and the phases of becoming, yet without revealing the essential secret.

With Hermetic texts as a basis—Western writings as well as those of the ancient sages—it is possible to reach a fairly clear idea of the Hermetic process *(Oeuvre)* in order to compare this to sacred teachings, in particular to those of the Pharaonic temple. Despite the obvious concordance, however, it could still be asked whether these

Hermetic texts, with gold as their bait, did not simply transmit theological teachings in a "seductive" manner.

This doubt has been removed since nuclear science demonstrated the instability of simple elements, thus annulling the absolutist argument which chemistry in principle opposed to the possibility of transmutation. It is evident that the transmutation proved by science has no relationship to theological principles; but the fact remains certain today for everyone that *there is a common energetic origin to all bodies,* and this brings us close to metaphysical assertions about the beginning of things.

The possibility of transmutation through a path of "genesis" is confirmed by a number of writings—from Pharaonic Egypt as well as from the transition time of Greco-Roman Egypt and even from fairly recent times in Europe. In accordance with all theologies, all these texts are founded on the certainty that *it is the divine Word, the Holy Spirit, which alone is able to animate matter,* and that therein lies the secret of origin.

The separation between these two concepts reflects the divorce of two irreconcilable mentalities. One of these concepts points to a kinetic energy immanent in matter as the starting point for the variety of types; the other calls upon an undefined cosmic energy.

With absurd reasoning, our science sees in the universe nothing but a closed circuit, an agglomerate and a decomposition of the selfsame matter. Such a view is certainly less reasonable than the admission of an undefined source of energy which becomes matter, although the latter solution poses a purely metaphysical problem. From there it is but a very small step to seeing a divine principle in the harmony of the world.

It is certain that the "ordinary" mind does not view things in this way and dreams only of making gold in order to become rich, without realizing that if a simple secret of manufacture were involved, gold would in any case cease to be of value.

Paradoxically, therefore, it is rationalistic science which justifies the possible existence of a sacred science based on an origin irrational in itself. Thus there exists proof of what is affirmed by sacerdotal science, and it demonstrates the genesis of the Great Work *(Grand-Oeuvre)* of the universe.

Hence there is a parallelism between the teaching of the phases of "becoming" of a perfect substance—spiritual in its origin and in its finality—and sacred teachings, whatever they may be.

Sacred science is like a grid, a colored background upon which all moments of the Pharaonic teaching can be inscribed. One of the *end* possibilities, the transmutation of elements, proves that the *beginning* announced by the texts must be true. The thing in itself is then of small importance since its entire history can be read and situated; thus the entire Passion of Osiris, and the more profound Passion of Christ, can be lived in oneself. Passion must be considered here not as suffering but as the joy of being able to envision resurrection beyond humankind. This principle pertains to every being who decides to pursue the true path.

To generate the *opus magnum* is to generate within us the liberation from our suffering and mortal condition, and, inversely, to search for this liberation is also to realize the *opus magnum.*

The possibility of making gold has always been used by sages to hoodwink fools, so that the "children of wisdom"—who cannot be deceived by selfish satisfactions—may be led toward the true path, which is the search for the real vision of the universe. Without the promise of gold, would the texts of master Hermetists have been disseminated, safeguarded, and respected by the ignorant?

We can now conclude that the foundation stone of wisdom is unspecified and belongs to none of the three kingdoms, yet its nature is to animate all. It is spiritual and may also, of course, be *directed* or *oriented* toward mineral (metal), toward plant, and toward animal. As it is *medicine* for the human body, so it is medicine for the metal: It eliminates all impurity, leaving only the purity of perfect equilibrium. Did the Lord Christ not cure leprosy?

The formula "Life-Health-Strength," which is always joined to the Pharaoh's name, is translated as a wish addressed to him, when it is He, the true King of kings, who *dispenses* life, health, and strength.

Following the path charted by sacred science, this is how the world appears: There is generation, that is, the development of matter as a fetal becoming; there is fixation into the corporeality of cosmic energy; there is an irrational source at the origin of things; there is a resurrection of spiritualized corporeality in a return toward the source, as corporal matter is but a transitory and relative aspect of an activity and re-activity of two natures sundered and issued from a cosmic Oneness: This final matter is the only true King.

Theology and science, then, reside in one single expression; therefore there exists a completely different relation of man toward universe, and hence the possibility of a civilization such as is found in Pharaonic Egypt, in ancient India, and in ancient China.

Accordingly, there are many revisions to be brought to our judgments regarding ancient peoples of whom only traces remain, such as the Maya and the Inca.

Instead of concerning itself with the decomposition of matter in order to find energy, instead of attempting to explain everything through the analysis of matter (its decomposition, its aging, its radioactivity), instead of pursuing this false track, the legitimate concern of science should be the search for the true source of matter, that source epitomized by this "word" which says it all—"God"—and in that light to study the becoming of forms that inhabit the universe.

To some, these statements will seem no more than a relapse, a regression to "old beliefs," to superstition, to the puerile stance—devoid of scientific spirit—of a time "happily transcended."

To this I reply: We are concerned with a proved reality and not a belief. I also mean to say that it is a veritable elite which forms the temple: a radiating temple and not a temple that imposes an exclusive dogma, restraining and contracting any impulse of expansion of thought or of the arts; a temple basing its theological teaching on proofs given by scientific demonstration. This demands the two paths of possible survival which lead quite naturally to theocracy, the myth being but a support to the people and a guide for the man wanting and able to elevate himself.

I earnestly anticipate the time when an enlightened being will be able to bring the world proof of *the mystery of beginning*.

There is much talk of the new age, Aquarius. This time is in preparation, but not yet come: With it will come this prophet who will establish a new world. Then there will no longer remain any doubt concerning the Pharaonic teachings, or about the words of the Gospels or the promises of authentic sacred texts.

It is said that Christianity, universal in character, is the last teaching brought to men, and the word of an epoch's ending. It is true that there is no higher teaching, but there is the constant beginning anew: One must always begin again, and it is due to this constant renewal that those who have not sinned against the Holy Spirit—meaning those who have not definitely repudiated the Spirit which makes and animates all—may come and go in order to discover the light at last.

The predominant idea developed in the Pharaonic *Book of the Dead* is expressed by its title *Book of Coming Forth by Day*. These teachings promise the "pure" that their soul will be allowed *to go* and *to come*, that is, to return to the terrestrial world. The "impure," on the

other hand, the "rejected ones" (those who have sinned against the
Holy Spirit), will know the second death, the definitive death, the
eclipse of the sun described in the *Book of Qererts* (the Book of
Caverns), the most dreaded of punishments.

Distances

More than three thousand years separate us from the flourishing
epoch of the 18th Pharaonic Dynasty, that of Amenhotep, the
Thutmosids, of Hatshepsut, the Amarnian experiment, and the
restoration of the cult of Amon with Tut-Ankh-Amon. Stepping back
in time is less impressive for us than comparing today's progress with
the state of things a mere fifty years ago. Here we can compare, there
we cannot. Inspired by a natural egotism, our complacency permits us
to go back not only 3,000 years into humanity's history, but with
paleoanthropology, to turn the clock easily back 25,000 or 50,000 years
in order to join the presumed moment when an anthropoid opened the
path toward a *Homo sapiens* capable of coordinating his thoughts.
Fifty thousand years—a conservative estimate as far as I am
concerned—have no significance for us.*

As to the history of the origin and becoming of thinking man, this
backward movement into time constitutes for the anthropologist only
a stripping, a sort of unclothing of the faculties, qualities, and powers
we have obtained over a hostile Nature. On the testimony of a few
bones and some rock drawings and figurations found in caves, we
undress morally and intellectually to the point of being no more than
cavemen. As long as the operation is purely subtractive, everything is
easy, since once and for all we accept that at a certain moment, all that
could have happened was that an animal phylum developed toward a
thinking human in order to end with our present superiority. For our
science, the difficulty starts with the possible motivations for the
various gestures and conditions making for the successive acquisitions,
such as upright posture or the change from a hairy animal into a naked
man in need of animal furs to clothe himself. . . .

To such a concept of paleontology one can compare the wisdom
tradition that speaks of the genesis of man in general through races
and subraces, in conformity with man's fetal evolution: The faculties
awaken successively just as the organs are formed in the embryo. In

---

*Since the date of this writing, paleoanthropological discoveries have continued to open new vistas of the
human past, forcing an ever-greater estimate of man's antiquity.—Trans.

that case, there exists a genetic vision of becoming, a genesis, like the genesis or growth of any other seed. At the origin there is a human seed just as there is a seed for any living thing. This concept is of course excluded from a rational science which denies the "mysterious" and "metaphysical" moment, as its reasoning must link everthing in a logical and mechanical manner.

An attempt is now being made to combine paleontology with genetics in order to construct a justifiable science of "evolution." Made in the name of the phenomenon of *mutations,* this attempt finds its weakness precisely in the fact that the causes of mutation are unknown. We are dealing here with a confirmed phenomenon; its causes, however, remain mysterious.

In fine: Subtracting is easy where life is concerned, but to add, in that case, is senseless. The arguments that motivate the multiple conditions demanded by the slightest step on the path from unreasoning animal to thinking man, end up taking refuge in statistics and... in calculations of probability.

Our tendency to judge the past on the basis of a comparison with ourselves (a perfectly natural tendency, moreover) conceives *duration* not as a factor separating an ancient civilization from ours, but rather as an evolutionary succession: Past civilization is held to be inferior to ours since it has preceded us! In fact, neither time nor space separates profoundly. In order to obtain true "divorce," there must be a difference of mentality. The state of mind separates or unites; we must search the state of mind for the mainspring of all behavior. This holds true for the phases of man's development as well as for the history of a humanity which differs from the humanity of today's history.

Whatever be the origin of humanity (and we shall return to this problem), we must first of all agree that diverse orientations in its development are possible. Necessarily, these orientations are conditioned first by the physical milieu within which evolution takes place, and next by the intelligent contact of humanity with natural phenomena. This contact can be more specifically cerebral or emotional; but it can also be intuitive, by which I mean consciously instinctive. The three aspects necessarily interplay, but the predominance of one of these contacts determines the different characters: the mental-intellectual, the religio-mystical, or else the "wisdom" character. The character is reflected in the mentality of a people, and particularly in the mentality of the leaders of that people.

Which mentality is preferable? Today, one would readily opt for the results from mental-intellectual contact as did the Greeks and, before them, the decadent Babylonians. All things considered, the result, and *end* susceptible of attainment, acts as a determining factor. These mentalities make for the only true separation between peoples and civilizations. Emotivity certainly predominates among black Africans, and their animism remains vitally incomprehensible to the rational mind; inversely, no reasoning can convince the devout animist who lives intensely on the physical level and remains in communion with the spirits of the dead, while the rationalist will create a scholarly way of thinking and a mechanistic science. The intuitive is much more rarely encountered than the emotive or the intellectual, but such were the Sumerians (as far as we can determine) and to the highest degree the Pharaonic caste of ancient Egypt, as their works and writings testify.

There is no more perfect divorce from the mentality of natural wisdom which prevailed in ancient Egypt than the one imposed in recent times by Western mentality. The latter is purely cerebral. They are two epochs, two humanities that cannot understand one another as long as they persist in judging each other by their respective frames of mind. This "distance" has not always been so precisely marked, however, and it is only the recent outcome of the Western orientation that shows a strict opposition between the two mentalities. For the Occident to reach this extreme and perfect intellectual definition, it had to be implanted with a seed that grew slowly and in spite of the apparent opposition of the Roman Catholic Church at a time when the latter tinged our entire civilization with religiosity. But it is precisely the evangelical character (revelation) that provokes the future development of a rational search; we will understand this better when discussing the nature of myth.

Pure and simple faith seeks no proof. But a day came when science counterbalanced this faith. In Scholastic times, during those interminable discussions, men dedicated themselves in secret—and on the basis of ancient traditions called "Hermetic"—to the search for a *science,* that is, for tangible proofs of the truths asserted by the Christic revelation. Most believers were confused by the historic human aspect by means of which these truths were spread, and they failed to understand the cosmic character of the images and parables of the Gospel. It was the aim of the few wise men who understood the universal character of this teaching (and in those times it was an obligation as well) to formulate eternal truth with Christic images and words, whence the attempt by Johann Andreae to form a Rosicrucian society around the myth of Christian Rosenkreuz. At all events, the

Rose of Sages around the symbol of the Cross is a reality for the precessional era of Pisces. Jesus Christ, divine incarnation, is Truth, and the science that so demonstrates is *the sacred science of all times, the sacred science and white magic of the temple.*

In the West, the few enlightened adepts of the Middle Ages were forced to hide. If they wrote—their duty always being to leave some testimony of the truth of their science—they could do so only anonymously, or perhaps under the protection of a personality powerful enough to assuage governmental and ecclesiastical suspicions. Believing themselves sufficiently strong to escape control of those two powers, the Knights Templar were led to the stake by their own audacity when those two villains joined forces against them. But man's curiosity cannot be squelched. A few principles of Hermetic science were circulating at large, and "profane" spirits with positivistic minds, ignorant of metaphysical causes, were gradually able to formulate a chemical and physical science. Not having been founded on the abstract realities of philosophy, this science took on a rational form. Thus the Hermetist's principle of Fire eventually became phlogistic, a fiery principle immanent in certain materials and rendering them combustible. This concept remained in vogue until Lavoisier demonstrated the fact that oxygen sustained combustion, combining as gas, burning, oxydizing the elements, and being susceptible of recovery: "Nothing created, nothing lost." With that thunderclap, science heralded the era of atheism, shaking the foundations of faith, henceforth opposed by the facts of reason.

The science that is the pride of our times is *very recent;* but the spirit of dialectic, that infernal temptation concealed in man's nature, dates from the beginnings of so-called "thinking" humanity. Dialectic is reasoning, and reasoning needs tangible facts. Armed with syllogistic logic, the same logic for which the old Scholastics had defined all possible combinations, it finally formulates only mechanistic thinking. In those Middle Ages, believers, after performing their devotions, had only to work and to discuss....

Devotions! In them resides the entire Western Middle Ages! God assumed human incarnation in order to suffer all the evil caused by the original sin; all is said, there is nothing further to seek, there is only prayer for the individual soul's salvation. In a definitive sense, each one is personally responsible for his own salvation or damnation. So says the Church. This ostracism excluding all research, be it even that of a sacred science, will provoke the reaction which I call the *science of evil:* for it is false. Its only possible consequences are an inhuman effect, it being purely technical and meant only for utilitarian aims exterior to man's intimate life.

The final destruction then becomes logical if only through the absurdity of a life without spiritual aim and the atrophy of the senses, which causes man to lose contact with his work.

We are far removed from Pharaonic times when science was a knowledge of causes; when work was the fusion of the artisan with his craft.

There has never been a greater distance between consciousnesses than there is in our time between Western mentality and the mentality of the ancient Egyptian sages.

2

The Deviation

To know the origin of matter and of existence—such has always been the essential preoccupation of thinking humanity. Theologies have answered these weighty questions according to their particular mentalities. In the Old Testament, Moses says: "In the beginning God created the heaven and the earth," which is a conclusion rather than an affirmation of origin, a conclusion imposed by the impossibility of devising a rational solution to the problem.

Through St. John, the New Testament says: "In the beginning was the Word, and the Word was with God, and the Word was God." This is a circular phrase, quite in the style of Euclid when he explains the geometric point: "The point is the intersection of two lines and the line is a point in motion." In other words, there is an irrational moment at the origin of things; this moment is *Logos,* the Word identified with its source of emission; it is the scission of a homogeneous state of oneness. For Judaism, God is definitely acting, creating. For Christianity, there is a mystery.

Pharaonic theology speaks of the origin through the Heliopolitan mystery: There is *Nun,* the primordial ocean; within *Nun* there is a fire which acts and produces *Tum,* the first earth or hillock which emerges from *Nun.* This fire is *Nun* itself. Therefore it is said: *"Tum,* by union with his hand, creates himself."[1] This image is reminiscent of St. John: There is a mystery, but, as we shall see further on, this mystery has a reality in fact, which fact the sage can demonstrate, even though unable to explain it. Thus Pharaonic wisdom identifies theology with sacred science: the experiment that demonstrates the reality of theological affirmation.

[1]See, Chapter 8, *"Myth."*

For Western history, through Greece, a mentality has developed whose cause, not whose source, resides in ancient Egypt. We will see below that Pharaonic Egypt remained absolutely faithful to a mentality which inspired the orientation toward a theology-science, but because this knowledge of causes was dependent on a private and restricted teaching, the Greeks searched for answers reason could accept.[2] Yet there is a *mystery* involved, an irrationality at the origin which makes rational philosophical construction impossible. Some of the first serious deviations date from there: They attribute a physical character to metaphysical principles which analyze the genesis born of the Heliopolitan mystery. When effects are visible, causes are sought. Experiment is the only demonstration of causes, and the mental transcription may be plausible and yet totally erroneous, just as it can sometimes be quite correct.

The influence and radiance of Pharaonic Egypt in antiquity were much greater than was previously supposed. Since the Middle Ages, our Occident has been blinded, particularly by the cerebration of the Greek Eleatics who preferred reasoning to experimentation. The beginning of this disquieting period of "arguers" can be situated with the Eleatic school around 550 or 500 B.C., a school founded at about the same time as the Pythagorean order, of mystico-religious character.[3] Those five centuries before the precessional passage from Aries to Pisces stand in curious correspondence with our sixteenth century, also five centuries before the next precessional passage from Pisces to Aquarius: Toward the year 1500, with the Renaissance, ancient Greece was again raised to honor in the West.

Greece, in its day, was using the tools of rationalism in an intense search for the lost word. No sooner had a doctrine seen the light of day than a rejoinder was being born, either a contradiction or an extolling of the idea expressed. To contradict, and to argue, have always been part of the intelligent and subtle temperament of the Greek.

In order to understand correctly this long period of philosophical attempts in Greece, one must place oneself in the setting of that time, when religious expression was reduced to the incarnation of natural principles in human form.[4] This simple humanization of the so-called

[2]The temples of Hellas, such as Delphi, Eleusis, and Delos, were founded on the same wisdom that was taught by the Pharaonic temples, and this Greece must not be confused with the philosophical lucubrations of emigrants from Asia Minor who came to people what is known as "Greater Greece," namely Southern Italy and Sicily.

[3]See Appendix I and Table 1, showing the principal Greek schools and a short notation on the Ionian school of Miletus pertaining to the "Naturalists" who were opposed by the Eleatics.

[4]When discussing myth, we shall see the fundamental distinction to be made between the anthropomorphization in Pharaonic myth and the humanization characteristic of Greco-Roman myth.

gods aroused the rebellion of Xenophanes, among others. But denying a religious expression and replacing it with nothing more than a rational doctrine invites other thinkers to discuss the fundamental value of such an affirmation and, of course, to search for other solutions, themselves open to discussion. There is a natural truth which makes itself felt but cannot be explained. This is why this Greek period of so-called philosophical disputes and doctrines could only lead to intellectual disorder and finally to outright negation of the divine, or to resignation.

When the temple, endowed with the wealth of its sacred science and its power of truth, is no longer in existence and can no longer orient and order, men have no choice but to negate, for no rationalization can replace revelation.

Thus it was that Xenophanes of Colophon, in the sixth century B.C., inaugurated the phase of religious revolt. The few authentic fragments of his teachings which have reached us represent the essential thought of this philosopher, but a great number of other thinkers have discussed, interpreted, and rectified this doctrine, giving a curiously *physical* character to purely metaphysical assertions.

Here are eight of the principal points of Xenophanes' doctrine:

1. There is one God only, supreme among gods and men; neither in form nor thought like mortals.

2. He sees all over, thinks all over, and hears all over.

3. But without toil he sways all things by the thought of his mind.

4. And he abides ever in the same state, moving not at all, nor does it befit him to move about.

5. Mortals believe that the gods are born as they themselves are born, and have perception, voice, and form like theirs.

6. But if oxen or lions had hands, if they could draw and fabricate as do men, the oxen would depict the gods like oxen, and the horses would depict the gods like horses; they would represent them with bodies according to their own form.

7. Homer and Hesiod have ascribed to the gods all things that are a shame and a disgrace among men; most often, they attribute them with such criminal acts as stealing, adulteries, and deception of one another.…

14. There never has been nor will there ever be a man who has clear knowledge of the gods, nor of all the things whereof I speak; for even if he does chance to say what is right, yet he himself does not know that it is so. There is nothing but opinion everywhere.[5]

---

[5] These fragments are numbered according to P. Tannery, *Mémoires pour servir à l'histoire de la science hellène*, 2nd ed. (Paris, 1930), pp. 147-148. Tr. after J. Burnet.

If on points 6 and 7 Xenophanes disavows the humanized myth, point 14 seems to reject all theology as being merely opinion, for only sacred science can prove a reality no longer dependent on opinion.

The true word has been lost.

According to Simplicios, Theophrastos had gathered together what was then known of the doctrines of Xenophanes of Colophon. The master of Parmenides taught that *God is one, not-engendered, neither infinite nor finite, neither in motion nor at rest; for the infinite and the immobile are non-being, whereas movement pertains to the plurality of objects limiting each other.*

Xenophanes here speaks essentially of the notion of divinity as reduced to oneness, excluding *the multiplicity of the gods.* His successors will discuss the possibility of multiplicity in a general sense. Xenophanes, on the contrary, *admits the plurality of objects* or things which limit each other reciprocally and have movement.[6]

On the basis of this doctrine of oneness, Parmenides takes a position tending somewhat more toward the physical; he again affirms *the unity of Being, uncreated, universal, one and only, immovable, and without end,* but he adds:

> Its name is All [that it is],[7] wherefore all these things are but names which mortals have given, believing them to be true—coming into being and passing away, Being and non-Being, change of place and alteration of color. But, since it is perfect within an extreme limit, it resembles the mass of a well-rounded sphere, equally distant from its center in all directions.[8]

Furthermore, declares Parmenides, in an offhand manner:

> There is Being and there is no non-Being; behold what I bid thee to proclaim.[9]

This affirmation of oneness as Being, excluding non-Being, and its identification with the whole, led to conclusions of a world entire and complete, full, and hence without movement. How not to react to such a concept which excludes what our senses confirm, namely variety and movement? We will return to this problem when considering Zeno's doctrine.

It remained for Leucippos and Democritos to elaborate an image of the world conforming more precisely to sense-supported reason.

---

[6]See Appendix 1, 2, Theophrastos, fr. 5 (Simplicios, in *Physics*, 5b). Theophrastos lived 371-264.

[7]Tannery's translation here differs from that of standard versions which convey the sense of "mere name."

[8]Extracts from the fragments of Parmenides, *Toward Truth*, tr. after John Burnet. See Appendix I, 3.

[9]Ibid.

We must remember that Xenophanes and Parmenides were antagonistic to the teaching of Pythagoras. Instructed in Egypt, Pythagoras speaks of *complementaries,* which his enemies turn into contrarieties. Later, when discussing Man, I will assert once again that the entire thought process of *Homo sapiens* is based on the faculty of negation. Affirmation can come only from consciousness of negation. In the reasoning of Xenophanes and Parmenides, therefore, there is a fundamental error because reason, whether excluding the evidence of the senses or affirming it (like Leucippos), definitely requires complementation.

In the negation of non-Being which affirms Being, there is the action of negating, which is a fact, hence a Being.

As to Pythagoras, numerous are the authors of antiquity who fought or excessively praised the Master and his school, which is why contemporary criticism rejects as fable most of ancient testimony.

From Pythagoras' own hand, no writing exists. It must be remembered, moreover, that from all these philosophers—Pythagoreans, Eleatics, and other Greeks yet to be cited—almost no original writing exists, and that many of the analyses of these philosophers' ideas were made from hearsay more or less mingled with opinion and interpretations.

Although certain modern critics have gone so far as to express doubt concerning the existence of Pythagoras, the arguments for his existence and for the value of his teaching are many. For example, when Xenophanes, in the fragments that survived him, derides the theory of metempsychosis, he is clearly aiming at Pythagoras, who, according to tradition, was his contemporary.[10] The declarations, first of Xenophanes and then of Parmenides concerning the unity of Being with the total exclusion of not-Being, later demonstrated by the specious arguments of Zeno of Elea, pose an antithesis to the Pythagorean teaching according to which "all is Number." Aristotle also devotes numerous commentaries to these authors.[11]

The first texts concerning the Pythagorean teachings are due to Philolaos, who affirms the existence of *one God, eternal, immutable, unmoving, itself like to itself, different from other things.*[12]

---

[10]Metempsychosis is to be understood as the reincarnation of the human soul. According to Ampère, "the dogma of metempsychosis is the belief in the immortality of the soul through a series of successive [human] existences."

[11]Aristotle, *Metaphysics,* I, 5, 6, and XII, 6; *Physics,* III, 4; *De Caelo,* II, 13, 293a, 23b, 20, etc.

[12]Fragments of Philolaos, from Philo, *De mundi opificio,* p. 24; in A. Ed. Chaignet, *Pythagore et la philosophie pythagoricienne* (Paris, 1873), I, p. 224.

Philolaos defines the world as a harmonious composite of finite and infinite elements, and he says that all things can be thought or known only through Number. The following words are also attributed to him:

> This is how it is with nature and harmony: the essence of things is an eternal essence; it is a unique and divine nature, knowledge of which does not belong to man.[13]

But as the world is formed of principles which are neither similar nor of similar nature, it would be impossible for the order of the world to form without the intervention of harmony. Thus *number,* as the Pythagoreans understood it, is the condition under which everything is determined and known, and harmony is the link between complementary elements whose nature differs. Harmony is here understood in its broadest possible acceptation; the musical octave is given as model and harmonic progression as illustration.[14]

The Pythagoreans thought of unity as the beginning of all things. From unity stemmed the determining duality which was in the same relationship to it as matter to the first cause. From these two elements, numbers result.

Aristotle attributed to the Pythagoreans the ten principles, which they ordered into two parallel series: limited and unlimited, odd and even, one and plurality, right and left, male and female, resting and moving, straight and curved, light and darkness, good and bad, square and oblong.[15] These fundamental principles, taken up later with fervor by the neo-Pythagoreans, were violently attacked by the Eleatics.

Most accounts of Pythagoras' life agree on the many voyages he made to the Orient, during which travels he acquired the basis of his philosophy and science. *It is incontestable that he journeyed to Egypt, as all authors concur on this point.*[16] Iamblichos specifies that Pythagoras remained for twenty-two years in Memphis and in Thebes, where the priests are said to have taught him mathematics and astronomy.

It is important to note that of the entire doctrine invented by the Eleatics, nothing remains, whereas every positive and fundamental teaching is ultimately attributed to Pythagoras and his school. Greek

[13]Ibid., p. 229.

[14]Ibid., pp. 230-231.

[15]Aristotle, *Metaphysics* I, 5.

[16]A. Ed. Chaignet, op. cit., p. 224. See also Appendix I, 4.

writers themselves affirm the "Oriental," meaning Egyptian, origin of these teachings. In opposition to the traditional teaching transmitted by Pythagoras, we find the grave deviation toward learned and academic thinking which will lead directly to total negation.

As to the fundamental and positive knowledge generally considered to be of Pythagorean origin, Paul Tannery's conclusions seem to be the most adequate; a severe critic, he can in no way be said to be prejudiced. According to him, the following geometric elements, Pythagorean in origin, were classified and gathered together in Euclid's *Elements:*

—The geometry of plane figures (Books I-IV)

—Theories of proportions applied to plane geometry (Book VI)

—Geometry of planes and solids (Book XI)

—Construction of the five regular polyhedrons[17]

For astronomy, which Pythagoras called *spherics,* the following information is also affirmed to be of Pythagorean origin:

—*The sphericity of the earth,* which was at that time disavowed by the last Ionians and later yet by the Atomists, Epicuros included.

—*The inclination of the terrestrial axis,* upon which their explanation of the seasons was based.

—*The rotation of the earth on itself, producing day and night.*[18]

—*The movement of translation of the earth "around the central fire," which was sometimes likened to the sun.*

Thus it seems that in the fifth century B.C., Philolaos, to whom we owe the disclosure of this data, was already teaching a cosmological system which certain modern scholars compare to that of Copernicus. Since it is known that the Pythagoreans affirmed the sphericity of the earth, its movement of rotation upon its own axis, and its movement of translation around a "central fire," it is possible to conclude that the heliocentric system of Copernicus has a very distant origin. This interpretation, however, has been vigorously refuted by Jules Sageret for the following reasons:

> The cosmology of Philolaos was and still is considered to be the heliocentric system itself, and has been attributed to Pythagoras. This is a legend whose formation postdates Copernicus. It is important to show its lack of

[17] See P. Tannery, *La géométrie grecque,* where the author attributes to Pythagoras all of Euclid's *Elements,* except for Books VII, VIII, and IX, Euclidian in style, and Books V, X, and XII, attributed to Eudoxos and Theaitetos.

[18] See G. Milhaud, *Origines de la science grecque,* p. 226. Cf. E. M. Antoniadi, *L'astronomie égyptienne,* p. 33: "The rotation of the earth upon its axis was professed by Hicetas, Ecphantos, Philolaos, Leucippos, Timaeus, Plato, Heracleides of Pontos, Aristarchos of Samos, and the Hellenizing Chaldean, Seleucos."

foundation, for if the knowledge of the heliocentric movement goes back to Pythagoras, one would have to assume a very long scientific development preceding him; the history of the evolution of the human spirit would take on quite a different aspect from what has been hitherto presented.[19]

Sageret, who would like to situate the beginning of the scientific world in Greece, is reluctant to admit to a very ancient science. But this is precisely the case with what we know today of Pharaonic Egypt. Before the "Greek miracle," there is indeed a very long period with a civilization possessing an elevated science on which the entire Mediterranean region had drawn. It existed side by side, furthermore, with the great Near Eastern civilization around the Euphrates, though the latter lacked the theological purity that could be found in Egypt. To this we may add the very ancient and learned Brahmanic and Chinese civilizations. The limited medieval vision of humanity's history is no longer acceptable today. It is not the world in general that began six thousand years ago, as had been wrongly deduced from certain sacred texts, but the historical epoch of Pharaonic Egypt, which begins toward the year 4240 B.C., the date at which the establishment of its calendar and system of Sothic cycles can be placed, a fact of the greatest importance.[20]

Professor Eduard Zeller, eminent defender of the Greek miracle, denies that Copernicus was inspired by Pythagorean doctrines when Copernicus himself affirms it:

> It is now universally recognized that Copernicus wrongly attributed to the Pythagoreans the doctrine of the rotation of the earth on its axis and the movement of the earth around the sun.[21]

Copernicus indeed cites ancient writers who inspired his discovery. Should he be forced to disavow them?

There is one point, however, that could partially influence Zeller's judgment: The Pythagorean system, inspired by the Pharaonic temple, goes far beyond the simple solar system of Copernicus, as is shown by certain allusions to the "central fire" which animates our own sun.

In order to judge this important question correctly, it would be essential to have access to the original works. Unfortunately, the earliest references concerning the cosmological system of Philolaos are encountered only in Aristotle, who, as an introduction to his own

[19]Jules Sageret, Le système du monde (Paris, 1913), p. 66.

[20]See Chapter 8, "Myth."

[21]E. Zeller, A History of Greek Philosophy (London, 1881), I, p. 453. Tr. Alleyne.

doctrines, briefly mentions the opinions held before his own time. It must be kept in mind that Aristotle rejected the whole of Pythagorean theories, particularly *the rotation of the earth, its movement of translation, and the natural analogy between the earth and the heavenly bodies which move around a central fire.* Seeing that Aristotle intends to show the absurdity of such hypotheses—which are clearly in contradiction with his own system, in which the earth is immobile in the center of the world—there is all reason to believe that he did not take great pains to present the doctrine of Philolaos in coherent form. It is indeed true that the Pythagorean system upsets the Greek conception of the world. For reasons analogous and of religious nature, the system of Copernicus in its day upset our own astronomy.[22]

> It remains to speak of the earth, to tell where it is situated, if it belongs to the class of things at rest or of things in motion, and of its shape.
>
> As to its position, there is some difference of opinion. Most philosophers—all, in fact, who consider the heavens as finite—say it lies at the center of the world. But the Italian school of philosophers known as "Pythagoreans" take the contrary view. For them, it is fire which occupies the center; the earth is only one of the stars, creating night and day by its circular motion around the center. They further construct another earth in opposition to ours, to which they give the name counter-earth.[23]
>
> All who deny that the earth occupies the central position believe that it revolves around the center, and not only the earth but, as we have said before, the counter-earth as well.[24]
>
> There are similar disputes concerning the shape of the earth. Some think it is spherical, others that it is flat and tambourine-shaped.[25]

The assertion expressly states that earth is not in the center, but that it revolves around a "central fire" in a circular motion. Such a theory stands opposed to the geocentric system then unanimously accepted.

Other fragments of Philolaos directly concerning this subject were transmitted by very late authors: by Diogenes Laertios (mid-third century A.D.), whose sources themselves lie in Theophrastos or Stobaios, the fifth-century-A.D. anthologist; by Aetios, a mediocre

---

[22]See discussion of Aristarchos of Samos, p. 29.

[23]Aristotle, *De Caelo,* II, 13, 293a, 15-25, tr. after J. Tricot.

[24]Ibid., 293b, 15-20.

[25]Ibid., 293b, 30. The reference is to Anaxagoras and Anaximander, for whom the earth was cylindrical in shape.

Peripatetic who might have been but a copyist himself, to whom the *Placita* are attributed; or else by Iamblichos, a Greek Neoplatonist who lived in the third century of our era.

> Philolaos was the first to declare that the earth moves in a circle.[26]

> Philolaos places fire at the center and calls it the Hestia of All, the house of Jupiter and mother of the gods, altar, bond, and measure of nature. Further, he poses a second fire, completely above, enveloping the world. He says that the center is by nature primary, and around the center ten diverse bodies perform their dancing chorus; these are the sky, the planets; lower down, the sun, then the moon below; beneath that, the earth, and below the earth, the counter-earth and finally, under all these bodies, the fire of Hestia, at the center, where it maintains order.[27]

There is every reason to believe that in these quotations, Aristotle had at his disposal only oral transcriptions of the theory he is attacking. Later anthologists tend to muddle everything. It probably concerns a double system, poorly understood, to wit:

1. *The heliocentric system,* which results from the affirmation that the earth is not in the center but turns in circles.
2. *The world system,* which poses Hestia, the Fire, in the center.

Today we know what the Greeks seem to have ignored. The fact is that ancient Egypt possessed a very complete solar, lunar, and Sothic calendar. The Sothic cycle is established on the coincidence every 1,460 years of the *vague year* of 365 days with the *Sothic* (or *Sirian*) *year* of 365¼ days. All civil acts were dated according to the vague year, composed of exactly 360 days plus the five epagomenal days consecrated to the *Neters:* Osiris, Isis, Seth, Nephthys, and Horus. [28]

The Sirian, or *fixed year,* was established according to the heliacal rising of Sirius, yet the interval between two heliacal risings of Sirius corresponds neither to the tropical year, which is shorter, nor to the sidereal year, which is longer. For it is remarkable that *owing to the precession of the equinoxes, on the one hand, and the movement of Sirius on the other, the position of the sun with respect to Sirius is displaced in the same direction, almost exactly to the same extent.*[29]

Calculations established by astronomers have demonstrated that between 4231 and 2231 B.C., the approximate duration of the reign of

[26]Diogenes Laertios *(Lives of Eminent Philosophers),* VIII, 85, in A. Ed. Chaignet, op. cit., p. 237.

[27]Stobaios, *Eclogues* I, 22, p. 488. in A. Ed. Chaignet, op. cit., p. 234.

[28]See Chapter 8, *"Myth."*

[29]See E. Meyer, *Chronologie égyptienne.*

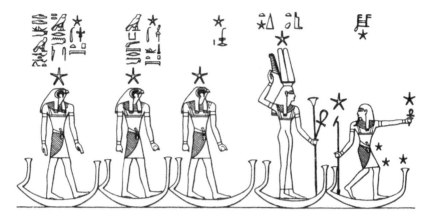

Fig. 1. *Sirius* (*Isis*-Seped.t) *preceding Orion and followed by Jupiter, Saturn, and Mars.*
Isis holds the *wadj* scepter and the *ankh*, the dilation or spiritualization of life. Orion holds the *uas* scepter, the flow of sap, while facing Isis and presenting life with the left hand. In other words, Orion offers the life that he draws from Sirius.

the Bull, *Hap*, the Sirian year was almost identical to our Julian year of 365¼ days. This period would cover the entire Ancient Empire, "and we cannot but admire the greatness of a science capable of discovering such a coincidence because *Sirius is the only star among the 'fixed stars' which allows this cycle.* It can therefore be supposed that Sirius plays the role of a center for the circuit of our entire solar system."[30]

Thus the double star of Sirius was chosen for these coincidences because it is the only star that moves the needed distance and in the right direction against the background of the other stars. This fact, known four thousand years before our time and forgotten until our day, obviously demands an extraordinary and prolonged observation of the sky. But there is yet other evidence: Sirius, the *Sothis* of the ancients which was called the *Great Provider,* is constantly evoked in the Pyramid Texts:

Isis comes to thee [Osiris] joyous in thy love;
Your seed rises in her, penetrating [*spd.t*] like Sirius [*spd.t*]. The penetrating [*spd*] Horus comes forth from thee in his name of Horus-who-is-in-Sirius [*Pyr.* 1635-1636][31]

[30]R. A. Schwaller de Lubicz, *Le Temple de l'Homme* (Paris, 1957), I, p. 719.
[31]K. Sethe, *Die altaegyptischen Pyramidentexte* (Leipzig, 1908-1922).

In the spirit of the temple, Sirius plays the role of the great central fire for our sun (which is the *Eye of Ra* and not *Ra* himself). It took our own discoveries in atomism and astronomy to suggest yet another characteristic of Sirius which coincides with what we are beginning to know about the atomic nucleus, made up of a positron (a giant star of very weak density) accompanying a neutron whose volume is exceedingly small in relation to the atom, but where all its weight is concentrated (a dwarf star of incredible density). In 1934, calculation still accorded the heavy companion of Sirius a specific gravity of 50,000 (whereas gold, for example, has a specific gravity of 19.3). This is an absolutely exceptional case with respect to other double stars and to our sun, which is generally accorded a specific gravity of 1.4 relative to water. But in 1953, according to new observations, it was possible to ascribe a density of 53,000 to this strange Sirian neutron which has not ceased to astound us.

> The companion of Sirius constitutes a remarkable exception: its mass is indeed far superior to what its absolute magnitude would assign it, and its density seems on the order of fifty-three thousand times the density of water, a fact since confirmed by other research based on the theory of relativity.[32]

The double star of Sirius—which for Pharaonic Egypt played the role of a central sun to our entire solar system—today suggests the existence of a cosmic system of atomic structure whose *nucleus* is this "Great Provider," the Sothis *(spd.t)* of the ancients. There might well be a need to revise our cosmology in the not-so-distant future.

But how were these things known to the Pharaonic sages? It seems undeniable that such a science filtered down through Pythagoras and his school, but remained occulted. This secrecy should not surprise us: We are familiar with the reaction of our Western world and that of the Roman Catholic Church in particular when Galileo and then Copernicus attempted to introduce the notion of a heliocentric system. Religion (be it Greek, Roman, or Christian) is conferred upon this earth's humanity. A heliocentric system, *entirely of mechanistic character*, represents a deviation from healthy mentality which for moral reasons demands a world in which the earth is central. The sky's appearance, moreover, pleads in favor of a geocentric system, perfectly sufficient for astronomical observations.

Elsewhere I have defended the religious point of view in opposition to Galileo; there is no reason to entertain the mass of

[32]*Annuaire astronomique et météorologique* (Paris, 1953), p. 291.

humanity with a fact that serves them in no way save to rob them of their confidence in life and create in them nothing but confusion. In a heliocentric system, man on earth is no more than a speck of dust in the universe, whereas in the geocentric system, he is the center of the world. The Pharaonic temple did not proclaim the heliocentric system either, but its entire calendar system proves that the ancient Egyptians were well acquainted with it. Moreover, they had evidence stemming from what I refer to as "sacred science" which made them understand the true system even better: Far from being simply mechanistic (cf. Laplace), it is actually bound to the principle of genesis, the law that presides over all becoming.

Despite the small success it found with Aristotle, the heliocentric hypothesis was taken up again by Aristarchos of Samos in the third century B.C. This doctrine, if we are to believe Plutarch, almost became his undoing, for the Stoic Cleanthes attempted to have him accused of impiety for daring to disturb Hestia's repose.

> Aristarchos of Samos composed a book consisting of several hypotheses in which the premises lead to the conclusion that the Universe is infinitely greater than had been declared. His hypotheses are that the fixed stars and the sun remain unmoved, that the earth revolves about the sun in the circumference of a circle, the sun lying in the middle of the orbit.[33]

Yet another text—one by Alexander of Aphrodisias, who lived in Alexandria during the third century B.C.—adds several curious details on the system of Philolaos so vaguely described by the more recent compilers:

> The Pythagoreans said that the bodies which revolve around the center have their distances in proportion, and some revolve more quickly, others more slowly, the sound which they make during this motion being deep in the case of the slower, and high in the case of the quicker; these sounds, then, depending on the ratio of the distances, are such that their combined effect is harmonious.[34]

What is said here concerning a "music of the spheres" has its origin in Pythagorean teachings on harmony. Pythagoras is cited by Kepler as being the source of his inspiration and as having led him to

---

[33] Archimedes (287-212 B.C.), *The Sand Reckoner* (Arenarios). Aristarchos of Samos, pupil of Straton of Lampsacos, is well known for having anticipated the Copernican system. "According to Plutarch's *De Facie in orbe lunae*, 923A, it is clear that Aristarchos also assumed the earth's rotation on its axis. . ." (M. R. Cohen, and I. E. Drabkin, *A Source Book in Greek Science*, [New York, 1948]).

[34] Alexander of Aphrodisias, *Commentaries on Aristotle's Metaphysics*, p. 542a, 5-18 (Brandis) in Cohen and Drapkin, op. cit., p. 96. Cf. Aristotle, *On the Heavens (De Caelo)*, II, 9, *The Harmony of the Spheres*, refutation of the theory according to which stars emit sounds that form a musical chord.

the magnificent and fundamental discovery of the laws that are the basis of astronomy. In his strange and honest work, *Mysterium Cosmographicum,* Johann Kepler (1571-1630) explains his thought process as inspired by the ancients.* He defends Copernicus and apologizes to the "guardians of the faith" for daring to defend a heliocentric system. He judged that if the ancients proclaimed it, there was no reason not to speak of it in our time: a specious argument from a man carried away by enthusiasm. His discovery, based on the five regular solids taught by Pythagoras, led him to formulate his three laws:

1. Planetary orbits are ellipses with the sun at one focus.

2. Each planet moves in its orbit in such a way that the time of describing an arc of the orbit is proportional to the area of the sector swept over by the radius vector.

3. The squares of the times of revolution of any two planets are proportional to the cubes of their mean distances from the sun.

This period which marks the beginning of our history of modern sciences and of the philosophy of the Renaissance is certainly a curious time. It appears as a kind of reflection (almost a reincarnation) of an analogous period from 600 to 300 B.C., rich as it is in men who left their names to history in all domains of thought: Nicolas of Cusa, Marsilio Ficino, Pico della Mirandola, who revived Platonism and Pytha-goreanism in Europe; Luther and Calvin, products of free thinking; Paracelsus, Jakob Boehme, the skeptical Machiavelli, Leonardo da Vinci, Copernicus, Galileo, Kepler, etc. The spirit of Pythagoras reappears, as does the revolt against religious ostracism, and the deviation from the pure [nonreasoning] path toward the path of the cerebrating mind. The history of the world is strangely cyclical.

But let us return to the Greek texts as we pursue the progress of what I consider to be the error of a purely rational mode of thinking.

In the wake of Parmenides, Zeno of Elea opens the gate which Abel Rey calls the beginning of scientific thought, by which he means purely rational thought. Later, Aristotle came to credit Zeno with founding the dialectic which was to dominate the mentality of the West. Plato, for his part, disliked Zeno; in his *Parmenides,* there is a dialogue between Parmenides, Zeno, and Socrates, showing the errors of an argument which, at the very least, could be called specious. Thus:

---

*The following statement by Kepler would be relevant here: "I have plundered the golden vessels of the Egyptians, in order to furnish a sacred tabernacle for my God out of them, far from the borders of Egypt" (May 15, 1618). (In Max Caspar's *Kepler* [London, 1959], tr. C. D. Hellman.)—Trans.

Socrates to Zeno: . . . Hence, if it is impossible that unlike things be like or like things unlike, it is therefore impossible that multiplicity exists; because multiplicity, once it is posited, cannot escape these impossibilities. Is this the purpose of your argument—to maintain, against everything that is commonly accepted, that multiplicity does not exist?[35]

As the dialogue proceeds, Socrates observes that Zeno defends the Parmenidean thesis and remarks that *while Zeno denies multiplicity, Parmenides affirms unity,* so that, although they speak differently, both *say the same thing.*

In fact, no particular argument is called for in the affirmation of unity. The contrary position, however, the negation of multiplicity, forces Zeno to ascertain the chain of reasoning that characterizes his mentality. In multiplying the arguments against plurality, he wants to demonstrate a *rational oneness* instead of a unity conceived in an abstract sense, remaining theological as in Parmenides' presentation.

Opposition to the Pythagorean philosophy can be clearly felt in the Parmenidean texts which uphold complementation. When Parmenides affirms the existence of Being and denies non-Being, in the final analysis he is formulating the postulate *"From nothing, nothing occurs."* This is the negation of mystery, of the irrationality of simultaneous Being and non-Being.

Zeno, in turn, takes a position opposing the Pythagoreans. He adduces other arguments and uses a classical Pythagorean datum of his time: *the definition of the point.* We quote Paul Tannery's interpretation of this definition:

For the Pythagoreans, *the point is a unit which has position,* in other words, a unit considered in space. It immediately follows from this definition that the geometric entity is a plurality, a sum of points, just as number is a plurality, sum of units.[36]

Tannery's interpretation of "unit-points" is rather surprising. The custom attributed to the Pythagoreans of noting the numbers up to ten by points—as in Pharaonic Egypt, where numbers up to ten are indicated by lines—is precisely aimed at defining the forms and functions of numbers and in no way signifies a material composition. Thus the number two, noted as * * , can only be a line, and three points * * * are needed, in addition to the line, in order to form a

---

[35]Plato, *Parmenides,* 127e. Tr. E. Diès, Collection Budé.

[36]P. Tannery, op. cit., p. 258. Further on, he adds that "mathematically speaking, the point is in no way a unit; it is pure zero, quantitative nothingness."

first compounded surface of triangular shape ∗∗∗ . Similarly, four
points can only form a square, and so on. The form is immanent in the
number, and the *possibilities* of grouping determine the *functions* of
numbers, such as duality, division, sexualization for the number two.
Thus the number three signifies the first triangular entity of which two
are needed to produce the first engendered surface, four. These
expressions are possible only through a numerical notation by points
or lines; they cannot be captured when numbers are noted by
conventional signs.

Was Tannery carried away by Zeno's sophisms when he felt
justified in considering these unit-points as a first concept of atomism,
when atomism is in fact a reaction provoked by Zeno's stand?
Pythagoras never committed such an error. Yet Zeno of Elea knew
how to argue. This is the man whom rationalistic science would today
still like to raise on a pedestal as the father of rational thinking. Zeno
was not afraid to pose the premises of an absurd hypothesis for the
purpose of reaching logical conclusions to his philosophic assertions.
In fact, Zeno remains logical to himself when he undertakes to follow
the rationalistic path; once he has set foot on this path, he pursues it
without noticing the by-ways that could lead him to reality. He
proceeds like a child who is told a marvelous bedtime story and
continues to ask: "And then what happens next?" and this "next"
continues in his sleep in another world where the laws of physics do
not play. Thus Zeno, the rationalist, begins to divide and will continue
to divide, unaware of the moment when the thing no longer stays the
same if divided once more, the moment when there appears another
complex which can no longer bear quantitative division but demands a
qualitative division where matter is energy.

Opposed to this academic thinking which Zeno typifies, there
stands the technical thinking of the Pharaonic mentality: There exists
the perceptible fact which shatters the hypothetical continuity of the
imagination's process of reasoning; not to accept this fork in the road is
to pursue the track of mechanistic science, which can be properly called
inhuman. But let us look more closely at the essence of Zeno's
arguments and the conclusions to be drawn from them.

In his *arguments against plurality,* cited by Simplicios, Zeno
proceeds by dichotomy and *divides to infinity any element whatsoever
of infinite plurality;* he thus manages to demonstrate that by reason of
this division to infinity, *the magnitude of each element of the plurality
is nil.*[37]

[37]See Appendix I, 5A.

This, however, is false reasoning. If a division to infinity is acknowledged, it means there will be no end to the dividing, and it is supposed that there will always be something to divide. Actually, Zeno here poses the principle of the mathematical point without quantity, a useful hypothesis for reasoning about a hypothetical world. In fact, today's physics shows that quantitative division *ad infinitum* is absurd, as at a certain moment, the "quantitative" molecule is composed of an energetic atomic complex. A development in physics was needed to demonstrate that a function cannot be indefinitely applied in the material world. *Sacred science starts from this mysterious but demonstrated reality which shows an energetic (spiritual) world preceding the material and quantitative world.*

The fact of an energetic, nonquantitative state immanent in the quantitative material aspect exists for our physics as well as for sacred science, and it is impossible to sunder these two states in order to consider one without the other. In all the arguments, the deviation consists in considering only one of these states to the exclusion of the other by submitting it to functions on a basis of continuity. Infinity is not part of this dualized world, and in the Pythagorean, or Pharaonic, spirit, the notion of infinity can be applied only to *absolute Unity* (God), that is, to *"the One whose name is unknown."*

In the second argument, Zeno reaches the conclusion that if there is a plurality, things will be both great and small, so small as to have no size at all, and thus nil in quantity, and so great as to be infinite.[38]

This amounts to confusing the function with the fact. The symbol $\frac{1}{n}$ designates a function in which, as the quantity is diminished, the divisor n is proportionately augmented; equilibrium is maintained in the sense of the infinitely small compensating the infinitely great. The problem changes when we apply this function to a quantity x in order to make it a fact, as Zeno does.

To the Pharaonic mentality, every value has its compensating complement. It is curious to note that this notion of equilibrium, of alternations, of the respiration that makes for life, is excluded in the arguments of the Greek philosophers.

In the third argument, Zeno finally demonstrates that if there is *plurality*, things must be *finite in number*, hence limited; but, applying his dichotomic method and the idea that plurality is a composite of *discrete points*, he concludes that things are *unlimited* because of the

---

[38]See Appendix I, 5B.

infinity of intervals between units. Thus, if there is *plurality*, things are *at the same time limited and unlimited*.[39]

Where did Zeno get those spaces between points? And what are those distances? If quantities are involved, these distances are measurable; if it is a matter of mathematical points whose magnitude is null, the argument is absurd.

In his four arguments against motion, Zeno also proceeds by dichotomy and manages to demonstrate:

1. *That it is impossible to occupy successively an infinite number of positions in a finite time* (Dichotomy and Achilles and the tortoise).

2. *That the fact of occupying a given position at a given instant leads to the conclusion that an object in motion is at rest* (the arrow in flight).[40]

These arguments of Zeno are not far removed from the principle of incertitude of present-day atomism, which indicates the impossibility of mathematically knowing situation and time simultaneously. taneously.

The most recent mathematical arguments lead into the same labyrinth with the invention, besides the two infinites of space and time, of a third kind of infinite, a *limited infinite* which is the basis of the transfinite. The example of Achilles and the tortoise is universally known, and it is precisely this paradox which constitutes the principal argument explaining the present doctrine of the transfinite.[41] The problem of Achilles was considered insoluble until the invention of differential calculus, which is founded on the deviation's very principle: The argument in the calculation is valid as far as the mathematical point is concerned, but must, in its application, become a determinate quantity.

It is curious to see men such as Newton, Leibnitz, and Descartes vying for the glory of having discovered a differential calculus based on the same arguments as Zeno's, and so precious today for launching spy-satellites and for raining deadly missiles on our neighbors, all mechanical applications made possible only by means of such scholarly mathematics. Obviously, the Pharaonic sages would have been quite incapable of making these calculations with their mathematics; but neither would the idea ever have occurred to them of inventing missiles in order to see what is happening in the universe.... Very

---

[39]See Appendix I, 5C.
[40]See Appendix I, 5, "The Four Arguments Against Motion," arguments I and II.
[41]See Appendix III.

likely they had other means of general investigation without needing these dangerous mechanical toys which are the glory of our deviate science.

Zeno's arguments have raised numerous polemics. Tannery calls attention to Zeno's affirmation of the existence of incommensurable quantities, as well as to the definition of the mathematical point, which is in no way a unit but a pure zero, a nothing of quantity. This position is opposed by those who consider that in a body, a surface or a line represents a totality of juxtaposed points. Thus:

> If Zeno's arguments are epitomized, it can be seen that they in fact amount to establishing, by means of the absurd, that a body is not a sum of points; that time is not a sum of instants; that motion is not a sum of simple passages from point to point.[42]

These conclusions call for a contrary reaction that considers the universe to be made of a multiplicity of isolated points called *atoms*. Once again, this is the nonsensical concept of the indivisible infinite.

Here is the conclusion drawn by Abel Rey, the rationalistic and enthusiastic Hellenist, from the arguments and "subtle reasoning" of Zeno of Elea:

> . . . our mastery consists in the integration accomplished by reason. This was seen by the Eleatic, and in his wake, by Greek science, and this much we owe it, down to the most empirical assertions of our science.
>
> The Eleatic perceived this through a certain mysticism of reason. If we had to find an epithet to characterize the system, that is the one we would choose. Parmenides, Zeno, and Milissos represent the mysticism of reason prepared by that mystique of countermysticism which is Xenophanes' philosophy. This school flourished in the face of Pythagorean mysticism, spread by the harsh and hard Doric race of Greater Greece, the race that built the temples of Paestum, that Eleatism of architecture. What mystic breath did it take to construct this vertiginous logic? What sense of mystery for this great clarity which transcends all appearances of ordinary life: path of salvation for thought which, like the other path, turns its back on any sensory and all too human path.
>
> To remain confined to human needs, as did Egyptian technique, or to remain separated from the great mystic efforts which strive to make us rejoin the depths of the real, as do Oriental techniques—this would never have ended up as science. Nor would the mere notations of human experience, nor the efforts to order them technically so as to be sparing of thought and to trace definite habits.
>
> It was necessary. . . to arrive at the idea of a system of things, of sciences that are farther along and more elevated than techniques: Science. And lastly, a

great mystic breath was needed to carry this science out of the perceptible and
beyond human measure: the mysticism of demonstration and of reason and, as
in Parmenides' first verses, the mysticism of truth for truth's sake.[43]

The author is correct, and he himself underlines precisely the
inhuman character of this purely cerebral science. Our nineteenth
century was able to exult in this fashion, but the latest stages of
contemporary science provide food for thought, and even the
nonscientific mass of humanity is beginning to tremble, faced as it is
with the effects of this glorified science.

It is not clear what Abel Rey means by the word "mystical" when
he applies it to the Eleatics who have come—as he himself brings
out—from Xenophanes' countermystical revolt against a purely
humanized myth. Rey uses the term "mystical" in a sense all too
frequently adopted in our day, to denote simply a mental exaltation.
There is nothing recondite about the Eleatic arguments. They are
within reach of everyone, whereas the term "mystical," in the author's
opinion, must be applied only to an experience outside of one's self in a
religious sense: an ecstasy.

As far as "Pharaonic technique" is concerned, Rey's thinking is
obviously confused, for we are dealing with *technical thinking* and not
with a technical outcome as is the case with our own science. To start
from positive fact in order to arrive at spirit and at God, such is the
Pharaonic path. To start from abstraction and from reason in order to
arrive at technique and at spiritual naught, such is the path of our
cerebral science.[44]

The Atomist Theory

After Zeno "demonstrated" the nonexistence of multiplicity in
order to proclaim a unity devoid of all abstract and theological
character, there remained for Leucippos but to prove logically that the
whole is composed of an infinity of particles. It is impossible to
separate Leucippos from Democritos; the latter is traditionally
acknowledged as the father of atomism. None of their writings have
survived, and we must turn to Aristotle (in *De generatione et*

---

[43]Abel Rey, *La jeunesse de la science grecque* (Paris, 1933), pp. 181-182.

[44]Cf. the plea against the error in today's thinking by Gustave Thibon in his Preface to Gilbert Tournier's
Babel ou le vertige technique (Paris, 1959).

corruptione, another text that comes down to us only in Latin) in order to learn the principle of this first doctrine of the atom.

It must be stressed that with atomic theory, we enter the domain of materialism. When Xenophanes and Parmenides fight against the humanized myth of Olympus, it is still a show of loyalty for a supernatural source which animates them. When Zeno intervenes with his sophisms, he deviates toward pure rationalism and thus opens the door to the materialist concept of the atomists, a neat trick in itself: *The whole is formed of a multitude of unsplittable particles and of infinitely diverse forms.* With this proposition, one is free to explain anything. Here is how Aristotle summarizes the Leucippos-Democritos doctrine:

> Leucippos [himself coming from the Eleatic school, and contrary to the Eleatics who proclaimed Oneness] believed he had sufficient reasons to establish a theory in accordance with the facts supported by sense-perception which would accord with production and destruction, motion, and the multiplicity of things.
>
> This much conceded to phenomena, he granted to the Monists that motion is impossible without the void and that the void is a non-being, and in no way participates in being.
>
> According to him, being, in the strict sense of the term, is an absolute plenum; as such, it cannot be "one," but is composed of an infinite number of elements which are invisible owing to their smallness.
>
> These elements move in the void (for the void exists); by their coming together they cause coming-into-being, and by their separation they produce corruption.
>
> They act upon each other according to their mutual contact, because the manner of this contact is not uniform; and, in combining and intertwining, they generate the universe.
>
> Indeed, from genuine unity there could never emerge a multiplicity, nor unity from multiplicity properly so called: That is impossible.[45]

From this text it is concluded that the atomists take into account the evidence of the senses and that they acknowledge multiplicity and motion; motion, in turn, presupposes the existence of a void. This theory recognizes the unity of being and the multiplicity of things.

> Nothing can be created out of nothing, nor can it be destroyed and returned to nothing. All change is but the aggregation or the disaggregation of parts [concept of *substance* later to be found with Kant].
>
> Nothing exists but atoms and the void: All the rest is hypothesis.

---

[45]Aristotle, *De generatione et corruptione,* I, 325a, in L. Mabilleau, *Histoire de la philosophie atomistique* (Paris, 1895), pp. 174-175.

The atoms are infinite in number, and their shapes are of infinite variety.

The differences in all things stem from differences in the number, size, form, and arrangement of their atoms. The atoms have no qualitative differences: they have no *internal states:* They act on each other only through collisions and blows.[46]

Here are some of Democritos' own words:

The sweet, the bitter, the warm, the cold, color—these exist in the mind alone; there is nothing, in reality, but atoms and the void.[47]

And a commentary by Philoponos:

Every element is a being in a literal sense; in such a being, non-being cannot penetrate, nor, consequently, can the void; and if the void cannot penetrate therein, since division cannot be brought about without the void, the elements are indivisible.[48]

According to Zeno of Elea, *the void is non-being and thus does not exist:* an elegant argument that loses its value as Leucippos and Democritos need the void in order to give the atoms room to move in. Oddly enough, it did not occur to them that there might be mediums of varying density, and that consequently the denser might take its place in the less dense by displacing it and thus move without there being a void. The arguments of these ancient philosophers always pose problems within absolute conditions even while rationalizing the relative. Seen from our vantage point, it can be said that they often had astonishing intuitions foretelling what modern science was later to clarify. But isn't our science the direct progeny of these premises as they were laid down by Zeno, Leucippos, and Democritos? Identical principles have identical consequences. When the ancients said that nothing becomes and that nothing is lost because all is but a game of particles combining and breaking up, they were asserting what Lavoisier maintained later on. The only difference is that the ancients based themselves on reasoning, Lavoisier on experiment.

Around 500 B.C., while admitting the necessity of a supreme intelligence to bring order into all things, *Anaxagoras of Clazomenae* already gave a mechanical explanation of the world. He saw it as

[46]Principal extracts from the doctrines of Democritos by Lange, in L. Mabilleau, ibid.

[47]Mullach, *Fragmenta Philosophorum Graecorum*, in L. Mabilleau, ibid., p. 80.

[48]L. Mabilleau, ibid., p. 184.

animated by soul as prime mover, triggering a series of mechanical effects:

> . . . for all things being intermingled, Mind supervened and arranged them all in separating them. The material principles are infinite in number and at the same time of infinite smallness.[49]
>
> The Greeks are wrong to recognize coming-into-being and perishing; for nothing comes into being or perishes, but rather mingles or separates from things that are. Thus they would be right to say "composing" rather than "becoming" and "decomposing" rather than "perishing."[50]

It is of little importance whether or not Anaxagoras influenced Democritos: All that matters is to emphasize that the atomist school eliminates a prime-mover intelligence as a kind of useless gear. *The universal mechanism* alone survives, ruled by *the law of necessity*. Isn't this the thesis upheld by Laplace at a time when our science, thanks once again to experimentation, demonstrated the marvelous arrangement of the "world system"?

Does progress consist in the experimental demonstration of what reason affirms as having logical existence? Do not syllogistic logic and experience share the same domain?

But it is the experimental demonstration of what syllogistic logic leaves unexplained that makes for access to the world of the true sacred science: *the incorporeal becoming corporeal.*

What can be reached through reasoning was reached by Leucippos and Democritos: a materalistic explanation of the universal phenomenon from which all mystery has been banished. Faith in a supranatural state or Being is replaced by ratiocination, with a consequent influence on the moral position.

Two paths are thenceforth available: either continued dialectical dispute in the exploitation of the masters' arguments, or a reaction against this materialistic option, a process which is indeed sketched out by Socrates, Plato, and Aristotle, who nourished the entire Christian Middle Ages and partially influenced Western thinking until the nineteenth century.

In this Greek period of the Eleatics and the Ionians, the search for truth employs reasoning that is often specious, sometimes magnifi-

---

[49]Philosophum, 8 (Diels, 384-385), in P. Tanngery, op. cit., p. 306. The material principles of infinite smallness are called *homoeomeries* by Theophrastos, who gives as examples water, fire, and gold, which are not engendered or perishable. (Simplicios in *Physics*, 6b.)

[50]Frag. 17 in P. Tannery, op. cit., p. 312.

cent. Seen as a whole, it is disquieting to compare this Occidental phase with the brilliant clarity of Buddhist thought in India and of Chinese Taoism shortly before the sixth century B.C. These philosophies, of course, are classified as "Eastern thinking" and, along with Pharaonic modes of thought, are referred to with a certain disdain by the scientific nineteenth century. But the three masters, Socrates, Plato, and Aristotle, assert faith in a divine principle, a "logical absurdity" which relates them to Oriental thought, although without reaching the conclusions that would permit them to avoid the deviation. Buddhism accepts several paths, including one which is apparently atheistic, but it does not fall into the error of a purely mechanistic rationalism. Lao-tse remains pure, bestows no name, and in a few words establishes the One and the multiplicity which springs from the One. In the search for sanctity or wisdom, the righteous path follows Nature, as every action evokes its reaction. Whatever the criticism raised against these Oriental doctrines, it must be admitted that they offer the solidity of a healthy moral basis. True, they never led to an era of glorious domination of the mind, an achievement that now seems to bring us back to Babel.

Returning from this easterly digression to the examination of our Western sources, we see that after the atomists, toward the end of the fifth century B.C., Athens was teeming with "professors of knowledge" or *Sophists*, usually paid to instruct the city's youth in rhetoric. Brilliant eloquence became the aim of master and student alike.

Plato and Aristotle despised the Sophists, accusing them of diverting dialectics from its true aim: the *good* and the *true;* of misusing it for personal ends, for power or fortune; of lying to achieve their aims. Indeed, the Sophists managed to maintain that truth is *relative* to the argument which sustains it, and that nothing is *absolutely* true. The search, therefore, is for "relative truth," for likelihood, or even for error—if it can be useful.

Two personalities stand out in that period: From the teachings of the *Ionian school,* Protagoras of Abdera draws the consequences of placing all faith in appearances as revealed by the senses, and therefore concluding with the relativity of ideas. Gorgias of Leontini, in Sicily, substitutes the *relative* for the absolute, and somewhat resembles Zeno of Elea in the form of his arguments which invalidate the truths of reason and reduce everything to appearances.

During this amoral and skeptical period when belief in God the eternal Provider was abolished, there came the successive arrivals of Socrates (468-400), Plato (430-347), and Aristotle (384-322).

Yet the facility of reason was soon to gain dominance over these teachings which still allow for the existence of an irrational moment. Epicuros takes up the ideas of atomism and formulates a law of conduct whose later application no longer conforms rigorously to the philosopher's ideas. A master's teaching must indeed be distinguished from the deviation his thinking undergoes when applied by the multitude. As a rule, the latter chooses what best corresponds to its mental sloth and its appetites. Thus the life of Epicuros has nothing in common with what "Epicureanism" eventually became.

Epicuros (342-270), in fact, lived according to what he taught his disciples. He showed his virtue through his gratitude and piety toward his parents, his benevolence toward all, his honesty, and frugality. He was satisfied with some bread and water; when, tormented by cruel pains at the end of his life, he courageously bore his final sickness, called himself perfectly happy and exhorted his friends to follow his precepts: frugality, peace of mind, and the refusal of all excess and agitation (cf. *Letter to Menaceus*).

For a better understanding of Epicurean morality, it must be kept in mind that Epicuros' immediate predecessor, Pyrrho (367?-275 B.C.), disciple of the Megarian school, taught the philosophy of *universal incertitude,* which envisioned everything from two contrary points of view: nothing affirmed, nothing contradicted. His wisdom consists in a suspended judgment between good and evil, justice and injustice. This results, for the conduct of life, in a kind of indifference or imperturbability, an *ataraxia* dictated by the impossibility of judging, and the acceptance of whatever happens, be it good or bad. This is reminiscent of Taoism, but Epicuros does not draw the same wise conclusions as Eastern philosophy, for along with his teachings on *ataraxia,* he postulates sensation as our only source of knowledge, and the materialistic system of atomism as the only reality.

The doctrine of Epicuros has been mainly transmitted by Lucretius (95-53 B.C.) in Latin, as most of Epicuros' Greek writings were destroyed at Herculaneum at the time of the eruption of Vesuvius in A.D. 79. In his *De rerum natura,*[51] Lucretius devotes the first two books to the atomic theory and the third to negation of the immortality of the soul.

Our starting point will be this principle: Nothing is ever divinely generated from nothing. [I, 150]

[51]Lucretius, *The Nature of the Universe.* Tr. after Watson.

Moreover, nature resolves each thing into its constituent elements, but does not reduce any thing to nothing. [I, 215]

Besides, whatsoever an existing object may be in itself, it will either act of its own accord, or undergo the action of other things upon it.... [I, 440]

Concerning the atom:

Since there is an extreme point [moment] in this elementary body which our senses are no longer able to perceive, that undoubtedly is without parts, and reaches the smallest degree of substance.... [I, 600]

...When the atoms are traveling downwards by their own weight in a straight line through the void, at quite indeterminate times and places, they swerve ever so little from their course, just so much as might be called the least *swerve*. If it were not for this *swerve,* they would all fall downwards like raindrops through the abyss of the void. No *collision* would occur, no shock would be produced, and thus nature would never have produced anything. [II, 220]

This invention of a *swerve* in the fall of particles is strange, and with Epicuros replaces the *affinities* he confused with free will (II, 285).

But the void can offer no resistance to anything anywhere at any time, but it must give way continually as its nature demands. Therefore, all through the unresisting void, all atoms must travel at equal speed despite the inequality of their weight. [II, 235]

Here Epicuros anticipates Galileo, and logic anticipates experiment. Then again comes an affirmation with regard to the mass of matter: *"Nothing is ever added to it nor is any diminution made from it"* (II, 295).

After having explained the variety of the atom's shapes as hooked or smooth and round, or as fluid, liquid, or rough in nature, and their varieties of combinations which define the properties of the composite bodies that stem from them, Lucretius writes:

Nature, therefore, changes all kinds of food into living bodies, and produces all senses of animate creatures.... So do you now understand that it is of great importance in what order the various atoms are arranged and with what others they are combined so as to impart and receive impulses?

But what is it, then, that strikes your mind, that puts it on guard and compels it to express diverse opinions, preventing you from believing that the sentient is generated by the insentient? [II, 880-885]

"By virtue of the arrangement of atoms, Nature transforms all foods into living bodies"; this kind of thinking continues to circle a problem stubbornly left unresolved because life cannot be explained mechanically. Life escapes equational logic; through man, it can even realize means that go against or beyond Nature.

Lucretius maintains that sensitivity refers to the soul, and the soul is extinguished at death. He asserts the existence of the plurality of worlds in an infinite universe and again confirms that all this happens without the intervention of the gods.

> Bear these well-known truths in mind, and you will immediately perceive that Nature is free, uncontrolled by proud masters, to accomplish everything by itself, spontaneously, without the participation of the gods. [II, 1090]

Book III is entirely dedicated to demonstrating that the soul is formed of extremely fine material atoms which dissolve at death. Thus the soul's immortality is denied and legends of infernal punishment are dismissed.

The device of a *swerve* in the fall of atoms or the notion of an ordering faculty in the shapes of these atoms without the slightest indication whence these shapes derive, all this seems fairly ill-conceived and poorly grounded. The principle of *ataraxia* is an expression of laziness rather than of wisdom. Down through the ages, investigations by materialist philosophers are characterized by a constant endeavor to eradicate the irrational moment from life and from natural phenomena; this abstract moment, incomprehensible to human intelligence, *which yet imposes itself on intuition.* As they always proved to be flawed, these explanations became wearying and resulted in a kind of resignation that became the stance of the Stoics. Their champion was Zeno of Citium, who lived from 362 to 260 B.C., which is about two hundred years before the precessional transition from the vernal point of the sign of Aries to that of Pisces.

In the Stoic pursuit of freedom, we find a curious similarity to the ideal of the revolutionaries of 1789, a revolution which was also situated about two centuries before the new precessional transition of the vernal point from the sign of Pisces to that of Aquarius. This brings to mind a similar great revolution which took place at the end of the Old Empire of the Pharaohs, about 2400 B.C., two centuries before the passage of the vernal point of the sign of Taurus into that of Aries.

In promulgating Stoicism (or the philosophy of the Porch), Zeno of Citium lent a certain solidity to his doctrine through the austerity of his habits, which was legendary in his own day. In his own conduct, he afforded to all a pattern for imitation in perfect consistency with his teaching.

Denying the abstraction of divine Intelligence such as taught by Plato or Aristotle, the only god recognized by the Stoics was *Reason* as immanent in phenomena and in destiny, which is cosmic law. The only reality they recognized was action, the manifestation of power pervading Nature and humanity.

The Stoics reproached Plato and Aristotle with limiting moral individuality; for them it was a matter of considering Man rather than the citizen, and Humanity instead of the city-state.

"I am a citizen of the universe," said Cicero, thus proclaiming no longer a narrow national interest but the idea of a cosmopolitanism common to all Stoics.

By means of the will, the Stoics sought the self-control that would render them independent of exterior forces and bring true freedom. But two different cases must be distinguished: those in which human will power can intervene and direct the activity in one direction or another (good and evil), and those which do not depend on human will, such as destiny, life, sickness, or infirmity. In the latter cases, the ills must be considered as affecting the body but not the will, which remains entirely free for man. If the wise man understands the necessary reason for things, he must merge his own volition with that of the Whole and cease to be enslaved: necessity understood and willed is true freedom.

Thinkers have always been tempted by this doctrine of submission to natural law, which we call "necessity." When Lao-tse calls this wisdom "nonvolition," it is said to mean *understood and willed* necessity.... Yet no contradiction is involved: In order to accept this attitude, a decision must certainly be taken. But must one not be already a sage in order to follow this doctrine? Otherwise, the latter would seem to be calling for a state of indifference, which is not wisdom but laziness. This has its echo in "Allah will take care..." or "God will provide..." As far as the vast majority is concerned, to trace a purely logico-philosophical path is to install a reign of egotism. They require an exemplary model, because words without images are reserved for those already conscious and capable of discernment.

Marcus Aurelius said:

Everything harmonizes with me which is harmonious to thee, O Cosmos!
Nothing for me is too early or too late which is in due time for thee. Everything

is fruit to me which thy seasons bring, O Nature: from thee are all things, in thee
are all things, to thee all things return.[52]

There is something sublime about this doctrine that preaches
independence and freedom through a merging with universal
necessity. Stoicism bred Roman jurisprudence, which was based on the
rights of *liberty* and *fraternity,* on the sense of justice and human
dignity that condemns all tyrannies, all servitudes, both civil and
political, and of course, slavery. In 1789 in France, this was called
equality, although in this case, the concept resulted from a revolt
against the abuses of the aristocracy.

Pushing his theories to the extreme, the Stoic considered suicide
not as an act of cowardice but as an affirmation of individual will
through free choice of life or death.

To sum up, in a troubled age of increasing corruption, Epicuros and Zeno
each posed to themselves the great problem which came to overshadow all other
things: "Where does goodness reside? And they both understood that the true
good must be in deliverance, in freedom.

But. . .

. . . . it is always a physical or logical freedom rather than the ideal of a truly
moral freedom.[53]

Rome was the capital of that world in which Epicureanism and
Stoicism reigned, a world driven to resignation by the futility of all
these dialectical searches for truth. This decadent world unconsciously
summoned up a directive responding to this call for fraternity
(cosmopolitanism?) and for the moral freedom which an inhumane
theory of rational freedom alone could never satisfy.

It was Christian soteriology that responded. A profound as well
as extremely subtle reason makes the Christian doctrine one of salvation. Something like the Islamic image of the "bridge of Sirah" can
be evoked here: The soul of the deceased must cross this bridge
separating salvation from damnation, a bridge no wider than a razor's
edge.

All philosophical arguments have resulted in the conclusion that
man can only find peace within himself and through his unwilled and

---

[52]*The Meditations,* tr. G. Long.

[53]A. Fouillée, *Histoire de la philosophie* (Paris, 1924), pp. 155-156.

conscious acceptance of the natural course of events. Thus the irritating problem of an irrational God has been eliminated and thus the history of God's human incarnation came to be taught. The problem of God is no longer irrational: The doctrine of Anthropocosmos presents cosmic man as well as universe incarnate in man. This ancient Pharaonic teaching now presented historically, hence concretely, will respond to both the demands of reason and the moral demands of humanity. The teaching of the apostles is suprahuman history, while at the same time pertaining to actual man. This is the answer to all anxieties and a good path from all points of view. The humanized myth of Olympus is eradicated and replaced by the historic fact of a suprahuman being.[54]

There is a single flaw characteristic of the Christian doctrine, with regard to human egotism and vanity: It poses its teaching as an article of faith but seemingly explains nothing concerning the history or "evolution" of the world. And from the first centuries on, controversy again arose in Byzantium regarding the nuances of a doctrine such as the Trinity; then in the West, from the ninth century on, there was argument concerning proofs of the existence of God. Since belief is necessary, does God then really exist? One does not doubt, one no longer dares to doubt the divine Christic incarnation, and so. . . how to prove God's existence? Obviously a ridiculous problem, but on the other hand, one believes in atoms as well, absurd though they be. Intellectualism—the Devil's laboratory—always feels obliged to imitate, if only by comprehension, the phenomenon of creation. This was the ambition of the fallen archangel. How could there be good without there being evil? To suppress one of the world's apparent poles would be to suppress the world altogether.

Having situated the origin of the great deviation toward materialism, this book does not aim at retracing the entire history of Western thought. Since the beginnings of Christianity, Platonic and Pythagorean schools were seen to flower once again, while Stoicism suffered a definite collapse. Following the schism created during the Council of Nicaea, the Christian religion, based on Apostolic and Roman Catholicism, established itself ever more firmly.

Then came the epoch when Islam, enriched by the works of the library at Alexandria (which influenced such Persian converts as Avicenna, Musa al-Khwarazmi, and Ibn Jabir), installed itself in Spain

---

[54]When speaking of myth, we will return to the characteristics of Christian doctrine.

with the last of the Umayyads and instructed many great men of the Middle Ages at the University of Córdoba. For it was the scholars of Islam who translated and commented upon the Greek writers whose doctrines were retransmitted to the Christians by Jews coming from Spain (e.g., Maimonides). It was in this way that the physics, metaphysics, and ethics of Aristotle, for example, penetrated into the West.

Albertus Magnus and Thomas Aquinas, both Dominicans, Saint Bonaventura, Roger Bacon—brutally persecuted by the Church—and Ramon Lulle, among others, were the great figures of that time. It is with them, and with Arnaud de Villeneuve, that the Hermetic doctrine was spread in the West. Sacred science could have fought against the deviation of the human spirit, were it not that its preservation is possible only through a temple-organization which selects men according to their moral qualities and their spiritual gifts. The seekers instructed at Córdoba in the science of *al-Kemit*[55]—whence *alchemy* derived its name—were not regarded very kindly by the Church: Arnaud de Villeneuve, recalled to Rome by the Pope in 1313, having taken a boat for this voyage from what is now known as the Riviera, preferred never to arrive. On the other hand, Master Albertus Magnus founded the first university at Paris, leaving his name to the Place Maubert in the Latin Quarter. The secret science of alchemy produced quite a few adepts (masters having total knowledge of this science), but countless clandestine seekers were disillusioned.

In the meantime, atomism continued to smolder like fire under the ashes. It would serve as a lifebuoy for disillusioned alchemists who no more understood the esoterism of Hermetic philosophy than the teaching of the Gospels.

In sum, it was Islam, particularly the Islam of the Maghreb and then later some of the Crusaders, who made the link between the Near East and the West. With the conversion of the Persians to Islam, knowledge originating in India, China, and Babylon came to be joined to the science drawn from Alexandria. What the Pharaonic temple had bequeathed to the world, however, was already deformed.

We may question the burning of the famous library at Alexandria, but not the looting and destruction of the library at the University of Córdoba after the Christian conquest of Islam in Spain. Destruction and the worst collective crimes have always been committed by

---

[55]*Kemit* is a name for ancient Egypt, referring to the fertilizing black silt deposited by the Nile's flooding. *Km* means "black" as well as "to complete, to accomplish" (in German, *vollenden, vollständig machen*), and *Km.t* means "the Black," Egypt.

humanity in the name of faith. Everyone is convinced that he possesses the only truth, but the great truth is accorded only to very rare men devoid of prejudice, exemplary in honesty and discretion. For truth at that level brings with it also a power not intended for everyone. We see today what evil has resulted from the vulgarization of ordinary knowledge, divulged under the aegis of a "liberal" orientation.

For want of alchemy, we now have chemistry and nothing else. Practical experiment replaces dialectics. Their real or symbolical meaning being inapplicable to this science, the terms of the Hermetic doctrine, having survived, are now searched for some positive significance.

Returning to the old formulas of the Greek philosophers, it could be declared that "nothing is created, nothing gets lost," and therein materialism found the proof of its affirmations. And so began the scientific era of the nineteenth century, supremely confident in its assertions. There also began the extraordinary flowering of scholars in the domain of the natural sciences as well as in medicine and chemistry. Following the admirable studies of Lamarck and Darwin, a theory of evolution was elaborated. Until the end of the nineteenth century, with its atomism and its mechanistic spirit, science considered itself to be all-powerful and, of course, justified in its atheism.[56]

The first doubts concerning Lavoisier's assertion, and therewith the first reaction against the doctrine of the immutability of matter, were cast by Henri Becquerel's discovery (the first observed effect of radioactivity) and Roentgen's X-rays. From that moment on, a flurry of discoveries gathered momentum toward conception in energetic terms of the preposterous material atom of the past. The Curies isolated the radioactive body called radium from pitchblende (oxide of uranium), and observed that the energy emitted is triple in nature and produces a new body called "emanation." Transmutation is thereby no longer a fantasy but a scientifically demonstrated fact.

But to say that the alchemists' dream has finally been realized is mere fantasy indeed, for there is no correspondence in contemporary science with what tradition expounds. Hermetic transmutation has absolutely nothing in common with the artificial and brutal effects produced by our modern physicist-chemists. Serious study of the texts of adepts (and not mere superficial reading) will confirm that fact. The results of modern science are the results of mechanical technique and not of genesis. There is no transition between false and true, between good and evil: It is all one or all the other.

[56]See Appendix II.

It might come as a surprise to the imagination of so-called occultists if I say that Albert Einstein perfectly exemplifies a master of black magic; a man of exceptional intelligence, selfless, good, human, musical, sensitive—and the first to deplore the evil that science wrought of his discovery. Yet his science served the search for a unitary formula.

Attempts have been made to relate the principles of unity of Pharaonic theology with this unitary principle as well as with the "point of the universe" which French scholarship has recently proclaimed. This is equally erroneous: Absolute Unity, *the Neter of Neters,* is an abstraction which can be proved but not understood, and the "universal point" is a definition, a complex, energetic body. Modern science, for all its brains, cannot escape from this vicious circle formulated by atomism and which has even tainted our biology: The great Pasteur (indeed humanity's benefactor) repudiates "spontaneous generation." Certainly there is no spontaneous generation if one wishes to consider it a chance occurrence, an unmotivated action. But if it is understood as a phenomenon resulting from an harmonic set of cosmic energetic influences, then one must accept it and search for its laws.

Today it is possible to suggest the following new orientation:

Is there a way to consider matter other than through the principle of atomism? Isn't it simply a convenient hypothesis? In reality, isn't it *the mass that comes into play,* besides the four qualities? Mass cannot be dissociated from density. What is the meaning of density? The quantity in a given volume. Is this a quantity of *atoms* or a "magnetic" quantity?

We are always dealing with two tendencies—two magnetic energies, attractive and repulsive; and two electric energies, likewise attractive and repulsive. Isn't the attraction the same, namely, magnetic, and isn't the repulsion always the same, namely, electronic? Hence two energies; the one attracts to itself, the other causes flight. The one that attracts carries weight. Are these not the same forces which, in physiology, make for the sympathetic and the parasympathetic nervous systems?

We know the magnetic effects in a mechanical fashion as reaction to an electric circuit and, inversely, we know an electric reaction around a magnetic effect. But here we are always dealing with bodies carrying mechanical or chemical energy and not with the energy itself. This dual energy must exist in the universe independently of any carrier, and realize bodily form through its junction.

This may be difficult to comprehend, but posed as "hypothesis," it would be much more fertile than the hypothesis of the material atom and could open the door to a science which would be vital and no longer inhuman.

It is foolish to explore materialism for a solution to the essential problem, which, in one guise or another, is always the problem of the existence of God. When an abstraction is involved, thesis and antithesis cannot become synthesis. The universe itself is entirely proof of God's existence, or else it is a composite of invariable elements; these are the only possible positions, but there are different ways of understanding the meaning of the word "God." This notion is arrived at either through pure and simple affirmation by posing God as origin, or as a conclusion drawn from a complete analysis of all we know concerning matter.

Though the atomist theory has a semblance of logic, it is actually pure fiction. Nevertheless, the absurd supposition of an indivisible portion of matter held sway for many centuries because it satisfies a mechanistic mentality. It took the discovery of radioactivity and its consequences in order to arrive at the understanding that with the end of the bodily form there comes the beginning of a new, purely energetic state. Although a compound state, this is still called an *atom* for the sake of convenience.

It is true that three principles dominate this primitive compound, and this first entity indeed carries two aspects of energy in action. To proceed with an investigation in the spirit of these premises would obviously lead toward the philosophic aspect of the problem, toward a metaphysical concept of origin. Rather than follow through in this direction, a warped mentality now demands a definition that will answer to the needs of the premises of physics, and thus it is the ultimate state called the "universal point" that seems to bring the solution.[57] But this means an atomic concept which defines the first state of matter as a volume. This satisfies all the analyses and suppositions of a science reluctant to abandon a material foundation, but gives no real solution to the problems of knowledge concerning matter and its becoming.

To think quantitatively about atoms—such is the gospel of that inhuman science beginning with Leucippos and Democritos; it is a desperate solution which lacks awareness of the principle of sacerdotal science. For the opposing point of view, there is Spirit or energy

[57]In this context, it would seem that the intuitive ideas of Henry Fairfield Osborn merit greater attention than they have received. See in particular the Preface to his *Origin and Evolution of Life* (New York, 1918).

without material support, and there is matter as an effect of the simultaneity of this energy which divides into complementaries and constitutes a proportion: such is the gospel of sacred science.

Atomism unavoidably leads science toward an inhuman concept of the universe with all the moral—or rather, *amoral*—consequences this entails. In offering a seductive richness of creature comforts, this applied science eliminates man's endeavor; mechanized, industrialized society makes humanity into a conglomerate of human atoms, particles devoid of any individual value.

3

Man

After the belief had been put to rest that God fashioned man from the clay of the earth, there was increasing preoccupation with regard to his origin; discoveries of bone remains and subsisting traces of human industry and art were the bases of the search. It rapidly became evident that the history of man cannot be dissociated from geological history. Lately, the study of genetics as well has been understood as a necessary factor.

Man appears on earth as do the geological strata, as plants and animals are born to it. Despite serious study, the problem of man's becoming has received no satisfactory answer. The nineteenth century believed that a rational concatenation could lead by transformism from earthworm to man. The folly of a materialistic evolution—like that of many other illusions—had to be admitted. For a long time, the current hypotheses were based on discoveries, in Java and in the Neanderthal valley, of bone remains that had belonged to beings intermediate between ape and man, or, more precisely, beings still closely related to the ape. The age of both *Pithecanthropus* and *Palaeoanthropus* was at that time estimated solely according to geological strata and the fauna they contained. The first-named accordingly belonged to the beginning of the Quaternary and the second to the mid-Pleistocene. But estimates of the dates of these strata varied considerably, particularly when they concerned the distant past. Thus the end of the Tertiary could date back from 100,000 or 150,000 years (Warren Upham) to 1,620,000 years (L. Pilgrim), to cite but the extremes. It is upon such vague ground that the age of man was estimated.

The latest discoveries in nuclear physics endow geology with several means for dating: *the strontium method* has permitted evaluation of the age of the oldest formations, those which go back more than three billion years; *methods using lead* (uranium, etc.) reveal the age of nonsedimentary rock between the Precambrian period and the Tertiary era, which began seventy million years ago; *the method based on isotopic relationships* pertains to marine sediments; and lastly, *the radioactive carbon-14 dating method* makes it possible to estimate the age of organic substances, but the latter procedure cannot date back further than 30,000 years, and therefore concerns only our immediate prehistory.[1]

It has therefore been possible to determine the beginning of the Quarternary sequence at approximately one million years ago, but it is precisely the chronology of that era, the era of man, which even today is most difficult to establish. For the moment, at least, we must therefore continue to refer to the "relative chronology" based principally on stratigraphy, the speed of erosion and sedimentation, the ice ages, the fauna, and the nature of the tools fabricated by man.

An astronomical method for situating the great glacial phases in time has recently been studied by Milankovitch. This method is based on periodic variations in the terrestrial orbit's eccentricity, in the obliquity of the ecliptic and in the displacement of the perihelion, as well as on considerations regarding the precession of the equinoxes. Charts of the variations in summer radiations for a given latitude show a striking similarity to the curves of glacial periods as defined by geologists. Based on these data, the earliest industries of worked flint in the Maghreb and in Europe, as well as a mandible of human aspect, were dated as pertaining to the lower Paleolithic, that is, approximately 600,000 years ago. *Pithecanthropus erectus* of Trinil and *Sinanthropus* of Peking were situated in the middle Pleistocene, and specimens of the Neanderthal type in Mousterian deposts (from 70,000 to 120,000 years ago?); but a large gap existed in these data, and doubt remained as to the degree of evolution that could be attributed to these all-too-rare specimens of an eventual and highly debated transition from animal to man.

It will be recalled that the famous discovery of the *Pithecanthropus* of Trinil in Java consisted solely of a skullcap, two teeth, and a femur. During the course of a year's excavations, these elements were found fifteen meters apart in a layer of ashes and tufa at the base of a volcano. The cranium, with its receding forehead, its enormous brow ridges, visor-shaped as with the gibbons, was far more simian than human, as were the teeth. In contrast, the femora testified to an

---

[1]The radiocarbon method has not proved reliable in all cases.

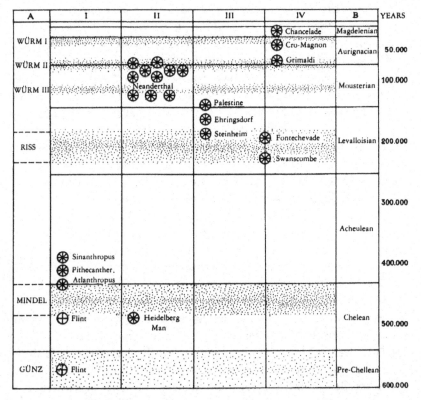

A	I	II	III	IV	B	YEARS
WÜRM I				✳ Chancelade	Magdelenian	
				✳ Cro-Magnon	Aurignacian	50.000
WÜRM II		✳✳✳✳✳		✳ Grimaldi		
		✳✳✳				100.000
WÜRM III		✳ Neanderthal ✳ ✳			Mousterian	
			✳ Palestine			
			✳ Ehringsdorf			
RISS			✳ Steinheim	✳ Fontechevade	Levalloisian	200.000
				✳ Swanscombe		
						300.000
					Acheulean	
	✳ Sinanthropus					400.000
	✳ Pithecanther.					
	✳ Atlanthropus					
MINDEL						
	⊕ Flint	✳ Heidelberg Man			Chelean	500.000
GÜNZ	⊕ Flint				Pre-Chellean	
						600.000

Fig. 2. *Synoptic Table of the Principle Types of Prehistoric Men.*
A. *Geological classification* of the Pleistocene by the great glacial periods: Würm, Riss, Mindel, and Günz.
B. *Archeological classification* based on variations in the working of flint.
I. *Archanthropians* of the Pithecanthropus type.
II. *Paleanthropians* of the Neanderthal type.
III. *Paleanthropians* presenting characteristics intermediary between Neanderthals and *Homo sapiens.*
IV. *Neanderthaloids* or *Homo sapiens* as well as two clearly Presapien types: Fontechevade and Swanscombe.
The dates, which are very approximate, are those of classical stratigraphy. This table aims only to show that the *Pithecanthropus-Neanderthal-Presapiens-Homo sapiens* filiation is impossible according to the geological strata revealing the age of the individuals.

upright walk. Had it been found alone, there would have been no hesitation in attributing it to a human being; "Such are the facts. If we possessed only the skull and the teeth, we should say that we were dealing with a great ape; if we had the femora alone, we should say that we were dealing with a man."[2]

Understandably, these debatable elements sparked many a passionate discussion between partisans and opponents of the transformist theory. For the former, the findings represented the *link* between ape and man; for the latter, no more than a giant form of ape. There is no objection to this latter hypothesis, as giant forms of animals did exist in this period, such as the giant pangolin which was found in the same geological strata as *Pithecanthropus* of Trinil.

Between 1929 and 1939, in the grotto of Choukoutien near Peking, the fossil remains of about forty individuals were found. Study of these *Sinanthropus* skulls revealed a close resemblance between these fossils and *Pithecanthropus* of Java, but while no utensils were found in deposits containing the latter vestiges, the grotto containing *Sinanthropus* yielded worked stones indicative of industry, as well as ashpits implying the use of fire. *Sinanthropus* provided proof of the only true distinction between animal and man: reason and intelligence, which incited these beings to fabricate tools and to make fire.

Thus both *Sinanthropus* and *Pithecanthropus* of Trinil were admitted at once to the family of *Hominidae*, despite certain very simian characteristics which had previously caused the foremost of ethnologists to hesitate in recognizing these beings as truly human.

Shortly thereafter (1939-1941), a Dutch geologist, von Koenigswald, made a new find in Java of pithecanthropines whose skulls and teeth, however, belonged to two subjects that were of greater height than any known human being or anthropoid. The smaller of the two was called *Pithecanthropus robustus* and the larger, *Meganthropus*. Sold among the remedies in Chinese pharmacies are "dragon's teeth" which often turn out to be fossil teeth. While browsing in such a place in Hong Kong, the same geologist discovered three large molars, even larger than those of *Meganthropus*.[3] The question was then raised: Given the great kinship of these giant teeth with those of a man, have we to do here with a *Gigantopithecus*, or rather with a *Giganthropus?*

There was then but one step to the thesis that man descended from a race of giants—as certain legends affirm—and some of the

---

[2]Marcellin Boule, *Les hommes fossiles* (Paris, 1921), p. 104.

[3]In 1956, new discoveries were made of giant jaws and numerous specimens of these teeth.

most eminent anthropologists did not hesitate to take it. Unfortunately, paleontology teaches that forms evolve in the inverse direction, from a relatively small size toward the definitive size; giant forms more generally signal *the end of a race near extinction.*

The view of descent from a giant apeman thus had to be abandoned. Would it not be possible, then, that our ancestors belonged to a race of which Pygmies would be the last representatives? Although this hypothesis more accurately conforms to evolutionary data, it was in turn excluded. And as there was refusal, furthermore, to see *Gigantopithecus, Meganthropus, Pithecanthropus robustus,* and *Pithecanthropus* of Trinil as the ancestral lineage of *Homo sapiens,* the problem remained intact.

The probability nevertheless persisted that in the beginnings of the Quaternary, there existed beings showing great morphological similarities to certain apes, but which could be considered *human* because they gave proof of intelligence through their handiwork; there also existed giant apes showing great morphological affinities with man, at least in the arrangement of their teeth. Verification of this last point, however, depended on the finding of at least several complete skeletons.

The preceding hypotheses were soon confirmed by two discoveries:

1. The discovery of *Atlanthropus,* represented by a number of fossil bones with human characteristics found in a deposit which contained tools of the Chelleo-Acheulean bifacial flaking technique and archaic fauna characteristic of the Lower Paleolithic. The conclusion was drawn that these fossil remains at Ternifine (Algeria) were the artisans of these pieces flaked according to the most ancient system known. They could be classified along with *Sinanthropus* as *Atlanthropus mauritanicus,* among the earliest vestiges of beings having engaged in human activity. Between these two species of individuals, however, notable dissimilarities were brought out, in form as well as in culture.[4]

2. The discovery of specimens of *Australopithecus* in South Africa, characterized by a biped walk, almost perfectly erect posture, and certain human traits, but still not to be considered anything but apes living in a countryside which was probably dry and desertlike.[5]

[4]Discoveries made in 1954 by M.C. Arambourg in the Ternifine deposits along with numerous other animal vestiges considered possible to situate in the early Quaternary. See J. Piveteau, *Traité de paléontologie* (Paris, 1957), p. 391.

[5]Discoveries made in the Transvaal between 1925 and 1952. See J. Piveteau, ibid., p. 288.

Thus one fundamental point is established: During the first half of the Quaternary, there existed beings strongly resembling apes and men, and presenting morphological characteristics common to both apes and men, so that a common stock would seem to be implied. It is impossible, however, to consider *Australopithecus,* still animal and of too-recent geological age, as a direct ancestor of *Pithecanthropus* or *Archanthropus.*[6]

Proof therefore now exists to the effect that man does not descend from the great anthropomorphic tree-dwelling apes, nor from the bipedal *Australopithecus.* Man and ape form two distinct branches, well characterized by their mores, their evolutionary mode, and above all by the presence in the former of an intelligence which is lacking in the other. But when and how does this moral sense and this intelligence appear? Until recently, it was only in the vestiges of a much more recent age that one could begin to recognize human beings closer to our direct ancestors; even at that, they could at most be said to have been closer to such possible ancestry only because *Neanderthal man,* who dates no further back then the Mousterian, in turn became surrounded by violent controversy. This is understandable for anyone who knows him by description.

"Neanderthal man" is a term which encompasses a great mass of documentation and owes its name to a site in East Prussia where a very simian skullcap was found. Later discoveries provided a large number of jaws, skulls, and skeletons belonging to the same type; the most complete skeletons are those found at La Chapelle-aux-Saints in 1908. In a deposit containing much worked flint of the Mousterian type as well as animal bones from the age of the mammoth, there were found remains of a skeleton *buried in a trench which appeared to have been intentionally dug for that purpose.* The considerable dimensions of the flattened cranium with enormous brow ridges, a sharply receding forehead, an elongated, forward-jutting head, a massive jaw, and a rudimentary chin—all show that this Neanderthal man presented certain characteristics of the chimpanzee. The arrangement of the teeth, however, is clearly human and the front nasal suture particularly so through the deep hollow at the base of the nose. If, in its details, the rest of the skeleton presents some resemblance to certain ape bones, the relative proportion of the limbs is definitely human. So is the relative brain capacity, casts of which show great simplicity in

<hr>

[6]See the demonstration of this impossibility in J. Piveteau, ibid., pp. 287 and 314.

convolution, however. Still, on the whole, the relation of these remains to anthropomorphic apes should not be exaggerated.

One disturbing fact remains: *This subject had been intentionally buried,* an act of ritual significance. It must be concluded, therefore, that in that region there existed an achieved man, a thinking man with a metaphysical concept of another life.

> The grave contained flint worked with remarkable skill, splinters of rock crystal and fragments of ferruginous sandstone. Close to the skeleton's feet...was found a black flint scraper....Near the hand was found a bovine hoof, its elements still connected, evidence of its having been placed there with the flesh intact and intended as nourishment, positioned within easy reach of the deceased, who was insufficiently disengaged from humanity to be able to go without food.[7]

Nevertheless, Neanderthal man differs completely from all human races, even the most primitive now existing; nor can he be compared to types very close to our present races, types which almost immediately succeed him: the *Grimaldi-Negroid* going back to the beginning of the Aurignacian, the *Cro-Magnon* type dating from the Aurignacian, and *Chancelade man.* From a morphological point of view as well as judging by their industry and art, these highly evolved men who almost coexisted with Neanderthal man could be considered his descendants *"only by admitting a mutation so considerable and so sudden as to be absurd."*[8]

Indeed, the Grimaldi-Negroids, dating from an epoch that borders on the Mousterian—and perhaps from the Mousterian itself— seem very likely to have been quite contemporaneous with the Neanderthals who, consequently, cannot be the ancestors of *Homo sapiens* but should be seen as a human offshoot representing rather a degeneration, as their sudden disappearance at the end of the Mousterian would seem to confirm.

It would not be irrelevant here to refer to the first three races known as *Homo sapiens* with which the most ancient specimens of prehistoric Egypt have been associated.[9]

The Negroids of Grimaldi[10] are represented by the skeleton of an aged woman buried side by side in a grave with a youth in fetal position, surrounded with the remains of sea-shell ornaments. The

[7]J. Piveteau, ibid., p. 499.

[8]M. Boule, op. cit.

[9]See Chapter 4, "Chorography of Egypt."

[10]Discovered in the Grotte des Enfants near Menton on the French Riviera. Subjects morphologically related to blacks are called Negroid, but their skin is not necessarily black. Thus the Bushmen are yellow-skinned and famous for the steatopygia of the women and their wavy hair.

very elongated skull is quite high and in volume at least equal to that of a modern Frenchman.[11] These individuals were of short stature (1 m 60 and 1 m 56), and the length of the legs in relation to the thigh, as well as a fairly forward-projecting jaw, cause them to resemble Negroids. On the other hand, certain steatopygous (fat-buttocked) figurines found in neighboring grottoes suggest their ultimate kinship with contemporary Bushmen or Hottentots; the Hottentot race, today completely vanished, is considered as having been composed of men distinctly superior to all African races.[12]

The types attributed to the Cro-Magnon race were, for the most part, buried in an outstretched position in graves and ornamented with necklaces, their bones colored a *bright red*.[13] The masterpieces of carving and painting that adorn their caves are well known.

This race was of great stature (1 m. 80 to 1 m. 90). Their dolichocephalic skull had a high dome and a brain capacity superior to that of a modern European.[14] "The skull presents to a marked degree all the characteristics considered as indications of an intellectual development of the most advanced kind."[15] On the other hand, ethnologists agree in finding an almost identical resemblance between Cro-Magnon and the Guanchos of the Canary Islands where "Verneau discovered modern islanders employing implements such as were once used by the ancient hunters of the Dordogne"[16] Let us note, lastly, that the Cro-Magnon had a fine, elongated nose, while that of the Grimaldi-Negroids was wide.

Chancelade man was very short (1 m 55) and his bones had also been colored with red ocher. The mode of his burial in fetal position, with the left hand placed beneath the head, the right under the left side of the jaw, recalls the treatment of Peruvian mummies.[17] The skull of this individual is dolichocephalic with a high, wide forehead, and "exhibits all the characteristics belonging to the higher races."[18] In

[11]Subdolichocephalic index, 68 and 69; volume, 1,580 and 1,375 cc respectively.

[12]Although the specimans found in the prehistoric sites of Egypt do not have wavy hair, the steatopygous figurines found there are also suggestive of the Bushmen. On the other hand, Asselar man, discovered in the open Sahara, was also very similar to the Hottentots and the Bantu.

[13]All the bone remains found dating from this period are colored red with oxides of iron and with ochers: at Paviland, at Brunn (Moravia), at Obercassel near Bonn, at Chancelade, at Hotaux (Ain), and at Menton. The numerous skeletons at Menton, moreover, were buried in grottoes known as "the Red Rocks."

[14]Cephalic index, 73.7; cranial capacity, 1,590 cc. (The average capacity of a contemporary European is about 1,350 cc.)

[15]A. de Quatrefages, *Hommes fossiles et hommes sauvages* (Paris, 1884), p. 65.

[16]M. Boule, op. cit., p. 291.

[17]In prehistoric Egypt, individuals were also buried in fetal position, but archaeologists make no mention of their bones having been colored red.

[18]Index 72, brain capacity 1,710 cc. See M. Boule, op. cit., p. 292.

sum, the small stature of this individual and the burial mode relates to that of the Eskimos, who are considered to carry on into our own times the Reindeer Age of prehistory. According to other ethnologists, Chancelade man is but a variation of the Cro-Magnon type. One fact is certain: While the first two types present a certain disharmony between their elongated skulls and rather square and large faces, Chancelade man has a "harmonious skull," a long, straight nose, and no prognathism at all. This subject thus bears all the characteristics of an intellectually endowed race, if one were to judge by the cerebral capacity, which far surpasses the mean size exhibited by contemporary Europeans.

A problem then arises, all the more irritating for its lack of rational solution: There was something like a hiatus between Neanderthal man and *Homo sapiens*, since the virtual coexistence had been determined in Europe of a still very primitive type, yet already possessing a certain moral sense, together with human types, related races of which are still found living in our day.

Little by little, discoveries of the highest importance made in Europe, the Middle East, and Africa have brought long-awaited answers:

In the caves of Mount Carmel and near Nazareth, a number of skeletons were found whose morphology presented numerous characteristics which relate them to the Cro-Magnon type: voluminous head, raised cranial dome, and brain capacity comparable to that of contemporary man. All the same, the visorlike brow ridges suggest one of the characteristics of the Neanderthal. It could have been concluded that this was an intermediate race between that primitive being and *Homo sapiens*, but it is nothing of the kind because the Palestine subjects were found in a deposit anterior to the Mousterian and they nevertheless manifest a superior stage of evolution. Therefore the Neanderthals cannot be seen as the ancestors of the Carmel remains but rather, as everything else allows us to suppose, a throwback of a regressive evolution.

Moreover, these facts are supported by different specimens found in Europe: *Swanscombe man,* for example, from the Mindel-Riss interglacial stage or somewhat later; the cast of this specimen's skull reveals *no notable difference from that of a modern man.*[19]

The *Fontechevade* skull, dating from the Riss-Würm interglacial

[19]See J. Piveteau, op. cit., pp. 588-591.

stage, is fairly close to the preceding specimen as far as date and morphology are concerned:

> Each one presents a thick cranial wall; they have the same width at the level of the asterion; their voluminous brain falls within the limits of *Homo sapiens*'s variations. From the absence of protruding eye sockets on the Fontechevade skull, it can be concluded that the same arrangement existed for the Swanscombe skull. . . . [While awaiting new discoveries,] one fact remains very well established: *Homo sapiens* does not derive from the Neanderthal who preceded him; for a long time he constituted a particular or presapiens series, evolving independently of the Neanderthal series. Long disputed, presapien forms are not a myth. They have existed. The few remains that we possess concretely prove the great antiquity of the phylum which culminated in modern man.[20]

Two general questions might well be posed here:

1. Does man appear everywhere on the earth's surface, or in certain particularly predestined places?

2. If the birth of man occurred in places particularly favorable to this phenomenon, was there subsequently only a single lineage or several races or types? In accordance with his geological center, man is still changing to this day, and thus *Homo sapiens* cannot be defined as following an absolute type.

To these questions, paleontology responds that man appeared much later in America, for example, while Indo-Malaysia and Africa are two centers or axes of evolution presenting two distinct lineages. And finally, Palestine and Europe furnish yet another lineage, called presapiens.

The situation of these principal centers of man's appearance brings us close to the esoteric tradition which speaks of the race of *Lemurians,* of a submerged or splintered continent (with Oceania, Indonesia, China, Ceylon, and Madagascar as remnants). There is also the tradition of the race of *Atlantis,* ancient vestiges of which have now been determined in western Africa; a wave of these people, having crossed south Saharan Africa, finally settled in the valley of the Nile (the legend of Gao, on the Niger, the city of a thousand golden domes, would be a souvenir of the passage of this migration).

Actually, man's development can be presented as a sort of fetal gestation determining races which are characterized by the development of certain vital centers, both nervous and sexual. Thus, according to the esoteric tradition, the Lemurians would be a human type still close to the androgyne (as is the fetus at three months) and the

[20]Ibid., p. 597.

Atlantis race, to the contrary, would be typically sexualized, producing large and strong men. The analysis of brain capacities alone does not seem sufficient to studying the development of *Homo sapiens.*

Furthermore, how can the appearance of man be judged on the basis of a few bones, without taking into consideration the various modes of burial, such as we still encounter them today: interment within the earth, cremation with the keeping of ashes, cremation with the dispersal of ashes in the Ganges at Benares, exposure of the corpse to scavenger birds (the Zoroastrian rite of the Parsees). Great efforts are made to preserve the idea of an *ascent* from animal to man, while disregarding the degeneration all things and beings undergo once they no longer receive new energy to maintain themselves. Esoteric doctrine presents the hominoid ape as the result of a cross between animal and human female. Should this be taken as a glib witticism or possible reality? In any case, we encounter infinitely more degeneration than perfection in the living world.

It is also true that climatological variation, be it only of a few degrees, can produce important effects on all life. A drop in temperature drives living beings toward other climates, just as the persistence of a higher temperature will witness the birth of new plant and animal worlds. These climatological modifications obey sidereal variations, and if the principal movements of our solar system are well known, others are less so. Such is the strange influence of celestial regions, such is the power of *Sirius*—that central sun of the Pharaonic sages—upon climates and on our entire solar system.

This very brief exposé of the most accurate findings of present-day [1961] paleontological and anthropological studies shows that the connection between *Pithex, Pithecanthropus,* and thinking *Anthropos* contains gaps impossible to fill with the theory of simple *transformism through heredity and adaptation.*

> As with all great creations of life, the appearance on earth of man, the accomplishment of hominization, bears all the characteristics of an invention.
>
> To sum up, the historical and geographical problem of locating the cradle of humanity certainly exists, and attempts can be made to determine the moment when the human species made its appearance on the globe.
>
> But it must be recognized that true beginnings can never be grasped by paleontology: The origins escape us. Such a gap is usually attributed to a lack of documentation which the luck of a successful excavation could someday complete. Yet here we seem to be in the presence of a fundamental law which nothing escapes that unfolds in the course of time.[21]

[21]J. Piveteau, op. cit., p. 327.

As to the evolution of the species, mysterious jumps occur which physiology and embryology attempt to situate in embryonic evolution by means of the phenomenon of *mutation.*

> It cannot be overly stressed that ontogenesis is the indispensable link between successive generations: It is the phase of active construction which may eventually see the manifestation of *mutations* unexpectedly appearing in the gonads of progenitors, and in the palpitating reality of reproduction, each phase of evolution represents the inscription of an amendment to the laws of development. Whatever be the problem raised by zoology, comparative anatomy, or paleontology, in the final analysis it will have to be reconsidered in terms of embryology. . . . [22] The embryology of vertebrates is one of the best explored. It is a considerable aid in the deductions of comparative anatomy and paleontology through the application of biogenetic law. Occurring in the domain of experiment, it makes it possible to deal with the nature of mutations which command phylogenetic transformations, to analyze the hold which they exercise on organogenesis, and to trust in the possibility of a natural explanation of evolution's mechanism.[23]

The specialized works concerning research on man's development reveal an extremely complex endeavor, and anthropology calls on many specialists: osteologists, paleontologists, geologists, zoologists, etc. When ethnologists then attempt to coordinate the research results of these different fields for a specific case, they are rarely in agreement among themselves.[24] But isn't this necessarily the fate of a rational science which ignores the sages' law of genesis and is obliged to make partial and specialized investigations unconnected by any *sense of synthesis?*

How is it possible, moreover, to judge man's state of consciousness in terms of the hominization of the animal? *All species, all races of living beings, have their specific seed.* Certainly, each kingdom owes its generation to elements realized by what preceded it. By the same token, there is a sequence from earthworm to man, *but there is no transition, no intermediary type, between beings "bearing the seed of their species."* There are jumps, considered to be *sudden mutations,* and this is where sacerdotal science situates its teaching: Knowing the function involved, it has no need of the multiple and unbelievable theories imposed by the materialistic approach.

Let us briefly summarize:

---

[22]P. Brien and A. Dalcq, *Aperçu de morphogenèse comparative et causale,* in *Traité de zoologie* (Paris, 1954), XII, p. 4.

[23]Ibid., pp. 30-31.

[24]See chapter 4 on the hypotheses regarding the origins of the ancient inhabitants of the Nile valley.

Vertebrates appeared in sweet water in which they were diffused and
differentiated. In the course of their transformations, some of them readapted
to marine life; others, abandoning their watery milieu, surfaced to dwell on dry
land.[25]

The basic types of *fish* date from the Silurian (the Primary). As
early as the Devonian, the great differentiation occurred among gill-
breathing types from which the fish, properly so called, emerged
during the Secondary, and at the end of the Primary, both gill- and
lung-breathing types giving birth to the *Batrachia,* which perpetuate
themselves to this day.

At the end of the Primary (the Carboniferous and the Permian),
the first *reptiles* likewise originate from the earliest amphibians and
diversify greatly during the entire Secondary.

Mammals, issuing from the *synapsidan reptiles* of the Permian, developed
during the Secondary. . . . But in the Tertiary, taking over from the reptiles, they
differentiated into powerful groups, many of which are already extinct or on the
way to extinction, while in the *primate* class, *man,* the last to appear, today
imposes his preponderance on earth.

Birds, which form perhaps the most specialized class of vertebrates,
separated from the *diapsidan reptiles.* Their beginnings go back to the Jurassic
(the Secondary) when they were represented by such *Sauria* as *Archeopteryx*
and *Archeornis.*[26]

In the course of this sequence of morphological stages
characterizing the great classes of vertebrate phylum, transformations
are produced which do not bear upon a single organ but on *the entire
organism* and lead to morphological and physiological changes. One of
the most characteristic examples thereof is that reptiles are, for the
most part, *poikilothermous,* while birds and mammals (which
descended from them) have become *homoiothermous,* having a
thermic regulation involving a radical change of the entire
metabolism. It is precisely these jumps from one class to another,
theoretically all taking off from a primitive beginning of vertebrates
dating from the Silurian, that now are explained as *mutations.*

We admit that present laws of development are also those which, during
geologic ages, governed the genesis of the innumerable individuals linking the
mesh of generations. . . .

We also admit that evolution occurs through sudden and hereditary

---

[25]Brien and Dalcq, op. cit., XII, p. 33.
[26]Ibid., p. 31.

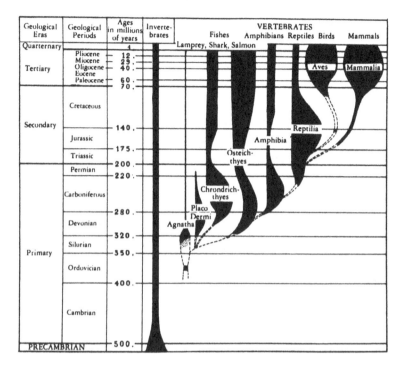

Fig. 3. *The Appearance of the Vertebrates* (adapted from A. S. Romer).

modifications in the morphogenetic organization of the eggs. However, we have postulated nothing as to the nature or the cause of these onto-mutations....[27]

Thus, though it was still believed even recently that the questions had been laid to rest once and for all, they are raised again today: How can the evolution of the species be explained? And what is the origin of man?

Let us recall the confrontation between our most eminent naturalists, Georges Cuvier and Geoffroy Saint-Hilaire, in 1830:

Cuvier, and then Louis Agassiz, defenders of *the theory of the immutability of species,* maintained that each species resulted from a special act of creation. For each species, Cuvier determined the "dominant characteristic," defined principally by the particular

[27]Ibid., p. 12.

nervous system; he thereby deduced the main branches, each one signaling a definite stage of evolution. Nevertheless, each branch is not the result of an evolution acquired through genealogical descent, but marks the stages of a plan preconceived from the beginning by the Creator. It is this plan which naturalists must research. The theory of immutable species accepts as a basic principle a kind of *continuous creation* and a succession of *spontaneous generations* which its detractors refuse to acknowledge, "creative power being independent, by its very essence, of all progress and perfecting."[28] One may remark that if the creation is subject to accidents, the preconceived plan is not thereby affected.

The theory of transformism is well known, advocated by Buffon, Lamarck, Geoffroy Saint-Hilaire, and developed by Darwin and then by Haeckel, and proof thereof was researched through paleontology in hopes of discovering intermediate forms between still existent classes.

Equally familiar is the law of patrogony, defined thus by Haeckel; "In the course of embryogenic development, each individual successively assumes the different forms through which his species passed in order to arrive at its present state, or, in short, ontogeny [the genesis of the being] is a rapid recapitulation of phylogeny [the genesis of the race].[29] This law is illustrated by the well-known example of the tadpole and the frog.

After a moment of triumph, the transformist theory is today quite shaken: No one has ever seen a mouse become a rabbit, even with time. Thus there are species characterized by a whole set of physiological particularities which remain identical within the same genus, no matter what adaptations occur during the course of the ages. It is useless, therefore, to employ Gaussian curves to research the sequence of growth in size or regression of certain members or certain organs, presumably under the influence of the milieu. Such a procedure allows for the computation of statistics, but does not provide the key to the passage of one class to another.

It is now admitted that the evolution of the classes occurred through successive mutations, that is, by sudden modifications of the genes. But this is to explain a fact by an unknown: Why the mutation? To what cause can the modification of chromosomes be attributed? To the heredity of individual acquisitions motivated by adaptation to the milieu, according to Lamarck's theory?

---

[28]Rémy Perrier, *Zoologie* (Paris, 1929), p. 83.

[29]Ibid., p. 84. Law formulated by Fritz Müller.

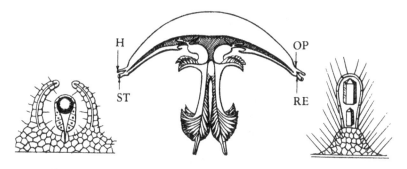

Fig. 4. *Schematic Cross-section of a Medusa.*
H = hood. ST = sensorial tentacles bearing statocysts. OP =
olfactory pit. RE = rudimentary eye.
On the right and left, two varieties of very enlarged statocysts
containing calcareous concretions.

First of all, it must be assumed that beings adapt to the milieu, and
furthermore, that they transmit their adaptations to their progeny.

If the first point is largely true, the second, on the contrary, would seem
hardly tenable. Today, the theory of acquired heredity is almost generally denied
for overwhelming reasons, both theoretical and experimental....[30]

The problem must be recognized, and if we are as certain as ever
concerning the evolution of living forms, we have never been less certain of the
mechanism that controls it.[31]

At present, it has been possible to trace the origins of the living
world as far back as the first or Paleozoic epoch; bacteria, algae,
sponges, jellyfish, and Annelida or segmented worms, are already
found in the Precambrian, and it is even possible to fix their age as
approximately 600 million years. Marvelous indeed, but in what way
does this help to resolve the problem of evolution?

In the schema of the passage from the primitive cell to the
Chordata, we find, after the Protozoa, the Coelenterata, among which
the jellyfish represents an advanced stage, although provided with only
two layers of embryonic cells; it possesses a nervous system, gastric
filaments, a digestive cavity, genital and sensory organs, all still in a
radial organization but with the principal functions represented. As to
the sense organs, each sensorial tentacle possesses an olfactory

[30]Jean Rostand, *Les chromosomes* (Paris, 1928), p. 268.
[31]Ibid., p. 277.

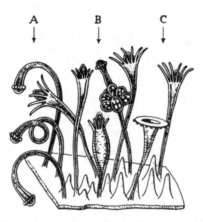

Fig. 5. *Colonies of Hydroid Polyps.*
A. Machozoids (defending fighters). B. Gonozoids bearing gamazoids or ovary in the form of a flower. C. Gastrozoids with more
or less dilated mouth.

indentation, a pigmentary trace or rudimentary eye, and a statocyst,
that is, a first sketchy indication of an inner ear to which we owe our
perception of equilibrium.[32]

As for the *Annelida,* they are already metamerized, each ring
being a complete individual, according to Haeckel, but the entire
ensemble is commanded by a brain, and represents the image of the
future chordate (vertebrate).

We recognize our ancestor, the amphioxus, by its first, still
cartilaginous indications of a future spine, like lines of force
congealing. Going backward, we are also familiar with the simple one-
celled amoeba which reacts sensitively without any nervous system,
sends out its pseudopodia from side to side, swallows, digests and
eliminates without any digestive organ, in brief, nourishes itself, lives,
and moves.

In the strange family of the polymorphic colonies of hydras, the
vital functions are distributed between the different individuals: The
gastrozoids have a mouth armed with tentacles; the others, the mobile
dactylozoids, rich in sensorial cells, serve as guardians and occupy the

. [32]Cf. R. Perrier, op. cit., p. 280. With the Acalephae, or free-floating, medusas, these organs are found on
the same individual, while on the Craspedota medusas, born on the hydras, there are sometimes found "ocelli,
or rudimentary eyes, with red or blue pigmentation, often even provided with a lens, sometimes with small
vesicles containing calcareous concretions which were long considered to be auditory organs (otocysts) but
would sooner seem adapted to the sense of equilibrium" (p. 262).

periphery of the colony. In certain species, the machozoids or "warriors" are in charge of defense, and finally, the gamazoids (reproducers) themselves present an immense variety. From these last are born either fixed individuals through offshoot budding, or the free-floating medusas.

Lastly, observation of this living world shows that *from the first animal form, all the elements—the Idea—of what the complete organization of man will be, are already given*. It would appear that man, ultimate creature of the animate terrestrial world, is prefigured.

This can be regarded in parallel to certain texts dealing with Hermetism which affirm that base metals are but abortions in a genesis extending toward noble metal.

All forms of base metal, meaning those which have not attained predestined perfection, would thus be comparable to the different animal classes which are likewise manifest in the genesis of the human fetus. The human stage once reached, any interruption at one of these phases would make for an abortion incapable of living; generated at lower stages, however, these intermediate entities live as do lead, iron, copper, etc., when extracted before their time from their mine or matrix of gestation. Therefore, of all the hypotheses suggested by the quest for an animal origin capable of giving rise to different branches, one of which would lead to man as having received the divine breath, the hypothesis looking toward primitive beings who develop human characteristics (as with the tarsier) seems best to conform with the natural evolutionary path.

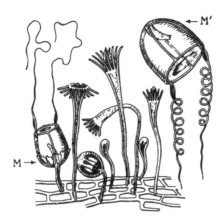

Fig. 5a. *Colonies of Hydroid Polyps.*
M: Medusa still attached. M': Detached medusa.

As in the case of paleontology, a materialistic orthogenesis for the evolution of the animal is inexplicable without the intervention of mutations. This mysterious phenomenon modifies the genes of the chromosomes and brings about the appearance of species and new races "adapted" to the milieu of their appearance. The phenomenon of life cannot be separated from the milieu in which it manifests itself. Evolution in general and geological transformations in particular, usually explained by submersions and climatological changes, obey the same laws that govern mutations. Earth as mineral is the province of chemistry; nothing, however, explains the appearance of geological strata. The molten rock and crystals attributed to the Paleozoic; the slate, sandstone, and shale of the Mesozoic; and the geologic layers formed by buried vegetation—all this is understandable. Less well understood are the layers of chalk or very pure limestone that have been explained as marine deposits. For the question remains: Where do all these minerals come from? This manifestation, which is a kind of mineral genesis, is as extraordinary as the appearance of a homoiothermal animal issuing from reptiles and poikilothermal amphibia.

For plant and animal life, there are adaptations to the milieu which can modify organs and organic functions, but cannot find any substitutes for them. Yet there exists no reason whatsoever for one species to become another, save a purely energetic influence acting on the gonads at a certain moment of disequilibrium during the conjunction of the male and female elements. Aren't these mutations "spontaneous generations" such as this phenomenon was described above? And this effect can be radical or partial; an animal state can be the very distant source of *Homo sapiens,* or could produce a being merely somewhat closer to man than to ape; but the disturbing fact remains that primates exist to this day, whereas none of the pithecanthropic beings considered as intermediaries between ape and man are any longer to be found. Should it be taken for granted that these intermediate beings could not outlive the birth of man? It would then be necessary to recognize the sudden appearance of man in the midst of an animal world hostile to his own life, which he would thus be forced to combat.

It has been four or five centuries since our civilization came to discover our planet, mistakenly believing that this is the first time humanity has taken cognizance of it. The history of man, more than being merely physiological, is the history of consciousness; a human

Fig. 6. *Spectral Tarsier* (Tarsius spectrum).
The unfortunate Tarsier, abandoned by scientists as the common
stock of man and monkey!

being primitive from our point of view and unlike contemporary man
could well have been richer than we are in true knowledge of Nature
and of her secrets, because he would have been instinctively more
united with her while endowed with a consciousness of this instinct: in
sum, a human being rich in that intuition which our cerebration has
stifled.

Consciousness

Broadly speaking, I distinguish three states of consciousness:
universal consciousness, innate consciousness, and psychological or
mental consciousness. Moral consciousness (conscience) is in fact a
sense of morality, be it acquired at random or innate.

Definitions of consciousness vary with almost every philosopher.
Essentially, consciousness requires at least a duplex state, a duality,
because it necessarily results from comparison. One God, absolute

unity, therefore does not exist; *He is,* but as soon as He becomes *conscious* of Himself—that is, the One divides into Two (or "the Word is uttered" or "God said...")—then *God exists* through the relationship between Himself and His creation. If we accept the hypothesis of a creation by supposing, as a beginning, the existence of a single thing, there would be a relationship between the Creator and this thing; there is consciousness for God, but as yet no consciousness for this thing which cannot recognize the pure abstraction of creative oneness. But as soon as there are two things, not the first thing divided into parts of itself, but two things distinct in their nature—the one earth, for example, and the other sky, one fixed and the other volatile, one male and the other female—then there is attraction and repulsion; there is choice, though as yet without decision; but since there is choice, there is affinity, which is the first and universal state of consciousness. Decision will come later, as it obtains only with the realization of the brain. Essentially, consciousness is but choice or selection by affinity, and the chemical affinity of bodies is the first manifestation—and the model—of consciousness.

Universal consciousness thus signifies the impulse toward the becoming of things, the separation of nonexistence from existence, the creative function; it is total consciousness, it is synthesis, just as the seed is the synthesis of the fruit that will issue from it. And all becoming, from the most primitive existence up to man, seems to be but the gestation of a fruit or the analysis of universal consciousness. In this meaning of the term, consciousness cannot *evolve* but can only successively manifest its finality to our sensorial and intellectual recognition. This it can achieve after embodiment of the various vital functions and after *a reversal of consciousness.* This *new and definitive scission of consciousness* renders the human animal conscious of itself, just as the Oneness of origin recognized itself, *thus negating itself within its own sole-singular Being.*

This reversal can only take place at the moment when all the functions of genesis are embodied, when they have become living organs; then *the faculty of negating* springs from the totality of vital functions, constituting reason, mental intelligence, and what is called "psychological consciousness." Mental faculties are the aim of human genesis alone, a liberation or *an unveiling of consciousness* imprisoned within transitory forms (mineral, plant, animal); yet these faculties are also the means which make possible the return to universal consciousness.[33]

---

[33]These statements will be illustrated by facts in the chapters on myth and the organization of Pharaonic life.

The forms which are gestated are but organs manifesting the generative function; in this gestation, the history of the kingdoms cannot be separated from human history: While each kingdom represents as a whole one of the essential functions, the latter are found reunited in man, the ultimate issue for this Earth.

Organic life is distinguished from inorganic life by the appearance of respiration, assimilation, vegetation, reproduction, and movement, all perceptible in the most simple monocellular animal. These are primitive vital functions, but they persist all the way to man. Tactile sensitivity, reaction to light, to taste (through choice of food) and to odor, exist with the first form of organic life. It can therefore be said that everything physically characterizing man has been conceived since the first vital manifestation, and the "evolutive" sequence from the animal kingdom to man is but an increasingly perfect organization of these characteristics.

Thus man is prefigured with the first corporeal manifestation and is virtually identified with consciousness; from the point of view of universal consciousness, manifestation is but a fall into the prison of matter. Therefore its liberation will be the travail imposed by this condemnation. This procession toward the organic incarnation of liberating phases forms the innate consciousness that each individual bears from birth. Under the signature of a class and its various kinds and species, each animal stage represents a formation or organic embodiment of a function. At each stage, an organ (or a function) dominates the totality of the organism, as does the eye with the bird, digestion with the jackal, scent (sense of smell) with the dog and the cynocephalus.[34]

For the individual, therefore, there is an innate consciousness proper to its species, but with man there is also an innate consciousness proper to the individual. This assumes, for the species, a seminal transmission, and *for the individual, transmission through a personal indestructible element bearing the characteristic inscription of its acquired consciousness.*

Instead of the purely materialistic evolution of a succession of animal types from earthworm to man, this doctrine presents the vital organization as an expansion of consciousness, and also explains the effort by which the human individual can transcend himself in his present state.[35]

As the force of gravity relates to bodies in the physical, so does

---

[34]These are the characteristics which the Pharaonic symbolique uses for the myth.

[35]See below, "Natural Excess."

universal consciousness relate to the form and spirit of the living being. It is always present, but all it asks is to be free of the veil which matter represents.

From the beginning, man is the aim, the perfect being capable of expressing all the possibilities immanent in universal consciousness up to the return toward the One which emanates this Word. *In mutations, as they are called today, the transitions from one form to another, more complete form are motivated: In a natural way, their orientation is toward the cosmically propitious moment, because mutations are the effect of an energetic cosmic influence commanded by the laws of harmony, and these influences are extremely variable.*

But one species cannot pass into another species without the integral decomposition of its first form: It is a general, absolute law that *a thing cannot change form without the destruction of its own form.* Thus *Pithecanthropus* will never become thinking man by means of seminal transmission. If, however, his organic form is entirely destroyed and decomposed, leaving nothing but the indestructible part of his being—which I refer to as the *fixed salt* that every being leaves behind after its destruction[36]—then this fulcrum can serve for the creation of a new being eventually to become a thinking man with cranial bones no longer fused. Therefore the Mosaic text can say: "And the Lord God formed man of the dust of the ground," because animal classes as well as species *are created.* They are created on a prepared foundation, this much is evident, but they do not become through seminal transmission; if that were so, there would be no evolution, no liberation of consciousness beyond simple adaptation to the milieu. It is understood that Darwin's *struggle for survival* serves for the selection of the most typical individuals of species and races, but this is only the exterior, exoteric aspect of the matter.

Natural Excess

In the course of the different evolutive stages, biology shows us the concretization of certain centers, organs, or forms. The particular development of certain nervous centers, such as the olfactory lobes in the snake,[37] visual lobes in birds, and the auditory center in fish, marks

[36]See *le Temple de l'Homme*, I, *De la conscience*, pp. 64-68.

[37]Regarding olfaction in snakes and the Pharaonic symbolism related to it, see *Le Temple de l'Homme*, I, pp. 678-696.

a phase of specialization in the evolution of the senses' development. For birds, the specialization is particularly notable in light of the fact that they have almost no *sense of smell,* a sense highly developed in snakes, which precede birds in the sequence of the classes.[38] Here again it is a matter not of addition but of a profound modification in the nervous system.

It is as if each class represented all possibilities of development, at times carrying certain characteristics to an extreme beyond any utilitarian ends that could be determined by simple logic. Thus the elephant's tusks are understandable, but not the totally curved tusks of the mammoth. We can understand the marvelous equilibrium of the supple panther's four limbs, as skillful at climbing as at leaping, but the excessive neck of the giraffe never ceases to amaze, nor does the kangaroo—the atrophy of its forelegs and the extraordinary development of its hindlegs allowing it jumps of six to eight meters. This is called a primitive mammal, and rightly so, in view of the strange birth of its young: Hardly larger than a nut and still in the phase of a small embryo, they find the marsupial pouch all by themselves, without the aid of eyes or feet. One can also cite the antlers of a reindeer, which reach such excessive dimensions as to compromise the animal's life.

Examples such as these, which can be classified as monstrous proliferations, are rather frequent. The lyre bird, for instance, admired for its beauty, knows not what to do with its very beautiful plumage, which is completely useless for flight or any other purpose outside of the mating season. *Uselessness,* that is indeed the only meaningful term that comes to mind when we reflect on the teratological proliferations affecting either isolated individuals, both plant and animal, or an entire species which maintains this new state. Yet physical nature has no place for the useless.

These phenomena can be systematically symbolized as follows: There exists for every specific being the radiation of a force emanating from a center, a vital flux whose rays terminate in the realization of the organs. The perfection of the organ will be the outermost circle to delineate this center of irradiation. It is possible, then, for one of the rays to go beyond this limiting circle and to make of this organ a supernumerary being, so to speak, useless to the equilibrium which is the formal harmony characteristic of this being.

This useless generation confirms the existence of a preconceived

[38]The kiwi, whose nocturnal life is oriented by its sense of smell, seems to be the exception among birds.

form for every being, a form measured by a harmony of proportions which attains perfection with man. Brought about through exceptional proliferation, the disequilibrium and disharmony obviously represent a kind of *surevolution* of one part of the being in question, a surevolution which manifests the possibility of transcending natural law.

This surevolution is monstrous only in relation to the normal—meaning natural—form and proportion of the species. The ancient Egyptians made use of instances of this sort (in plants, particularly the lotus) for signifying precisely the meaning of the Sed festival, a festival of regeneration and of a qualitative exaltation that only sacerdotal science could envision. Although as a rule strictly confined within the limits of our expectations, Nature herself thus shows us the way of transcending quantitative frontiers; clearly indicated is the existence of a preconceived aim for the bodily state.

As to the possibilities of consciousness, Nature further teaches us how to glimpse them; to be avoided is the error of burdening the instances presented to us with an explanation conforming to our own way of thinking: The fact must be seen in itself such as it confronts us.

Mention should be made of *gestures* that go beyond the normal life of the animal and indicate a primitive consciousness of natural magic. Hence the particular dances between certain male birds, sometimes opening with bows and mock battles which are followed by rounds and steps, ending with stamping accompanied by vibrant gestures and trembling, until the subject is thrown into a kind of ecstasy. In the case of the double snipe, the birds form a long line and their song, beginning at one end, is taken up successively by each of them. Another phase of the concert begins with several sustained notes followed by a rapid succession of piercing notes while the excited bird throws back its head in ecstasy.[39] Displays such as these which lead to an extreme state of excitement are of course explained as the need for sexual stimulation; it is surprising, therefore, to see certain males, *after* coupling, jealously maintaining their dance space—which they continue to use even without reason for further intervention of sexual stimulation—and abandon their progeny to be raised by the females only.

These movements which provoke a sort of mystical catalepsy bring to mind certain dances among black people, the Whirling Dervishes, and the Moslem's *zhikr* which involve the pronouncing of

[39]See E. A. Armstrong, *La vie amoureuse des oiseaux* (Paris, 1952), p. 262.

ritual words *regulating the breath* and accompanied by gestures, often in increasingly rapid rhythm, the entire exercise being pushed to the extent of provoking ecstasy and physical insensibility. It seems that the *sense of excess* exists in Nature, expressed by exaggeration of the forms themselves or by gestures and attitudes.

According to the saying that the exception proves the rule, monstrous proliferation demonstrates the preconceived plan of living beings. But gestures such as the examples just cited are extraneous to the normal life of the animal; they confirm a natural and instinctive orientation toward the search for a supracorporeal consciousness. This search for ecstasy (of which catalepsy, in this case, is but an external effect) constitutes a ritual common among peoples of very old culture. The continual repetition of a gesture or word is intended to fascinate the mind in order to give free expression to the "understanding,"* be it psychic or higher. In our "civilized" world, litany plays the same role, but to much lesser effect. Already evidenced in the animal world, rituals of this kind exist among all peoples.

The symbolique of ancient Egypt shows the deeper significance associated with the endeavor to eliminate the mental plane. Upon the *Neter's* head, as on that of the King, a band or diadem is placed, marking off the cranial skull cap, that part of the brain which commands personal decisions. This separation leaves these beings with the vital centers of the encephalon only, so that they may be inspired by spirit alone.[40]

But here again, one must not imagine outlandish causes and effects: The true spirit is harmony. To remain within and in touch with natural harmony is obedience to God and to the *Neters.* Animal life and particularly the life of wild animals frequently offers us teachings worth retaining. If man is the preconceived aim of Nature—and it is difficult to think otherwise—all the types, all the evolutionary phases of Nature, are as instants in man's gestation. The animal world manifests and "gest-ates"† all the natural possibilities which are within man: physical surevolution as well as the means of a surevolution of consciousness; or again, the intuitive communion between beings manifested by the elephant, for example, when the animal "intuitively" (?) hears the distress-call of one of its kind at great distances away. The elephant (Ganesh) plays a vital role in Hindu symbolism. The symbols of great religions must not be disregarded as

*French *entendement.* No satisfactory English term exists, as *entendre* bears the connotation of *hearing* as well as of *understanding.*—Trans.

[40]See *Le Temple de l'Homme,* I, *Le Diadème.*

†The author refers to an untranslatable Hermetic cabala involving etymologies.—Trans.

we reach the end of the present age. Knowledge can still be gleaned from this symbolique so fully expressed in the animal kingdom.

Among birds in particular, one observes many gestures *which serve no purpose and consequently have only a symbolic meaning.* For example, *Sterna hirundo:* At mating time, the couple makes its courtship flight, the male bearing a fish in its beak; then the two birds perch. The male offers the fish to the female and then demands its return; mating is not completed until the fish has changed beaks several times. The symbolic character of this custom becomes even more evident when one observes this series of gestures performed *without* the fish, showing that the latter does not serve for food.[41]

The multiple gestures of mating, dances, and songs are well known; during their performance, the male exhibits himself in all his glory, and a most extraordinary example of this is the following:

> Among Birds of Paradise, it is observed that the male constructs an arbor or passageway with vertically arranged twigs, with the entrance and exit facing each other; he arranges it on the ground, in a little forest clearing, while the real nest is made later in the branches of a tree. In front of the arbor's entrance and exit, he arranges a sort of terrace which he decorates, according to his species, with little bones or snail shells, fresh flowers which are usually white, or various objects...as many as possible of blue, each species always having a marked preference for a particular color....
>
> Sometimes he decorates the interior walls of the arbor with a gray, brown, blackish, reddish or blue substance composed of crushed grasses, bark or cinders, etc., amalgamated with saliva.... As this construction nears completion, the female of *Ptilonorhyncus*[42] arrives. She installs herself within in order to calmly observe the male's parading which takes place on the terraces: There he dances, strikes extraordinary poses, emits series of strange cries and, with symbolic gestures, seizes in his beak the ornamental objects he has amassed around him and presents them to the female as if for her admiration....
>
> Included in the behavior of the Birds of Paradise [*Ptilonorhyncus* of the species *Violaceus*] we find dances and special postures, vocal sounds and symbolic gestures, in addition to a special construction of artistic conception which seems strongly to heighten the sexual excitement not only of the male who jealously guards his arbor, but also of the female who installs herself within it in order to witness the male's performance.[42]

Conclusions

Man's origin is unknown.

Following new discoveries of bone remains and perhaps of tools fabricated by *Homo sapiens,* paleontology can situate man's

---

[41]See Brien and Dalq, op. cit., XV, pp. 710-711. *Sterna hirundo* = the sea swallow.
[42]Ibid., pp. 555-557.

appearance at new dates, but this does not resolve the essential problem of origin. Efforts are made to erect a rigorous genealogical tree, establishing simian and human branches, but there is a gap between the branches and the trunk. Thus, along with the eminent biologist Jean Rostand, we must recognize that the cogwheels of the ontological "mechanism" remain undiscovered.

For our rational materialistic science, it is indeed a matter of finding a material sequence in the becoming of the living being, a search which will some day be recognized as absurd.

Biology shows us that all the sensitivities and all the vital functions which characterize the bodily life of man have been inscribed in living matter since the beginning. Man is *preconceived,* and all of nature is like a womb in which the human being gestates through phases arrested into typical and independent beings, quite as metals are described in Hermetic texts: Base metals are arrested phases in the metallic gestation, the preconceived end of which is the female lunar silver and the male solar gold. Arrests in universal gestation are characterized and *bear the seed of their species:* they can perpetuate themselves in their form, but they can never pass from one form to another solely by the seminal means of reproduction. This is why the ape will never become man. Passage from one phase (or form) to another during gestation demands that nothing interrupt this gestation; this means that the milieu must not vary and the supply of energy and nourishment must not cease.

This continuity is comprehensible for the gestation of metal in the mineral matrix and for the gestation of the organism in the animal womb. But though a prematurely born animal evidently is not *viable,* intermediate living forms *subsist* in the parallel suggested by the universal gestation of man. These forms are alive and capable of reproducing: They are finished types.

We observe that metal requires the mineral as a gangue-matrix for its gestation. The mineral for its part is but the combination of metallic or metalloid elements, including some which are clearly premetallic, as for example arsenic and silicon. Metal itself, in its first form as hydrogen, was preceded by phases of becoming (energetic phases, in this instance). For there is always a state of being serving as basis for a new state of being. Thus it is with the kingdoms: The vegetal can only develop from a mineral ground, and the animal requires plant life as foundation.

If there were no variety, gestation would occur without a womb and would go straight to the fruit *preconceived in the instant of inspiration* or impetus. In Christianity, this moment of inspiration is

the annunciation made to Mary. In ancient Egypt, it is the moment
called *theogamy*, when the odor of the god penetrates the palace
represented by *Mut* (maternity) *in the* (lunar) *barque.*[43]

If there were but a single moment of inspiration, there would be
only one lineage, but it is the multiplicity and inequality of these
moments which make for varieties. These moments of inspiration
can occur at any time, in relation with the cosmic harmony of energetic
sources, the principal and most direct source for our earth being that of
the sun.

There are no "miracles": All organic bodies, as well as certain
mineral compositions, are susceptible at the moment of their
decomposition to an orientation toward a new form through the
influence of cosmic energy. In this event, these new bodies constitute
characterized beings who will follow their own destinies. This is how a
new being is grafted onto the similar nature that precedes it when its
first form is destroyed. It is true that while progression is possible
toward the final preconceived type, there can also be regression if the
activity at that moment falls amiss and finds itself in disharmony with
the nature of the being in its state of transition. By "in transition" is
meant what a simple chemical reaction suggests: When, for example,
into the medium of a liquid chemical composition, another chemical
body is introduced which is susceptible to combining with one or
another of the bodies in solution, a moment arrives, unsituated in time,
when one or another of these bodies is molecularly liberated *in
transition* between the first compound and the new one. At this
instant, the molecule is exposed to all possible energetic influences,
and it is here that the appearance of organic life could be situated.

The appearance of *organic life* on our globe, in the geologic epoch
of *geochemical* formations, poses a problem similar to Homo sapien's
appearance following the development of the animal.[44]

The moment of *transition,* the result of the destruction of a given
state, is the moment that can produce natural mutations of the genes.
Nature thus aligns the individually viable varieties, forming the linked
phases of what in its finality will become man. These are *creations.* The
law of cosmic harmony (all stellar influences) commands: It is the
divine Word that orders because the true God is harmony, a puissance
which we ascertain but do not understand.

Thus man could not be *created* until all the vital forces were

[43]See Chapter 8, "Myth."

[44]See Appendix IX.

realized in *individually finished and functionally specified organs*. The puissance which makes for natural genesis and which never rests, can then no longer devise further additions and is able only to maintain the acquired state. All new creation henceforth can only be the beginning of what might be called a *return,* an "energetization" of bodily forms. In mineralogy, therefore, we see bodies which have acquired the greatest atomic weight burn themselves out in intense energetic radiation until they have returned to their primeval state, such as uranium to lead. These are natural cycles which are perpetually beginning and running their course as long as a new and higher creation does not intervene; and this exalted creation can only be a power of negation conscious of the final state of corporeality that has been acquired. A structure such as this accommodates more complete and subtle images, images concerning the process of *becoming* in general, as well as *Homo sapiens*'s origin.

There is a normal course from jellyfish to ape; there is *an abnormal moment, a "reversal," between ape and man. Homo sapiens* does not emerge from ape, but the complete physical being which certain apes represent as the end result of the animal lineage is indispensable for the *creation of man* "in the image of God," just as a torch is necessary to bear the light, the fire that illuminates and shows up all things while devouring the torch that carries it.

4

Chorography of Egypt

Before beginning to study the myth and examine the symbols covering the walls of the temples planted along both banks of the Nile, and in order to approximate as closely as possible the basic mentality that presided over the execution of these gigantic works, we must consider a psychological element that is as indispensable as the archaeological data: the influence imposed by the typical character of a region upon its inhabitants, an influence which can never be erased by time.

Whatever the particular mixture of people and even of beliefs, the same terrain will always exert the identical influence: The earth makes the man. Thus, in Egypt, we observe the influence of *Hapi*, the Nile, the lone river, calm and meditative, having slowly carved its bed through immense deserts. It is preeminently the land of the one and only God, and the majestic peace of the Nile inspires religiosity. From Cairo, however, the Nile divides into several branches and constitutes the Delta, Lower Egypt. While the people of Upper Egypt with its unique river have remained simple, faithful to their religious and mystical traditions, the people of Lower Egypt are inconstant, covetous, and turbulent. And indeed, the intellectual Greeks, with their reasoned and subtle approach, settled in the Delta, while the first Christian mystics found refuge in Upper Egypt, around the Thebaid, close to the vestiges of temples and tombs asserting life eternal.

Yet there is another important aspect to be considered: While it is certain that populations are impregnated by the character of the new land occupied during migrations, the fact remains that the racial essence does not change. As the problem of the region's influence must be taken into account by the archaeologist, so the racial question becomes the ethnologist's concern.

We are therefore led to envision the broad lines of certain problems which, although seemingly of different order, are yet intimately related through the myth: prehistory and the search for origins, on the one hand, and on the other, the political division of the territory into two kingdoms, South and North, subdivided into forty-two nomes or provinces.

These questions can be studied either *historically* or *symbolically*; yet whatever the point of view, certain undeniable facts must be briefly set forth before the various interpretations can be summarized.

On the basis of the earliest known texts, we can ascertain that there existed in Egypt a religion whose nature is such as to upset the currently held conception of a combined monotheism and pantheism, joined by zoolatry. On the basis of such a definition, numerous historical interpretations have been evolved, with the aim of reconciling the various "systems" by determining the anteriority of one over the other. Since the Pharaonic conception links these apparently conflicting elements into one whole, the problem finds no irrefutable answers when placed in an historical context.

Study of the texts shows, in fact, that since the Ancient Empire, there is an affirmation of faith in a one and only God, eternal and nameless; the *Neter of Neters,* boundless and incomprehensible. Parallel to this vision, there exists a pantheon composed of a considerable number of *Neters* or principles.

These *Neters* belong to several "theological systems" taught in different, well-defined locations: Heliopolis, Memphis, Hermopolis, and Thebes. Each nome, furthermore, dedicates a cult to a local *Neter* and often even to a triad of principles. Taught concurrently is the myth of Osiris, mythical king of Egypt, killed and cut into pieces by Seth, his brother, who in turn took over dominion of the land. This brought on the interminable conflict between Horus and Seth, since Horus, the son of Isis and Osiris, claimed his father's heritage from the usurping Seth.

Before Menes and the unification of the country, tradition tells us that the Empire was divided into two kingdoms: the land of the South attributed to Seth, and the land of the North attributed to Horus, each kingdom with its capital. This myth has been interpreted historically, with the final victory of Horus over Seth as a conquest of the southern land by a king from the North. By generalizing this historic conception to the whole of the pantheon, it has been thought that originally each nome had been a small independent state with its own theological system. In the struggles between these states, victory of one over the

Fig. 7. *Nile Gods Bearing the Symbols of the 2nd and 3rd Nomes of
Lower Egypt.*
Base of the colossus of Amenophis III. Karnak, Eighteenth
Dynasty.

other was thought to have resulted in the supremacy of the victorious
Neter: in short, a political conquest masked as a religious conquest.
And thus, a king native to Heliopolis is supposed to have finally unified
Egypt. Proof of this theory is that Atum, the Heliopolitan *Neter,*
was considered supreme *Neter* of the Ancient Empire.

Of course there exists a fact contradictory to this interpretation:
Ptah of Memphis is *at the same time* the supreme *Neter* of creation.
This is therefore no longer a matter of absolute supremacy. The
historical version evades this difficulty by stipulating a "syncretism" or
a fusion of several "philosophic systems" under the authority of the
most powerful.

The problem is further complicated by the coexistence, during the
entire historical period, of the three mysteries of the theology as well as

all the local *Neters,* and this demands further explanation. An emblem relative to the local *Neter* belongs to each nome. What can be the significance of these emblems, whose origin goes back to prehistory and which represent animals, plants, mountains, objects, and other symbolic signs? Certain authors have found in these ensigns the totem of ancient tribes disseminated along the river at a time when the land was not as yet organized into first a double, then a single kingdom. And as the people involved are considered to have been primitives, the conclusion remains that the choice of emblems could only have been dictated by superstition or fear. This explanation might be justified, if need be, for the crocodile and the snake, but does not account for the symbol of the bucranium attributed to Hathor, of lightning to Min, or of arrows to Neith, for in these instances we are dealing with symbols which no historical reason can justify. These cases are ascribed to *fetishism,* which amounts to putting one word in place of another.

Whether historians present a thesis of totemism, fetishism, syncretism, or the religious or political conquest of territory, none of these hypotheses justifies the selection of the animals attributed to a specific *Neter* in relation to a particular site. And yet, objects dating from the most remote period are found to represent certain symbols whose configuration remains unchanged throughout the entire

Fig. 8. *Boats Bearing the Symbol of Hathor's Horns.*
Red paint on white ground. Prehistoric bowl.
(F. Petrie, *Prehistoric Egypt*)

historical period. These facts demand that the origin of such symbols be sought in a very distant past, inviting investigation into what is known of Pharaonic prehistory.

Traditions and Legends Concerning the Prehistory of Egypt

The most valuable document is the *Royal Papyrus of Turin* which gave a complete list of kings who reigned over Upper and Lower Egypt from Menes to the New Empire, including mention of the duration of each reign.[1] Coming before this royal list, the first columns of the papyrus were consecrated to prehistory, meaning the reigns that preceded Menes. They were laid out in the following manner:

In the first column was a list of ten *Neters,* with each name inscribed in a cartouche, preceded by the royal symbols of Upper and Lower Egypt (the bulrush and the bee) and followed by the number of years for each reign. Most of these numbers are missing.

In the second column was found a list of kings having reigned before Menes and the duration of their reign. The remaining fragments establish that nine dynasties were mentioned, among which the (venerables) of Memphis, the venerables of the North, and finally the *Shemsu-Hor,* usually translated as the "Companions of Horus."[2] Fortunately, the last two lines have survived almost intact, as have indications regarding the number of years:

... venerables Shemsu-Hor, 13,420 years
Reigns up to Shemsu-Hor, 23,200 years (total 36,620)
King Menes

It can thus be understood that the ancients considered their prehistory to go back 36,620 years before Menes. If this king's accession is placed at the time of the calendar's establishment in approximately 4240 B.C., the origins would date back about 40,000 years before our era. This date, of course, is considered by modern historians to be exaggerated, and they dismiss such figures as fabulous. Although the number of years may vary with each author, the ancient

[1]Found intact, the Papyrus of Turin was shattered into bits during its transport to Italy. For its history and description, see Meyer, *Chronologie égyptienne,* p. 147, and Maspero, *Histoire ancienne de l'Orient classique,* I, p. 255, 4.

[2]See discussion below on the meaning of the "Companions of Horus."

chronologists do bear witness to a tradition ascribing great antiquity to Egyptian prehistory:

Diodoros of Sicily[3] reports that according to several chroniclers, gods and heroes ruled Egypt for 18,000 years. Thereafter, the land was governed by mortal kings for 15,000 years, bringing the time span of history and prehistory to a total of *33,000 years.*[4]

Manetho grants 15,150 years to the divine dynasties and 9,777 years to all kings having reigned before Menes, giving a total of *24,927* years to prehistory.

According to George the Syncellus, the Egyptians possessed a certain tablet that they called an ancient chronicle and that mentioned thirty royal dynasties preceded by the reign of the gods, comprising a period corresponding to twenty-five Sothic cycles of 1,461 years, that is, *36,525* years, a period supposedly referring to the fabled periodic revolution of the zodiac.[5]

After mentioning 340 generations of kings and high-priests who ruled over Egypt, Herodotos adds several strange and controversial words:

They also said that during this long succession of centuries, on four separate occasions, the sun moved from his wonted course, twice rising where he now sets, and twice setting where he now rises.[6]

Instead of condemning this "fairy tale" as proof of the Egyptians' feeble astronomical knowledge, would it not be better to seek for an understanding of its meaning? Doesn't the rising refer to the vernal point? In modern language, this would mean that the vernal point had twice been located in the same constellation of Aries, and that it also passed twice in the opposing constellation of Libra. This would grant the duration of one and a half precessional cycles to the entire historic and prehistoric periods, or approximately *39,000 years.*[7]

In the list of *Neters* who ruled Egypt during the mythical period, the Turin Papyrus enumerates [Ptah,], Ra, [Shu], Geb, Osiris, Seth,

[3]Diodoros of Sicily, *The Library of History*, Book I, 44.

[4]This reading has been challenged: it could be (5,000 + 10,000) + 18,000. for a total of 33,000 years: or else (10,000 − 5,000) + 18,000, which makes a total of only 23,000 years, as Diodoros writes in Book XXIII.

[5]See E. A. Wallis Budge, *A History of Egypt* (Oxford, 1902), I, p. 129.

[6]Herodotos, *History* II, 142. Tr. Rawlinson.

[7]This duration is approximate because *the duration of the precession varies slightly with time;* the value of 26,000 years corresponds to the year 50 of our era, and diminishes by 11.4 years per century (Annuaire de Flammarion, 1953).

Horus, and then Thoth, Maat, Horus. But the best information concerning the myth relative to divine domination of Egyptian territory must be gathered from later accounts:

> One of the first acts related of Osiris in his reign was to deliver the Egyptians from their destitute and brutish manner of living. This he did by showing them the fruits of cultivation, by giving them laws, and by teaching them to honor the gods. Later he traveled over the whole earth, civilizing it without the slightest need of arms, but most of the peoples he won over to his way by the charm of his persuasive discourse combined with song and all manner of music.[8]

According to Diodoros (I, 14-23), Isis discovered the use of wheat and barley, formerly wild, and Osiris invented the domestication of these cereals, whence the custom of offering the first fruits to the *Neters*. Osiris taught man the growing of all sorts of fruits, discovered the grapevine and taught its cultivation, the use of wine, its preparation and preservation.

Osiris also erected golden temples to the gods and built the first cities, but it was Hermes (Thoth) who first established a common tongue, named the objects, invented letters, and instituted the cult of the gods. He gave man the first principles of astronomy and music.

It must be stressed that there is an element of truth to these legends, since recently discovered vestiges of plants at prehistoric sites confirm the antiquity of cultivated wheat and barley; clay seals covering the corks of innumerable wine jars found in the tombs, stamped in the name of the First Dynasty kings, testify that in those early times the grape was cultivated and wine produced, with careful record kept of different vintages and harvest years.[9]

Plutarch continues his narration of the Osirian myth, which, as we shall see, is directly related to the symbolism of territorial division during the entire historic period:

> Typhon (Seth), during the absence of Osiris, attempted nothing revolutionary because Isis, who was in control, was vigilant and alert; but when he returned home, Typhon contrived a treacherous plot against him and formed a group of conspirators seventy-two in number. He had also the cooperation of a queen from Ethiopia who was called Aso.[10] Typhon, having secretly measured Osiris' body and having made ready a beautiful chest of corresponding size artistically ornamented, caused it to be brought into the room where a

---

[8]Plutarch, *Isis and Osiris*, 13; in the *Moralia*. Tr. Babbitt.
[9]We shall speak below about the symbolic names given to vineyards.

festivity was in progress. The company was much pleased at the sight of it and admired it greatly, whereupon Typhon jestingly promised to present it to the man who should find the chest to be exactly his length when he lay down in it.

They all tried it in turn, but no one fit it;[11] then Osiris got into it and lay down, and those who were in the plot ran to it and slammed down the lid. . . . Then they carried the chest to the river and sent it on its way to the sea through the Tanaitic Mouth. Wherefore the Egyptians even to this day name this mouth the hateful and execrable. Such is the tradition. They say also that the date on which this deed took place was the seventeenth day of Athyr, when the sun passes through Scorpio. . . .

Osiris was then twenty-eight years old, or in the twenty-eighth year of his reign, a number related to the length of the lunar cycle.

According to Plutarch, "Pans and Satyrs" who lived in the region of Chemmis, the marshes of the northern Delta, spread news of the deed, throwing the people into panic. The tidings reached Isis, who was then in Coptos. Greatly anguished, Isis wandered everywhere, inquiring about the fate of the chest, and in her travels reached the Tanaitic Mouth.[12]

The chest, cast up by the sea, was set down at Byblos at the foot of a tamarisk tree. Now this tamarisk, having grown to massive stock, enfolded the chest and concealed it within its trunk. The king of the country, Melcarthus (the Phoenician Hades), admired the great size of the plant and gave orders to cut off the portion that enfolded the chest (which was now hidden from sight), and used it as a pillar to support the roof of his palace.

Isis, ascertaining these facts by divine inspiration, came to Byblos. Among the multiple vicissitudes of her travels, the story is told of her transformation into a swallow which hovered around the pillar with a wailing lament until the day when she revealed herself to the king and the queen and was granted that the pillar be cut open and the chest removed, to be taken by her back to Egypt. She hid it not far from Buto, in a secluded spot; but Typhon, who was hunting by night in the moonlight, happened upon it. Recognizing the body, he divided it into fourteen parts and scattered them, each in a different place.[13]

[10]Aso is said to be the personification of the burning winds of the South.

[11]It is said that Osiris was more than 5 meters, that is, 10 royal cubits, in height.

[12]Here Plutarch interpolates an episode concerning the birth of Anubis, born of the union of Osiris and Nephtys. He interprets this union as the inundation of the Nile (Osiris), whose waters spread far away to those who dwell in the outermost regions of the dry land (Nephtys), leaving as proof the melilot plant. Anubis became the companion of Isis and was dedicated to guarding the gods.

[13]The number of parts varies according to the narrator. Diodoros speaks of twenty-six.

Fig. 9. *Osiris in his coffin, in the tamarisk tree, watched over by Isis at his feet and Nephthys at his head.* Temple of Dendera.

Isis sought for them again throughout all of Egypt, and as soon as she found a part, she gave it to each city as if it were the entire body, causing a tomb to be raised in its honor. This is why, in many nomes, a Serapeum is dedicated to one of Osiris's members: the head at Abydos, the ear at Sais, the dorsal spine at Mendes, the left leg at the island of Biggeh near Philae, and so on.

The only part of Osiris's body that Isis failed to recover was the male member: Typhon had thrown it into the river and the lepidotus, the sea bream, and the pike fed upon it—whence the sacred horror inspired by these fish.

When Osiris returned from the nether world, he undertook to train his son, Horus, for combat[14] and it was thus that Horus prepared to reconquer Egypt, which was under the subjugation of the usurper Seth. Numerous battles took place. After one of his victories, Horus delivered Typhon in chains to Isis, who released him and let him go. The interminable combats were renewed until Hermes (Thoth)

---

[14]Horus, raised in the marshes of Buto by Uatchit, serpent-divinity of the Red Crown, was born of the union of Osiris and Isis "before they emerged from the belly of Nut," according to Plutarch.

persuaded the Great Ennead to declare Horus the legitimate heir of Osiris, and the power over the Two-Lands of Egypt was finally accorded to him.[15]

> As for Isis who consorted with Osiris after his death, she became the mother of Harpocrates, untimely born and weak in his lower limbs.[16]

Harpocrates (a transcription of the Egyptian *Her-pa-herd,* "the infant Horus")—represented as a newborn baby, finger on his lips, emerging from a lotus—was according to Plutarch, the personification of seeds just beginning to sprout, and according to others, the rising sun.

Plutarch himself interprets this legend and explains its symbolism by reducing it all to the climate and annual rhythm of the Nile's flooding:

> Of the stars, the Egyptians think that Sirius, the Dog Star, is the star of Isis, because it is the bringer of water. They also hold the Lion in honor, and they adorn the doorways of their shrines with gaping lions' heads, because the Nile overflows "when for the first time the Sun comes into conjunction with Leo"....[17]
>
> As they regard the Nile as the effusion of Osiris, so they hold and believe the earth to be the body of Isis, not all of it, but so much of it as the Nile covers, fertilizing it and uniting with it. From this union they make Horus to be born...and the seasonable tempering of the surrounding air is Horus, for the watery and saturated land best nurtures those exhalations which quench and abate aridity and dryness.
>
> The outermost parts of the land beside the mountains and bordering on the sea the Egyptians call Nephthys....
>
> The insidious scheming and usurpation of Typhon, then, is the power of drought, which gains control and dissipates the moisture which is the source of the Nile and its rising; and his coadjutor, the Queen of the Ethiopians, signifies allegorically the south winds from Ethiopia....
>
> The story told of the shutting up of Osiris in the chest seems to mean nothing else than the vanishing and disappearance of water....
>
> When Isis recovered Osiris and was watching Horus grow up as he was being made strong by the exhalations and mists and clouds, Typhon was vanquished but not annihilated, for the goddess who holds sway over the Earth would not permit the complete annihilation of the nature opposed to moisture,

---

[14]For details concerning these battles, see G. Lefebvre, *Romans et contes égyptiens* (Paris, 1949), p. 178, "The Contendings of Horus and Seth," after a manuscript dated from the reign of Ramses V, but probably a copy of a Middle Empire version.

[16]Plutarch, op. cit., 19.

[17]Plutarch, op. cit., 38. Cf. Aratos, verse 351. Concerning Sirius and the calendar, see Chapters 2 and 7 and Appendix VIII.

but relaxed and moderated it, being desirous that its tempering potency should persist, because it was not possible for a complete world to exist, if the fiery element left it and disappeared.[18]

Plutarch's interpretations certainly contain an element of truth. Examining the various essential themes, we note that during the entire historical period of Egypt, *the sun was situated in Leo* for the heliacal rising of Sirius. This is why the ancients, as early as the Fifth Dynasty, fashioned the temple gargoyles in the form of a lion head, a fact that seems to confirm their knowledge of the zodiac.

The assertion that the Nile flows out of Osiris is confirmed by the legend which the priests of Bigeh related when they showed the tomb of Osiris: here can be found one of the two sources of the Nile, "the pure water of Bigeh," the fertilizing water of the Nile, attributed to Osiris as the principle which favors fertilization, whence his identification with the flood waters themselves. He was *"the Great Nile who creates wheat with the water that is in him, and causes trees and flowers to germinate with his perspiration.*

In his season he is reborn, and his limbs are renewed with each year."

His left leg was buried in the *Abaton,* or tomb of Osiris, signifying "the inaccessible." The priests thought that this leg was the seat of one source of the Nile.[19] The *Abaton* was represented "under the aspect of a mountain hollowed out by a cavern in which sat Osiris as the Nile, guarded by a serpent," holding in his hands two vases overflowing with water (the symbol of Aquarius). In the shape of a human-headed bird, the soul of Osiris perched on the branches of a nearby woods. Placed in these woods were 365 offering tables to which a high priest, serving for one month at a time, brought a daily offering of milk and water.[20] Every *ten days,* Isis herself came with an offering of milk in order to "rejuvenate" Osiris. It is also said that Horus, in the form of a crocodile, conveyed the dead body of Osiris to this site.[21]

At other sites, the tomb of Osiris is a "hillock" surmounted by a tree.

The identification of Seth—or Typhon—with the dessicating principle is confirmed by the attribution to him of desert lands and all desert animals: antelope, gazelle, etc. These are ritually sacrificed in the search for the *Eye of Horus,* ritual object of the cult inscribed on all

---

[18]Ibid., 39-40. All these legends are allegories concerning sacred science.

[19]When the zodiacal signs are projected onto the human body, the sign of Aquarius is attributed to the leg.

[20]See A. Erman, *La religion égyptienne* (1904), p. 433.

[21]We recognize here the *decans* (ten days).

temple walls. Finally, the association of an Ethiopian queen with Typhon can find a geographic interpretation in the fact that the southern lands, attributed to Seth since remotest antiquity, comprised not only the twenty-two nomes of Upper Egypt, but also a large section of Nubia and all the deserts of Libya: scorched deserts and fiery South.

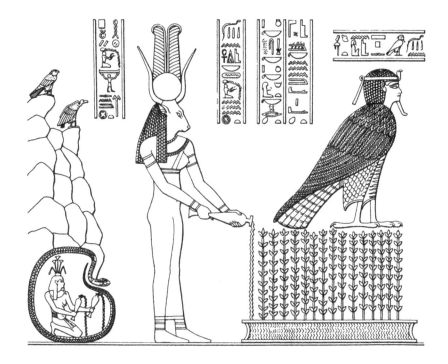

Fig. 10. *Configuration of the Sources of the Nile at Bigeh.*
North wall of the temple adjoining Hadrian's Gate, leading to the Nilometer. Philae.

Concerning the growth of Horus in the marshes and the humidity of the Delta, this also is geographically exact since the Delta—or Lower Egypt—is attributed to Horus. In contrast with Upper Egypt, which is totally devoid of normal rainfall, it is a fact that the Delta is very humid, particularly in proximity to the sea.

Plutarch's interpretation of the legend of Osiris, though charming and based upon real climatological facts, does not explain the formation of the myth; the latter is unjustified on the mere basis of these geographical facts. It is interesting, however, to point out the passage immediately following the above quotation:

> ...One would hardly be justified in rejecting that other account, to the effect that Typhon, many ages ago, held sway over Osiris's domain; for Egypt used to be all a sea, and, for that reason, even today it is found to have shells in its mines and mountains. Moreover, all the springs and wells, of which there are many, have a saline and brackish water, as if some stale dregs of the ancient sea had collected there.
>
> But, in time, Horus overpowered Typhon; that is to say, there came on a timely abundance of rain, and the Nile forced out the sea and revealed the fertile land, which it filled out with its alluvial deposits.[22]

Here again, the tradition related by Plutarch rests on a basic truth which can be verified and completed by contemporary geological facts. It refers to two distinct episodes in the creation of the Nile Valley as shown by its substratum.

The *sandstone* which covers all of Egypt and extends very far toward the West into the Libyan deserts and to the south of Nubia forms two distinct layers: *the lower layer* contains a bed of silicified leaves and trees such as can be seen a few kilometers from Cairo, close to the *Red Mountain*. Although Plutarch does not mention it, the ancients certainly knew this petrified forest, as it was situated close to the quarries where they mined the precious red sandstone, in great demand for the construction of certain monuments and statues.[23]

The upper stratum of sandstone contains sea shells and marine mollusks, confirming the fact that after having been covered with forests, *this part of the continent used to be all a sea,* as Plutarch says. But at this epoch, which precedes the Tertiary, the contours which were to delineate Egypt did not as yet have their definite form. Still, during the Miocene, the primitive Nile irrigated a part of the Libyan desert;[24] it was only toward the beginning of the Pliocene that the present valley of Egypt was formed in which the Nile settled, abandoning the Libyan plateau.

But the epic of the Nile was far from over; its encroachments and withdrawals still modified the aspect of the continents. Also, toward the middle of the Pliocene, the Mediterranean engulfed the valley, flowing in as far as Aswan like a narrow fjord; deposits left on the riverbanks

[22]Plutarch, op. cit., p. 40.

[23]For example, the sanctuary erected by Hatshepsut at Karnak to house the sacred boat, as well as numerous colossi, are made of this crystalline sandstone, which itself reportedly contains remains of petrified wood.

[24]The beginning of the Miocene dates back some 29 million years. The ancient mouth of the Nile was situated more than 100 kilometers south of the Mediterranean shores, at the same level as Wadi Farag and the Moghara Depression.

The beginning of the Pliocene dates back 12 million years.

testify to this fact. Finally, the time arrived when, according to Plutarch, *the Nile forced out the sea, and revealed the fertile land, which it filled out with its alluvial deposits,* a victory that is situated as occurring toward the end of the Tertiary. Since then, in obedience to considerable variations from the movement of withdrawal and the alternation of the rains, the Nile carved its bed deeper and deeper while leaving traces of its successive beds in numerous levels—or terraces—bordering its banks and upon which many flint "workshops" have been found.

Thus the valley of Egypt was formed, but the mouth of the Nile was located at the level of Cairo and the Delta did not yet exist. It was only during the Quaternary that the Nile, after having carved its bed, leveled off and formed the Delta with alluvial deposits about thirty meters in thickness. According to Herodotos, the Egyptians thought that at the beginnings of their history, all lands situated north of Lake Moeris were but marshes:

> What the Egyptians say about the configuration of their country seemed to me very reasonable. For anyone who sees Egypt must perceive, if he has only common powers of observation. . . . that the part of Egypt (the Delta) to which the Greeks go in their ships is acquired country, the gift of the river. The same is true of the land above the lake, to the distance of three days' voyage, which is exactly the same kind of alluvial land.[25]

Then, after having described Egypt in its entirety and having given its dimensions from the sea to Elephantine, Herodotos adds:

> The greater portion of the country seemed to me to be, as the priests declared, a tract gained from the water by the inhabitants.[26]

Herodotos compares the ancient gulf formed by the future Egypt to the Red Sea, and estimating that this gulf could have been filled up within 20,000 years, or perhaps only in 10,000 years (in fact, it is a matter of about one million years), he inquires and then concludes:

> I give credit to those from whom I received this account of Egypt and am myself, moreover, strongly of the same opinion.[27]

In sum, it would appear that those who informed Herodotos had, as he says himself, a rather precise idea as to the formation of their soil.

[25]Herodotos, op. cit., II, pp. 4-5.
[26]Ibid., II, p. 10.
[27]Ibid., II, p. 12.

In any case, there was an unbroken tradition concerning an alluvial origin for the Delta and the existence of a maritime gulf before this ushering in of earth by the Nile. A great civilization must have preceded the vast movements of water that passed over Egypt, which leads us to assume that the Sphinx already existed, sculptured in the rock of the west cliff at Gizeh, that Sphinx whose leonine body, except for the head, shows indisputable signs of aquatic erosion.[28]

We have no idea when and how the submersion of the Sphinx took place. Both ancient and modern texts concerning this monument are rare and remain evasive. No Greek traveler makes mention of it and Pliny devotes only a few lines to it after having described the Pyramids:

> In front of them is the Sphinx, which deserves to be described even more, and yet the Egyptians have passed it over in silence. The inhabitants of the region regard it as a deity.[29]

It is known that the great hollow carved into the rock around the Sphinx was filled up several times during the course of history by sand dunes which submerged all but the head. A commemorative stela erected between the paws of the Sphinx recounts how Thothmes IV (1425 B.C.) had the sand cleared away from it during the first year of his reign. Wishing to perform an act of worship to Harmachis once while he was out hunting, the king stopped and drew near to the Sphinx:

> ...Now, a great magical power had existed in this place from the beginning of all time and it extended over all the region.... And at this time, the Sphinx-form of the most mighty god Khepera came to this place and the greatest of Souls, the holiest of the holy ones, rested therein.[30]

The sun being at its zenith, Thothmes IV became drowsy, and the Sphinx spoke to him, saying:

> Behold me, O my son Thothmes... the sand whereon I have my being hath enveloped me in on all sides; say unto me that thou wilt do for me all that I desire.[31]

---

[28]It is maintained that this erosion was wrought by desert sands, but the entire body of the Sphinx is protected from all desert winds coming from the West, the only winds that could effect erosion. Only the head protrudes from this hollow, and it shows no signs of erosion.

[29]Pliny, *Natural History*, XXXVI, p. 17. Tr. Eichholz.

[30]E. A. Wallis Budge, op. cit., vol. 4, p. 80 et seq. Stela of the Sphinx.

[31]Ibid.

It is thus that the Sphinx was liberated from the sands, but according to Maspero, it seems that this was not the first time:

> The stela of the Sphinx bears, on line 13, the cartouche of Khephren in the middle of a gap. . . . There, I believe, is the indication of an excavation of the Sphinx carried out under this prince, and consequently the more or less certain proof that the Sphinx was already covered with sand during the time of Cheops and his predecessors.[32]

A legend affirms that even in Cheops' day, the age of the Sphinx was already so remote that it was impossible to situate it in time. This Sphinx is a human and colossal work. There is an enigma about it that is linked with the very enigma posed by the Sphinx itself. The account

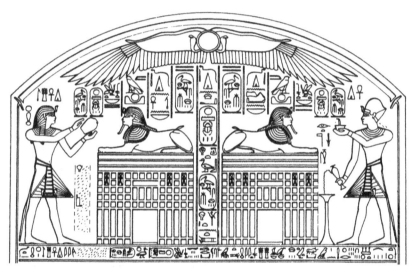

Fig. 11. *Stela of the Sphinx of Gizeh* (upper section). Thothmes IV, Eighteenth Dynasty.

of Diodoros is the only document that sheds any light on the Nile's flooding of the valley during a remote epoch when the land was already inhabited by a great people. This took place during the reign of Osiris, after this *Neter* had founded several famous cities:

> Then it happened that the Nile, at the time of the rising of Sirius which is the season when the river is usually at flood, breaking out of its banks inundated

---

[32]G. Maspero, *The Passing of the Empires* (New York, 1900). According to other Egyptologists, Khephren, inspired by a rock in the shape of a lion, carved the Sphinx there! But they forget that the Sphinx is carved in a cavity excavated by human hands and eroded by water.

a large section of Egypt, particularly that part where Prometheus was governor. Few inhabitants escaped from this deluge.[33]

Observe that in the myth, Osiris represents the waters of the West and of renewal. Rather than seeing a simple symbolization of the territory in the mythical legends of Osiris and Horus, as Plutarch does, would it not be wiser to see them as the traditional description of the great events which formed the land of Egypt? Then the reign of Osiris would evoke the flowering of a great civilization become legendary, which preceded the destruction by the waters of the river. The myth's death and resurrection of Osiris would admirably motivate the fact we have just described. Following this destruction by the flooding came the reign of Horus.

The Osirian principle is that of karmic religion—whose profound significance we will later examine—while the revelation of Horus is reserved for the intimate teaching of the temple, for those who have renounced the illusions of this earth.[34]

The Materials

It is important to stress the particular choice made by the overseers of the work in the selection of materials destined for the construction of a temple dedicated to a particular *Neter*. In order to obey a symbolism dictated by Nature, they would never hesitate to transport monoliths weighing hundreds of tons for almost 1,000 kilometers on the Nile, because their symbolic usage was conditioned by the particular nature of the genesis of each kind of stone. Therefore we must also glance at the principal stones utilized in the construction of Egyptian monuments.

1. *Stone of igneous origin: diorite, basalt, syenite, black or red granite*, which are found in the Sinai Peninsula and mainly at Aswan at the level of the First Cataract. Here the Nile rages between huge rocks of dark granite for more than ten kilometers from the island of Philae to that of Elephantine. From the neighboring quarries of Aswan also come the numerous red granite obelisks dedicated to Ra, the sun, which stand before the pylons of the temples. In the temple of Luxor, for example, each of the two obelisks was set upon a base, also of red granite, upon which two groups of four sun-worshiping Cynocephali (baboons) were sculptured in the round.

---

[33]Diodoros of Sicily, op. cit., I, p. 19. Prometheus is to be equated with Ptah.
[34]The theme of the two theologies is developed in Chapter 9, "The Two Ways."

Granite is called *mat* and its hieroglyphs are followed by a determinative depicting a kind of vase. And granite is so much associated with its place of extraction, that is, the first nome of Upper Egypt, that the name of the metropolis of its nome, *Abu* (meaning "elephant"), is also followed by the distinctive determinative of granite.

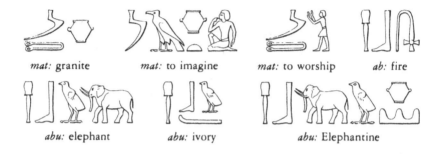

| *mat:* granite | *mat:* to imagine | *mat:* to worship | *ab:* fire |

| *abu:* elephant | *abu:* ivory | *abu:* Elephantine |

Fig. 12

The word *mat* designates granite in general and perhaps most particularly red granite, because when black granite is meant, the color is usually stipulated. This same word *mat,* determined by a man holding his hand to his mouth, means "dream, discover, imagine, conceive"; determined by a man in the posture of worship, it means "praise, adore." As to the word *abu*—designating elephant, ivory, and the isle of Elephantine—its root is *ab;* when accompanied by the determinative for fire, the latter designates a temple brazier.

Granite, coming from fire, is also employed for certain doors or for colossi. At Luxor, for example, the colossi standing or walking in the name of Ramses (birth of the Sun) which surround the first court of the temple are of *red granite. Black granite* was chosen for carving the seated colossi in front of the pylon: *"that of the west is carved from a block of black granite chosen in the quarry so that the red crown is found to be carved in a vein of red traversing the block."*[35] On the sides of each throne seating the other two black granite colossi at the second entrance to the temple is the representation of the Nile gods uniting the Two-Lands, as well as the *black cubit,* identical in measure to the cubit of the Rodah Nilometer and to the two *basalt* cubits of Dendera. Black granite was also chosen for sculpting the splendid statue of Thothmes III bearing, in the manner of a Nile god, offerings of plants

[35]*Le Temple de l'Homme,* III, p. 43.

and domestic fowl carved with incredible precision, considering the hardness of the material.[36] Lastly, the quartzite walls of Hatshepsut's "red chapel" depict ritual scenes, while its black granite foundation is entirely devoted to descriptions of the territory: the symbols of the nomes supported by the Nile gods, villages, fortresses, and provinces.

Black diorite was chosen for carving the celebrated "Palermo Stone" on which the list of kings of the Ancient Empire is inscribed, registering for each reign the level of the high Nile in cubits, hand breadths, and fingers, year by year, as well as the important events of each reign such as the arrival of products from Punt during the rule of Sneferu or those from the Sinai Peninsula during the rule of Sahura. In short, it is a veritable chronicle going back to Menes, including as well the census of cattle, an accounting of gold and fields, and the principal religious or traditional festivals.

In *black basalt* (volcanic rock) are the fragments of cubits whose surfaces, besides their subdivision into palms and fingers, bear precious indications concerning the length of Egypt, the height of the Nile's spate, and the flood level at three essential points: *Abu* (Elephantine), *Per-Hapi* (near Old Cairo), and *Behedet* (the marshes of the Delta).

Thus the selection of material for each object or statue conveys, through its *symbolique*, an orientation concerning the basic meaning to be sought. Here the color black, which is that of Atum's hillock at the origin of the world, is related to the entire land of Egypt, *Kemit*, the Black Land, and its fecundity. This is a beautiful example of *symbolique*.

2. *Sandstone*, which is found throughout the territory as far as Nubia, is the material most frequently employed for important structures. But a distinction must be made between the temple hewn from rock—extracted from matter, as at Abu-Simbel—and the constructed temple, defined by the material. Sandstone is a sedimentary deposit composed of different aspects of silica reduced to sand and agglomerated. It can be more or less colored by salts of aluminum or iron. Therefore it is a substance originating from *fire* (the quartz), ground and transported by *water*. Being a result of alluvial deposits, sandstone symbolizes *earth*.

In Egypt, a distinction is made mainly between two kinds of sandstone, that of *Gebel Silsileh*, gray-rose in tone, and that of *Gebel*

---

[36]Found at the foot of Hatshepsut's southern obelisk at Karnak (Legrain Cat. No. 42056). Now in the Cairo Museum.

el-Ahmar (the Red Mountain), which is composed of red quartzite more or less packed with pebbles and remains of petrified wood.

As a curiosity, we cite an extraordinary and little-known use of quartzite in the infrastructure of two Thirteenth Dynasty pyramids, a dynasty about which almost nothing is known.

In a pyramid of unfired bricks dressed with limestone, erected in the name of *Khenzer User-ka-ra,* the burial chamber is made of a monolith of very fine-grained and extremely hard quartzite weighing about sixty tons, hollowed out in such a way as to leave a place in the bottom for the sarcophagus and the chest of Canopic jars.

In the other pyramid, which is anonymous, the funerary chamber, first covered with limestone and in two places with granite, contains a quartzite monolith of about 150 tons. Carved in the shape of a trough, this enormous block, like the aforementioned, was worked so that the sarcophagus and the chest of Canopic jars projected from the mass of stone. Three enormous blocks of quartzite formed the roof.[37]

3. The third kind of stone that plays an important role in construction is *white limestone.* This sedimentary rock contains numerous layers of flint nodules horizontally deposited, the whole overlaid with beds of sandstone along both banks of the Nile from Esna to Cairo. It was from these high cliffs that the ancients excavated the pure limestone for the royal tombs of Thebes, for example, working the flint nodules as easily as the soft limestone. *The fact that extant monuments show no flint nodules broken away from their cavity reveals the existence of tools capable of easily slicing through them and, consequently, of a surprising technique and method.*

The limestone is called *the white stone,* and that of Turah (near Cairo) was particularly renowned under the name of *white stone of Aân,* designed in the writing by an eye underlined with a stroke of kohl. This is the material utilized for the splendid, newly discovered "stepping-stone" walls surrounding the pyramids of *Zoser* and *Sekhem-Khet,* which date from the Third Dynasty. It is also very likely that this same limestone of Aân was used in the construction of *White Walls,* the name for the city of Memphis where the temple of Ptah was located.

In the prehistoric period, limestone was employed to make pear-shaped maces the image of which is used to designate the color *white, hedj,* in the hieroglyphic writing. White limestone was also selected for

---

[37]See J. Vandier, *Manuel d'archéologie égyptienne,* II, (Paris, 1952-1958), pp. 202-208.

Perfect white stone of Aân   Ankh uas   Ankh
                                          milk   alabaster

Fig. 13

the monument to the Sed festival of Sesostris the First at Karnak (Twelfth Dynasty), and this fact prompts its comparison with a certain mace of white limestone belonging to King Narmer and depicting the first known ceremony of the Sed festival, dating back to the First Dynasty.

In the construction, limestone symbolizes *Air*, as if it were vegetal matter.

Among the buildings of the Ancient Empire, mention must be made of the descending passageway connecting the pyramid of Unas situated on the plateau, with its "temple in the valley."[38] This passageway, 666 meters long and 6 meters 70 wide, was entirely paved and its adjoining limestone walls were covered with magnificent bas-reliefs representing all manner of religious, craftworking, and agricultural scenes. It should be remembered that it was in the pyramid of Unas that the religious texts concerning afterlife, known as the *Pyramid Texts,* were first discovered, carved on the walls of interior chambers. The burial chamber is lined with limestone on only three of its walls, the west wall and the ends of the north and south walls encasing the basalt sarcophagus being made of *alabaster.* The hearses blocking the corridor are of *red granite.*

Alabaster probably originated from limestone in a liquid or muddy state, whence come its gray, brown, or rosy whorls floating in it like veils, as if this matter were in a state of *becoming* from a more terrestrial state toward a more subtle, flowing, state that could be compared to cream rising to the top of milk. It is curious, in this connection, to note that *ankh uas* (the sap of life) is one of the designations of milk, and that *ankh* (life) sometimes also serves to designate alabaster or some object executed in this material.

But the term most specifically designating alabaster is *ches,* a phonetic group which, depending on the determinative, can also mean an edible grain, or something precious. Alabaster is frequently qualified as clear or pure, followed by the name of its place of origin, the most famous being *Hat-nub.*

[38] All the pyramids were constructed on the plateau and connected by a long causeway to a temple located in the valley.

Hat-nub, "house of gold," is the name of an important alabaster deposit in the Arabian Mountain, located about twenty kilometers southeast of Tel el-Amarna. Since the Fourth Dynasty, the Egyptians went there to seek the beautiful translucent alabaster necessary for their monuments. It is important to note this appellation of "house of gold" for an alabaster quarry, as gold is never found in a limestone mine. This is evidently an allusion to a phase of the Hermetic opus, and it is not without interest to remark that the term *Hat-nub,* chamber or castle of gold, serves to designate:

—the funerary or sarcophagus chamber in the tombs;

—the workshops where the temple statues of the *Neters* were carved and decorated with precious metals;

—the spot where statues of Osiris were placed in the Serapeum of the most important temples and where several ceremonies of the *Neter's* resurrection took place during the month of *Khoiak* (Christmas).

Among the famous monumental masterpieces in alabaster is the sanctuary of Thothmes III at Karnak, designed to house the sacred boat of Amon; each of its walls is made from *a single piece of alabaster* eight meters in length.

4. *Unbaked brick* made out of Nile mud which is very rich in vegetal matter. In the constructions, it symbolizes *water;* texts of the foundation ritual call it "marriage of earth and water."

When the symbolism so demanded, there was no hesitation in building with hard stones upon foundations of unfired bricks. The surrounding wall of the courtyard of Nektanebo at Luxor, for example, is made of unbaked bricks curved inward so as to form archways in both floor plan and elevation; the northwest angle of this wall is worked in stones resting on brick.[39] Certain pyramids are made of sun-baked brick with a facing of limestone, such as that of *Khenzer User-ka-ra* mentioned earlier. Inversely, unfired brick is found surrounding a core made of stones, as in the pyramid of Sneferu at Mêdûm.

The predynastic temple of Medamud, consecrated to Gemini, is made of two mounds of unfired brick surrounded by walls and headed by a double pylon, all built in this same material coated with limewash.

Brick plays an important symbolic role in the ritual of temple foundation, which obeyed very ancient specifications. All the plans always refer to a *divine book;* thus the temple of Edfu was rebuilt under the Ptolemies according to the *"book of foundation composed by*

---

[39]See *Le Temple de l'Homme,* II, Plates 47-49, and III, Chap. X.

Imhotep, son of Ptah" (Third Dynasty), a book descended from heaven to the north of Memphis. The temple of Dendera followed *a plan recorded in ancient writings dating from the Companions of Horus* (and hence an allusion to prehistory). Further, Queen Hatshepsut says that in the execution of her obelisks, she made no move that was not directly dictated by her father, Amon.

Fig. 14. *Hatshepsut Molds the First Brick, Four Times.* Karnak, Eighteenth Dynasty.

The King, the inspired one, consecrated and crowned, having abstracted himself from his "private thoughts," transmits the divine will to men through the phases of the Empire's genesis. Therefore, the King, assisted by the *Neters,* is represented at all the ceremonies of a temple's founding, the essential scenes of which are as follows:

The King and Seshat, mistress of divine books, each tap a mallet upon a stake which they are driving into the ground. This scene, known as "stretching the cord," consists in determining the *orientation* of the temple according to the circumpolar stars at a specific date of the year. It is also said that Thoth is there with his books, that Ptah-Tatenen measures the ground, that Neith utters the protective formulas, and that Selkit lays her hand upon those works destined for eternity....

Then the King ploughs a furrow with the hoe four times; he scatters the contents of a bushel-basket, shapes the first brick *uniting earth and water* four times, for the four corners of the temple, and after having circled the temple with incense, the King *gives the house to its Master*.[40]

The construction of the temple takes place after very scrupulous selection of materials according to the symbolic intention, and it is also according to the king's command, with the assistance of the *Neters,* that the quarry is chosen from which the stone is to be extracted.

The choice of the veins running through the stone, of faultless masses for blocks which are often enormous and, as with alabaster, extremely fragile, certainly implies a profound knowledge of the life of rock. The stones are never taken by attacking the mountain from without, but only in interior masses which have never undergone erosion, and immense caverns hollowed in the mountains by Pharaonic quarrymen can still be seen today.[41]

To this effect, here are several words carved on the rocks of Wadi-Hammanat which are rich in gold, under Ramses IV, relating to the prospecting of quarries in the mountain of Bekhan.[42] There it is said of the king:

Excellent in wisdom like Thoth, he (the king) *perceived the words of the house of sacred writings*.... In order to visit the quarries, then, in obedience to the *Neter's* desire, he commanded *the scribe of sacred writings* and the prophet of the house of Min (of Coptos) to search *Bekhen* mountain for the material destined for *the great and marvelous monuments of the "Place of Truth."*

This is an instance of a royal theocratic act.

Next, a large expedition leaves for the mountain, led by the first Prophet of *Amon* and including a chief artisan, three overseers, quarrymen, stonecutters, draftsmen, and more than 8,000 men mobilized for these undertakings.

---

[40]See *Le Temple de l'Homme,* III, p. 116, "Donner la maison à son maitre," an example of symbolique.

[41]For the construction of the Gothic cathedrals, the stones were likewise sought from the interior of the rock formation.

[42]Stone extracted from this mountain is a gritty schist of dark, brilliant color and very hard. See H. Gautier, *Dictionnaire des noms géographiques,* VI, p. 119.

Survey of Prehistoric Egypt

The progressive drought that transformed the great forests of North Africa into steppes and then into immense deserts during the Quaternary wiped out all traces of life, plant as well as animal, except in the areas surrounding the rare waterholes. Thus almost nothing is known about the Paleolithic period apart from several rock stations found between the First and Second Cataracts. The petroglyphs representing long processions of elephants allow us to conclude that the population which carved these images were contemporaneous with the dense forests necessary to the life of these animals, a period estimated to date back about 20,000 years.[43] The figurations of ostrich, giraffe, and gazelle are the most recent and would correspond to the Magdalenian culture of Europe (between 9,000 and 14,000 years ago).

The most important Neolithic sites are *Merimde-Beni-Salame,* the *Fayum* in the north and *Tasa* in the south (polished stone and no copper objects). Excavations there provide the basis for concluding that these places were occupied by hunting and farming people manifesting very advanced craftsmanship in textiles, ivory ornaments, and innumerable tools worked in flint and the hardest stones. The burial ritual appears to differ somewhat in the north and south: At Merimde-Beni-Salame, the bodies were lying in fetal position on the right side, with the head to the south, the face turned eastward, while at *Tasa,* personages in the same position had the head toward the south but facing *west,* a burial mode encountered, with the same orientation, during the periods that followed in Upper Egypt and Lower Nubia. This involves a symbolique related to the land of *Lower Egypt* (Merimde-Beni-Salame) and that of *Upper Egypt* (Tasa, Badari, el-Amrah, etc.), and not to people of different cults.[44]

The most important objects discovered at these sites are *basalt vases* indicative of a drilling technique that made possible the boring of the hardest stones, and *cosmetic palettes* still containing traces of red ocher and malachite that reveal the use of makeup, which is found throughout the entire historic period. Wheat, barley, buckwheat, and flax were cultivated. The barley grains found in the silos of the Fayum

[43]See Dr. E. Massoulard, *Préhistoire et protohistoire d'Egypte,* pp. 91-95, *Institut d'Ethnologie* (Paris, 1949). Dunbar would have these figurations date from the end of the Aurignacian, in which he situates the disappearance of the elephant from Egypt. For the age of these periods, see Willard F. Libby, *Radiocarbon Dating* (Chicago, 1955).

[44]It is fitting to point out that for reasons which could not be other than symbolic, the corpse in certain instances was cut into pieces—in the image of the myth of Osiris—and the parts of the body probably disposed according to a determined orientation.

pose an interesting problem: In order to have obtained a variety of barley identical to that now cultivated in Egypt, the wild barley from which it is derived would have to have been cultivated for a very long time, so that *the origin of agriculture would be much anterior to the Neolithic A period of the Fayum.*[45]

These grains were submitted to radiocarbon testing, which showed them to date from about 4,200 to 4,600 B.C. Hence the origin of agriculture in Egypt must certainly be much anterior to this date.[46]

The discovery of elephant bones in the Fayum again poses the problem regarding the date of this animal's disappearance from North Africa.

Three successive civilizations are classified in the *Predynastic* or *Chalcolithic* period in which copper objects appear:

—the *Badarian* and the *Amratian,* remains of which are encountered only in the south of Upper Egypt, directly succeeding the *Tasian;*

—the *Gerzean,* originating in the Fayum, which succeeded the two previous civilizations in Upper Egypt but, according to several indications, would have been contemporaneous in other parts of Egypt.

The *Badarians,* determined by radiocarbon as having existed from about 3,800 to 4,100 years before our era, were very refined. Not only was their pottery the most beautiful and well made of the prehistoric period, but the numerous ivory ornaments—combs carved with bird heads, rings, bracelets, minutely worked figurines,—all testify to their taste for adornment. They used makeup which was kept in ivory vases or horns, and which they scooped out with spoons also made of ivory. One of their tombs alone contained some 5,000 to 6,000 beads of enameled steatite, *the first known example of glass paste,* imitating turquoise almost to perfection. This lapis lazuli paste, capable of scratching glass, is very siliceous, and requires very high temperatures for its manufacture. These beads, similar to those of the historic period, were used to make necklaces, bracelets, and girdles. Also dating back to this period is *the first endless screw* (Archimedes' screw) carved in ivory (one cannot but wonder how), as well as straight or curved needles containing eyes, and the first known examples of *casting* and of *hammered copper.*

The *Amratians* brought a new variety to the technique of

---

[45] See. E. Massoulard, op. cit., pp. 30-43.

[46] See Willard F. Libby, op. cit., pp. 77-79. When dates can be otherwise acertained, they tend to show radiocarbon dating to be *posterior* to them.

enameling by applying it upon a core, such as a jewel in the shape of a bird made from this material. The hard stone cosmetic palettes take animal shapes: hippopotamus, antelope, turtle, etc., among which *Hathor's symbol* is noticed. Needles, pins, and other small copper tools are numerous, and *the first objects in gold and silver,* beads and vase lids, are found in these sites, dated by radiocarbon to about 3,700 to 3,950 years before our era.[47]

The statuary provides numerous examples of figurines, more or less stylized or realistic, and several instances of steatopygous (fat-buttocked) figures raise the question of race: The subjects of these two civilizations are all dolichocephalic (long-headed) and their hair is brown or black, braided or wavy (curly hair is an exception). But while the Badarians have a large nose and are beardless, the Amratians, with their aquiline nose, appear to have a short, pointed beard,[48] and one of the elements of their dress seems to have been the Libyan "sheath" with a long cloak and sandals.

These types of men, the one hairless and the other shaggy, recall the old Hindu tradition that speaks of the former as a people originally from *Lemuria* (a continent submerged, with the exception of certain islands—Madagascar, Indonesia, Ceylon, etc.), who were reputed to have been beardless, that is, sexually still in a phase of determination (the third race), while the *Atlanteans* (the fourth race) were sexually determined and the men bearded. According to this view, traces of Lemures would remain on the eastern coast of Africa, while populations of the western region would hark back to Atlanteans.

The *Gerzean* civilization, encountered in the Fayum, in the south of Upper Egypt, along the Red Sea and in Lower Nubia, aside from several innovations is very much like its antecedents. The flint tools attain a perfection that will never be surpassed, in Egypt or elsewhere. Besides the admirable knives which are sometimes more than forty centimeters in length, it is sufficient to mention several very thin and carefully polished flint rings presenting a technical problem of great interest because any percussive work would inevitably have shattered them. The first example of *cast copper* is found and the first specimens of *lead* and *iron* work, such as a *falcon* formed with a thin leaf of lead applied to a wooden core. Gold and silver objects are plentiful and artistically decorated, as, for example, the handle of a flint knife made of two sheets

[47]See Tables 2 and 3.

[48]The Badarians have been compared to more recent predynastic civilizations as well as to the Dravidians and the Vedics; the Amratians to the Eskimos and Ainus as well as to modern white races and, above all, to the ancient peoples of western North Africa. But the place of origin of these populations of the Nile Valley is still much disputed.

of gold stitched together by a gold thread, with one side bearing the image of two intertwined serpents similar to the caduceus. The famous ivory knife handle from Gebel el-Arak is an example of great sculptural skill. Depicted on one side is a combat between what are probably Libyan personages; on the other, a Mesopotamian framed by two lions: The proportions of the figures are perfect and could not be considered as "primitive art."[49] It is useless to seek a Mesopotamian origin for this piece whose symbolique imposes itself: Egypt is the very knife which separates the East (Mesopotamia) from the West (Libya). During the epoch of Seti I, furthermore, the canal marking the Egypto-Asiatic frontier at Zalu was called *"the water of the cutting."*

The *symbolism* of a great many objects is clearly manifested by amulets in the shape of lions, jackals, falcons, flies, frogs, bulls, crocodiles, etc., such as the Egyptians continued to wear throughout the entire historic period.

Fig. 15. *Boat Carrying an Elephant, Symbol of the City of the First Nome of Upper Egypt.*
Red painting on white bowl done before firing.
(F. Petrie, *Prehistoric Egypt*)

Among the many games are marbles as well as the prototype of Pharaonic chess which made use of the hieroglyphic sign *men,* meaning "foundation." Lastly, Gerzean pottery, made from quarry clay, is strongly characterized by its red-on-white figures which are painted before firing. The most common motifs are of boats propelled by oarsmen and surmounted with two cabins, one of which is fitted with a pole decorated with pennants and emblems bearing the *symbols of the Pharaonic nomes:* the bucranium, for example, symbol of the seventh nome of Upper Egypt, and the elephant, designating the name of

---

[49]See plate 2, the knife from Gebel el-Arak.

Elephantine. The elephant's presence on these boats and the continuity of its symbol to designate the metropolis of the first nome of Upper Egypt brings to mind the epoch when the elephant lived in that country. Indeed, either the symbol was imported by people coming from the south, an assumption which makes little sense, or else the original naming of Elephantine after this animal goes back to a remote epoch when Aswan was not yet the arid desert of today. The forests had already disappeared by the beginning of the historical epoch. Thus a tradition must have been transmitted regarding the existence of an entirely different kind of life in this area. This would serve to prove either that a race of men lived there since the time of the forests, or that this was transmitted by legend. In any case, the fact remains that men coexisted with elephants in this region at a period dating back, according to Dunbar, beyond 20,000 years.

The origin of the Gerzeans is very much debated. Ethnologically, the fact of dolichocephalism excludes the possibility of a Mesopotamian origin knowing that the mountain people of these countries are specifically brachycephalic. Nevertheless, an indisputable artistic influence on certain details evokes the idea that several elements originating in Mesopotamia penetrated through Wadi-Hammamat toward Coptos, the main center of prehistoric sites. On the other hand, the majority of Amratian artistic remains clearly relate to the making of the later objects found in all West Africa. On the basis of certain fat-buttocked figurines, it is not out of the question that a so-called "Negroid" element (such as is encountered in Malta, Menton, and in Africa) was at that time mingling with the natives who were peopling part of North Africa as well as the Nile Valley, and of which the Bushmen are the last representatives.[50]

Ethnological studies have indeed revealed four racial types as composing the predynastic population: a Cro-Magnon type, a Negroid type (such as the famous specimens of Menton), a Mediterranean type corresponding to the contemporary white races, and, lastly, a mixed type. With rare exceptions there are no *blacks* properly so called. The specimens from the beginning of the dynastic period mark a distinct augmentation of Mediterranean elements to the detriment of the Negroids. Are we dealing here, according to the tradition, with the conquest—or reconquest—by the *Shemsu-Hor* of the territory then occupied by mixed populations who took refuge on the banks of the Nile?

---

[50]See previous discussion. The term *Negroid* does not at all mean *Negro*. This term encompasses certain particularities concerning the proportions of the limbs and a faint prognathism, but has nothing to do with the skin color, which may be white.

The term *Shemsu-Hor,* incorrectly translated as "Companions of Horus," literally means *Followers of Horus* in the precise sense of "those who follow the path of Horus," that is, the "Horian way," also called the solar way or *paths of Ra.*

This epithet applies to superior beings who produced the race of Pharaohs, as opposed to the majority of people who follow the common way, the way of Osiris. These *Followers of Horus* bear with them a knowledge of "divine origin," and unify the country with it.

One fact is certain: the mode of burial in fetal position, characteristic of the entire prehistoric period (the precessional cycle of Gemini), did not disapper immediately, and under the First Dynasty, near a tomb of archaic character, a royal functionary was found buried in an elongated position.[51] Certain instances of burial in fetal position, as well as objects called "predynastic," have been found in Ancient Empire tombs.[52] These facts seem to indicate that it is rather reckless to classify systematically all Badarian, Amratian, and Gerzean, etc., sites as "predynastic." The customs and mores of these populations, as well as numerous objects, are indeed very different in usages and style from those of the historical epoch. But it is not impossible that the peoples dominated by the *Shemsu-Hor* preserved their customs and beliefs during a relatively long period of time before totally adapting to the religious directive of sovereigns who brought them a sacred science.

However imprecise the radiocarbon dates—most often posterior to the true dates—they make it possible to ascertain the coexistence of so-called predynastic populations with those of the beginnings of the historic Pharaonic Empire. The Gerzean remains testify to the existence at that epoch of a population long in possession of agricultural knowledge and a craftsmanship of incontestable perfection, but offering no evidence of a writing system, apart from a few pottery signs. In the First Dynasty tombs, on the other hand, there is the sudden appearance of a complete writing and tokens of a high science.

The First Dynasties

Until the great discoveries made in 1954 at Heluan and at Sakkara of grandiose royal tombs from the first dynasties, it was still possible to

[51]See Walter B. Emery, *Great Tombs of the First Dynasty,* I, pp. 98-99.
[52]See Sir W. M. F. Petrie and J. E. Quibell, *Naqada and Ballas,* No. 95; for example, see Tomb 524.

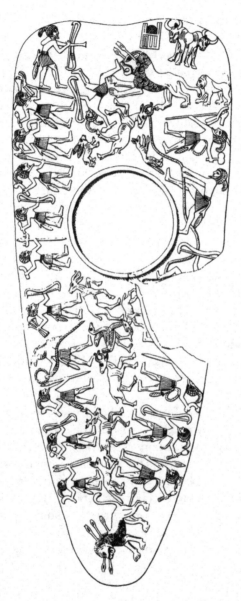

Fig. 16. *So-called Prehistoric Palette found at Hierakonpolis, one fragment of which is in the Louvre and two others in the British Museum.*
Above, from right to left, the emblems of Horus are shown. The personages wear the ritual tail, a characteristic of the Pharaoh.

speak of the beginnings of historic Egypt in terms of a primitive architecture in sun-dried bricks, comprising only a few rare stone pavings. But even if these tombs of kings and private personages have all suffered considerable plundering, they reveal that:

—Since the First Dynasty, the nobility had stone tombs: The burial chambers were made of huge blocks of white limestone painstakingly fitted together, and the superstructure of unfired bricks formed step walls carefully coated with white plaster.

—Walking staffs, fans, chairs, beds, and chests were of common usage; the legs of the bedsteads were admirably fashioned out of ebony or ivory in the shape of bull-hooves.

—The linen garments show surprising regularity in weaving—comparable to those made by modern machine—and incredible fineness of thread: *"It is difficult to believe that it was spun with a simple spindle. To tell the truth, it seems that spinning is another of the mysteries of the ancient Egyptians, and the mind still gropes in vain to find its solution."*[53] Second Dynasty stelae testify, moreover, that these textiles were dyed in red, green, blue, and white.

The results of these excavations show that the Egyptian civilization of the Archaic period was much more advanced than previously supposed...[54]

The discovery at Sakkara of immense tombs (more than fifty to eighty meters long) dating from the First Dynasty in the names of kings also found in the small structures at Abydos, again raises questions that had been considered as settled. Sakkara can now be considered the true necropolis, and the rudimentary tombs at Abydos simple cenotaphs. Although burned and plundered, these tombs still yield a great many clay stoppers sealed in the name of each king, as well as ivory plaques used as labels on the wine jars. One of the most amazing details of the tomb of Uadji (third king of the First Dynasty) is *a ledge surrounding the entire superstructure on which was placed an arrangement of clay bull heads fitted with real horns.* The interior of the superstructure of another tomb formed a vast recessed chamber, entirely covered with painted frescoes, *the most ancient ever found.* But, given the fact that no bodies of any First Dynasty kings have ever been discovered, either at Abydos or at Sakkara, the problem of their final resting place remains unsolved.

[53]Zaki y Saad, *Fouilles de Hélouan. Les grandes découvertes archéologiques de 1954,* in *La Revue du Caire,* Special Issue 1954.

[54]W.B. Emery, op. cit.

Earlier discoveries at Hierakonpolis (the former capital of the South) and at Abydos (the Thinite capital) had already revealed the existence of cities and fortresses constructed of unfired brick on the edges of the Libyan desert. Not far from Ballas, a great number of ovens still containing grains of wheat and roasted barley reveal that the use of *beer* was already known; these ovens are meant for the malting of grain used to make a light beer. The enamel industry was enriched by several colors: the Horus name of King Aha (first king of the First Dynasty) *in brown enamel is inlaid in the blue enamel* covering the entire surface of a round vase.

Rock crystal was used not only for arrowheads but also for vases, the fabrication of which raises a problem as yet unsolved. Even if the exterior polish can be explained, the hollowing of potbellied rock crystal vases—several examples of which were discovered at Sakkara—remains incomprehensible. Likewise the procedure involved in the making of the extremely thin and perfectly spherical crystal vase found by Zaki Saad at Heluan.

Perfection was attained in *copper working* and encountered in a vast variety of objects such as the pitcher with the tubular spout in hammered copper, covered with thin silver leaf. As for jewelry, we cite only the bracelet of King Djer, made of twenty-seven elements each having the shape of a palace-facade crowned by a falcon. Thirteen gold parts, poured molten into a mold and then chiseled and burnished, alternate with fourteen turquoise elements.

It must be borne in mind that these few examples of objects testifying to a very high civilization are but poor vestiges found in tombs which had been plundered over and over again during several millennia.

The hieroglyphic writing is perfected and completed. In the tomb of an official of King Djet—or King "Serpent" (fourth king of the First Dynasty), two scribe's palettes were discovered with their cups bearing traces of red and black ink. Also dating from the same king is a fragment of accounts. The tomb of Hemaka, grand vizier of King Den (fifth king of the First Dynasty), yielded a cylindrical wooden case completely covered with inlaid aromatic woods and containing a roll of black papyrus. This same tomb also contained a large number of disks in stone mosaic of surprisingly beautiful craftsmanship which are believed to have been used as spinning tops.

According to tradition, King Djet (third king of the First Dynasty) composed works on anatomy and built temples and palaces.

We are reminded here of the famous surgical papyrus whose archaic style confirms its very ancient origin. It is considered to go back to Imhotep, who personifies the great sage of the Third Dynasty. This document, which reveals a profound knowledge of the human body as a result of long observation, was possibly already very old by the Third Dynasty.

We find gestures proving the existence of the *foundation ritual* as far back as King "Scorpion" in the prehistoric age. Details concerning the ritual, revealed by the votive maces, the Narmer Palette and the Palermo Stone, suffice to confirm that from the first kings of the First Dynasty, the *fundamental bases of cult and royal ritual, the organization of the territory, sciences, and arts were already in full force.* Examples of this are the ceremony of the Sed festival which serves as proof of a perfect knowledge of sacred science, *the procession around the wall, the procession of the bull Apis,* all of which remain a tradition throughout the entire historical period.

On an ivory tablet belonging to King Den, *the sign of the year* encloses two of these ceremonies, indicating the existence of *a perfectly constituted calendar at this epoch.* It is due to this calendar, already in use *before* the third millennium, that the annals of the first kings can be composed by the Fifth Dynasty, year by year, with reference to months and days.[55]

For one of the First Dynasty kings, the Palermo Stone relates the celebration of the festival of Sokaris and the Djet festival pertaining to the cult of Osiris, a sojourn in the temple of Sais consecrated to Neith (in Lower Egypt) and then at Hierakonpolis (capital of the South), as well as the first known census of cattle, goods, and subjects.[56]

Again we remark the existence of vineyards whose most famous vintages were dutifully noted under each king (First Dynasty).

> King Djet: Vineyard of the beverage of Horus.
> King Den: Vineyard of the beverage of Horus' body.
> King Aâdj-ib: Adoration of the body of Horus.
> King Smer-kha: . . . of gold of Horus.
> King Qâ: The gold of Horus' body.[57]

Since the tombs contain sealed jars bearing these names, it is very likely that they were carefully selected wines which were consecrated to the temple cult.

[55]The present attempt by German Egyptologists to situate the institution of the calendar in the year 2780 instead of the previously accepted date of 4240 is not justifiable, since this calendar was already in use at least by the year 3000. And the establishment of a lunar and solar calendar related to the Sothic cycle would demand very long periods of observing the heavens.

[56]To these indications must be added mention of the height of the Nile's spate, which was observed in three essential points of Egypt, implying the existence of a system of measurement and survey.

[57]R. Weill, *Recueil de travaux,* XXIX, pp. 50-75.

Fig. 17. *The Narmer Palette.*
The King wears the white crown of the South in the gesture of
"ritual massacre of the prisoners" with the white mace *hedj.*

In conclusion, it must be said that it is impossible today to establish an exact chronology of the dynasties. It is impossible to clarify historically the origin of the Pharaonic sovereigns. To the contrary, it is certain that from the beginning of the so-called historical period with the first known Pharaohs, there existed a complete writing, a carefully established calendar, a social order, a census, a perfectly ordered myth and cult, all things that obviously testify to a long civilized epoch preceding the historical period.

On the other hand, no monumental document allows us to connect this state of affairs to a "prehistoric" period during which a cataclysm seems to have occurred.

An epoch of such destruction, between the ending and the beginning of a time, can only be explained in the light of similar crises. The existence of precisely such a period is observed at the end of the precessional epoch of *Taurus* (the Eighth to the Tenth Dynasties), as well as at the end of the epoch of *Aries*, at the moment of passage into the Christian era; and again we see the beginning of an identical crisis during the present epoch of passage from *Pisces* to *Aquarius*. The same symptoms characterize them: a democratization that casts into oblivion the achievements from the time of the kings and repudiates a religious metaphysics; the social disorder, moreover, is often accompanied by climatological and telluric disturbances.

Rationally, it is not comprehensible how the sole fact of the vernal point aiming at a constellation (that is, a region of the starry heavens) can produce such phenomena by passing into a new sector. The fact nevertheless remains and can be verified.

We must imagine a similarly grave crisis for the same reason during the passage of the vernal point from *Gemini* to *Taurus,* a moment that is situated toward the year 4200 B.C. The first dynasty known as historical is very probably situated about 700 years later (during the second decan of Taurus), about 3500 B.C. Starting with this First Dynasty, we observe an established cult dedicated to the principle of the *Bull;* the cult previously dedicated to the *Twins* (Gemini) as evidenced by the mounds on the virgin soil of Medamud, as well as the custom of burial in the fetal position, cease from that time on.

In parallel with this hypothesis, we observe a similar sudden and glorious renaissance at the beginning of Amon's cult of the Ram at the time of Sesostris III, toward 1900 B.C., about three centuries after the transition from *Taurus* to *Aries.*

Similarly, the definitive establishment of Christianity in the year 325 A.D., under Constantine, with the proclamation of Christianity as the

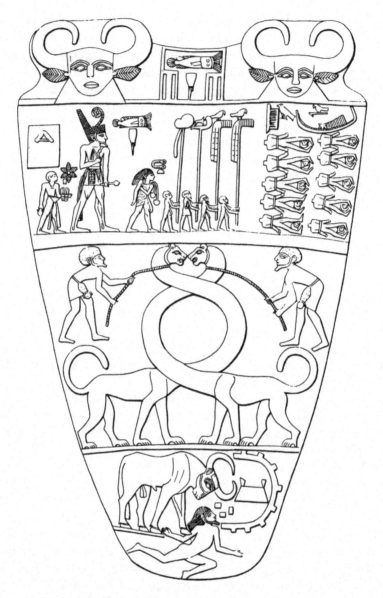

Fig. 18. *The Narmer Palette.*
The King wearing the red crown of the North is preceded by the
scribe and four emblematic banners.

state religion, and the closing of the temples of Egypt at the time of the Council of Nicaea, established the separation of Roman Catholicism from orthodox Catholicism after long and difficult discussions on the interpretation of the Gospels. Mention must also be made of the serious disturbances which took place in Egypt at the end of the Ptolemies, before the passage of the vernal point.

Adopting this principle—distinctly astrological in character—would certainly illuminate all that disturbs historians about the beginnnings and upheavals of this great land of Egypt, so mysterious to our rationalist mentality.

While historical facts confirm these strange religious and social movements, they do not explain the relation that could exist between these phenomena and the sole fact of transition of the vernal point from one celestial region—signed by a group of constellations—to another.

We lack the knowledge of zodiacal influences upon the vital phenomenon, although it seems that such a science must have existed. Indeed, for what reason or through what reasoning would this zodiac have been established, ascribing a planetary, elementary, and psychological character to each sign? This is certainly not just a random result, nor is it a result of systematization or vain speculation. It is true that men of wisdom have affirmed the proved existence of a systematic arrangement of the zodiac on the basis of sacred science. This zodiac has existed at all times: it was known in China, India, Chaldea, Egypt, probably among the Mayas...and even in our Middle Ages as figurations of zodiacal signs on the porticos of medieval cathedrals testify.

5

Symbolique and Symbol

The symbolique includes imaged writing as well as gestures and colors, all aimed at transcribing in a functional manner the esoteric significance of a teaching whose inner meaning remains inexpressible by any other form. "Symbolique" and "esoterism" are two words not often correctly understood. What can be said clearly and described objectively has no need of symbol. What is visible, tangible, or objective, however, can hold an irrational or an esoteric idea. This aspect of the object demands a symbol which can sometimes be replaced by parable.

Irrationality is not to be understood here in the mathematical sense, as for example, the "root of two," or the number corresponding to the coefficient *pi*. These are numbers that never find their term, fulfilling only a geometric function: the diagonal of a square and the diameter of the circle; they are only mathematically indefinable. This is not esoterism, nor does it contain an inner meaning such as intuition alone can apprehend.

The situation is different when one speaks of the original "Trinity," of the "divine Trinity"; Catholic dogma says "Three persons in One," which is also irrational and unimaginable, an abstraction which the triangle can *symbolize*. Here there is symbolique. It pertains to an unobjectifiable fact and a creative function at the same time. Hermetic art often and in different forms evokes this original state, more especially by the word "chaos." It can therefore be said that the symbolique is the means of evoking the intuition of a function which eludes rationalization; it therefore applies only to theogony, to theology, to sacred science, in fine, to knowledge of a world of causes.

This definition can be illustrated in many ways by Pharaonic images and figurations, stories and legends, but might be more comprehensible at first if exemplified by a work based on the teachings of the Gospels. The purely symbolic Isenheim altarpiece, now in the Museum of Colmar in Alsace, is a splendid example, and a unique and affecting work. The painting is attributed to Matthias Grünewald,[1] but it is the adept who inspired this painting, probably Guido Guerci, preceptor of the Antonins of Isenheim, who here commands our deep respect.

When a painter faithfully represents a scene or gesture described in the Holy Scriptures, this is but a transcription and not a symbol, even if the moment is rendered according to the artist's personal interpretations (as with a descent from the cross by Rembrandt, for example).

The Isenheim altarpiece shows the crucifixion surrounded by scenes and gestures which make sense individually but are purposely anachronistic or illogical in their function and in relation to normal tradition. Thus it is John the Baptist, historically long dead by the time of the crucifixion, who points at Christ on the cross. Mary Magdalene, the sinner, is posed as a supplicant before the crucified man whom she prepared for burial by annointing him with precious unguent; yet the vase or *crucible* still containing this *precious balm* is placed in front of the cross. This ointment is, in fact, the central and essential object of this entire symbolique. The painter has not neglected to give the sinner golden hair and a robe of reddish gold, an unusual color which only an adept can be supposed to have inspired. At the feet of John the Baptist, a lamb holds a small short cross in its *right* front leg, an anomaly because this cross, symbol of John the Baptist, is usually raised on a high staff and held by the *left* foot. Moreover, from the lamb's left (heart) side, a stream of blood flows into a chalice, an image of very specific symbolic value.

Next to Mary Magdalene, this masterpiece depicts Mary, mother of Jesus, collapsing in anguish, pale and dressed in *dazzling white*. She is supported by John—Christ's favorite disciple—curiously garbed in bright red: the red supporting the white, reminiscent of the *white Pharaonic crown placed in front of the red crown.*

The crucified Christ, of abnormally large size in relation to the other personages, has a body marked by that hideous disease, unknown in our time, which was known as "Saint Anthony's Fire" or "Mal des Ardents"[2] which the Antonins of Isenheim *knew how to cure.* The charitable Order of the Antonins claimed the protection of Saint

---

[1] Matthias Neithardt or Gotthardt, known under the name of Matthias Grünewald (1470/1480-1528).

[2] This disease was *gangrenous ergotism,* cased by the ergot of rye. It is to be noted that rye is harvested in *autumn* and the kind that is called "Saint John's rye," sown in June, lasts throughout winter.

Anthony, fourth-century hermit of the Egyptian desert. This Order was widespread in Europe and had houses in Alsace, at Isenheim and Strasbourg.

Two accents should be noted which stress the significance of the images of Saint Anthony: The left panel of the painting shows the saint, very richly dressed, holding the symbol of the *Tau* in place of a cross; this is the *Tau* of Saint Paul[3], it is the Coptic *Tau*. Saint Anthony's *Tau* is exactly the cross of life, the Pharaonic *ankh* without its female oval. Saint Anthony pays no heed whatsoever to the poisonous breath of the monster who spreads the disease with a breath that penetrates the window by shattering it. On the right panel, Saint Sebastian is represented as pierced with arrows, a symbolic reference to a particular date.

Everywhere the emphasis is placed on the opulence of Saint Anthony, on the color red by means of his outfit (coat and cap), and through the monsters, all red, which assail the saint in order to tempt him.[4]

The extraordinary colors and some particularities of this painting are striking enough for this work to serve as an example of symbolique. The many anomalies depicted guide us in seeking a significance, an enigma such as perhaps can be put in parallel with certain Hermetic texts, for example, the writings of Count Bernardus Trevisanus (1406-1490) who refers to "Babylonian dragons" obviously familiar to everyone (?)...or to a singular passage from the hieroglyphic figures of Nicolas Flamel (1330-1417).

This is good and true symbolique as is the Christic Passion in general when the Lord says: "Hitherto...have I spoken unto you in proverbs; but the time cometh, when I shall no more speak unto you in proverbs, but I shall show you plainly of the Father,"[5] and that marks the beginning of the Passion.

We have already found the principle of the Passion in the legend of Osiris. Transcribed by the myth, its two great phases are separated: the Passion properly so called, with Osiris, and the resurrection with Horus. The "practical" meaning unfolds through the behavior of the various

---

[3]The church of St.-Paul-Outside-the-Walls in Rome is in the form of a *Tau*.

[4]Those who have not been privileged to see this work at the Museum of Colmar may refer to the *Petit guide pour le Musée Unterlinden à Colmar*, Ed. Alsatia, Paris-Colmar, by L. Kubler, Curator of the Museum; to the *Retable d'Isenheim*, Ed. Alsatia, Colmar, by L. Sittler, and to the *Retable d'Isenheim*, coll. *Orbis Pictus*, Payot, Lausanne, Switzerland (containing color plates).

[5]John 16: 24-25.

Fig. 19. *Saint Anthony holding the Tau, and the Infernal Being blowing "Saint Anthony's Fire"* (Mal des Ardents) *at him.* Isenheim Altarpiece, left panel.

Neters who enter into play: It concerns a teaching that aims at attaining liberation for the immortal being trapped in a mortal body.

In Christian symbolique, the aim is different: God is *humanized,* and for resurrection through death, the teaching of the Gospels demands this display of the human body on the cross,[6] this body

---

[6]In the painting, Christ bears the stigmata of St. Anthony's Fire on the yellowish-white body of a corpse which is both theologically irregular and distinctly symbolic.

Fig. 20. *Saint Anthony, richly garbed, pays a visit to the poor and emaciated hermit Saint Paul.* (Isenheim Altarpiece, third side, left part.) Tradition has it that this image contains the plants that cure "Saint Anthony's Fire." Note that it is Saint Paul who is teaching and Saint Anthony who receives the teaching.

incarnating all human suffering *as an example.* In truth, it pertains to *man crucified in space,* cosmic man, the anthropocosmos filling the four orientations of the world and fixed on this cross by the three manifested principles (the three nails). The crucified Christ of this altarpiece bears the stigmata of the terrible "Mal des Ardents." The meaning of this can only be that He also cures this disease. Intended here is not a symbol of resignation that would lead one to believe the Lord accepted death from this sickness. The incarnation of the divine Word is offered to a fallen world in order to show the way to redemption. But who has "erred" and been condemned to mortal life? Was it the first man? Or is it man in general when he enters the road of return? Is not error immanent in creation itself? If there were no division into Adam and Eve, there would be no "fault" or double way.[7]

[7]See Chapter 9, "The Two Paths of Liberation."

In this symbolique there is a deeper intention, inexpressible by mere words because it pertains to the law of genesis in general. This symbolique speaks both of knowledge concerning the royal opus and of the process of the human being becoming suprahuman. The particular in the universal also includes universality in the particular, and this reversal, real as it may be, is unimaginable.

Indeed, the beginning, the very first manifestation, is in essence divisible into two aspects. These are complementary but they are also opposed, as are male and female, creating the "fault" which must be expiated by death in order to resuscitate immortality within unity. But this is a *possibility* only, not a *necessity*. "Male and female created He them" (androgynous), says the Mosaic Genesis in speaking of Adamic man. Hence, if this Adamic state *did not undergo division*, man would be king of the world "in the image of God."

In the *N'Domo*, the first initiation among the Black Bambaras,[8] the male is considered as androgynous until circumcision, the severed foreskin then signifies femininity; once separated, there remains only man as male. Circumcision, the reason for which is claimed to be one of hygiene, here turns out to be a *symbol* related to an essential metaphysic; its hoped-for effect: ". . .and be fruitful and multiply. . . .as the sand which is on the seashore. . ." But the *King* is created perfect; in principle he has nothing in common with the multiplication of the "kingdom of this earth": yet if the "essence," the breath of divine inspiration were not divided in man as well, there could be for him no animated procreation. Only through the breath of life which IS and also *exists,* can mortal being hope for immortality after his Passion.

The teaching of the Gospels is complex: Christ, King of the heavenly kingdom, equally reveals the man of earth. Symbolique.[9]

Besides the inscriptions carved in stone, Pharaonic Egypt left many writings on papyrus and allegorical stories all designed to transmit an aspect of knowledge. There are also a great many examples of symbolism, but these should not be confused with symbolique, defined as a functional symbolism.[10]

Descriptions symbolic in character are always based on some historic fact; the aim is to present a *rational* development, readable as a more or less fantastic or fabulous story while at the same time transmitting a particular teaching. It is obvious, moreover, that the

[8]See Zahan, *Société d'initiation Bambara* (Mouton, Paris-La Haye).

[9]See Chapter 9.

[10]Definitions given in a lecture on Symbolism to the Society of Symbolists in Paris, 1956.

writings or images carved in the temples convey more than a simple profane meaning. As a first important example of Pharaonic *symbolique*, we will present an account of a strange battle of conquest in the land of the *Kheta*, also known as the *Settiu*, or Seth-beings.[11]

The theme of the famous "Battle of Kadesh" has been treated by Egyptologists as purely historical fact. A battle of Kadesh certainly did occur, as the Pharaohs always had to defend their frontiers against belligerent nomads and attempted invasions.

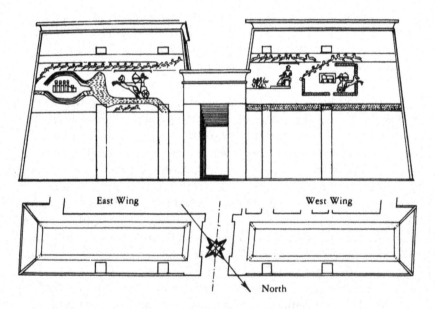

Fig. 21. *Arrangement of the Battle of Kadesh on the Pylon of the Temple of Luxor.*

Nevertheless it may well be asked why this particular "battle of Kadesh" is the subject of those grandiose compositions in the name of Ramses II[12], or again, why this battle of Kadesh in particular is related by Ramses II.

[11]In the war annals of Seti I at Karnak, there is a play on words between the *Kheta* and fire, *kht*.

[12]Location of figurations: exterior (north) facade of the temple of Luxor pylon; outside (south) wall of the great hypostyle hall in Karnak; interior (north) facades of the two pylons of the Ramesseum; interior (north) wall of the hypostyle hall of the temple of Abu-Simbel (entirely hewn from the western moutain bordering the Nile in Nubia). The Ramesseum is the funerary temple of Ramses II, situated on the left (west) bank of the Nile, while the temples of Luxor and of Karnak are on the east bank.

It is well established that this battle can be situated at Kadesh, in a bend of the Orontes River, during the fifth year of the reign of Ramses II. What is difficult to understand, however, is why the king, after having single-handedly vanquished the immense army of the Kheta and all their allies, must continue to fight against them for fifteen more years only to agree to a peace treaty granting all advantages to the conquered and, finally, to marry the daughter of the Kheta chief.[13]

Fig. 22. *The Seated King and the Encampment.*
Pylon of the Temple of Luxor, west wing.

The temple of Luxor gives a general idea of the significance of this battle on the west side of the pylon where two successive configurations are carved in superimposition. The first composition shows the solar king seated on his golden throne, his face turned toward the west (sunset) and the king in his chariot charging toward the occident and drawing his bow in that direction, toward the night.

The second composition shows the image fronted about so that the enthroned king now gazes eastward. He is depicted as larger than in the first representation, a fact not without significance. In the first

[13]As related in the temple of Abu-Simbel, the battle of Kadesh took place in the year 5 of the reign of Ramses II and the peace treaty was signed in the year 21 (1278 B.C.).

Fig. 23a. *The Battle of Kadesh:* Fortess of Kadesh.
Pylon of the Temple of Luxor, east wing.

composition, the king's east-west direction is comparable to the daily
precession of the sun; seated and drawing his bow, and smaller than he
will next be shown, the king symbolizes the setting sun. In the second
image, the west-east direction symbolizes the nocturnal path of the sun
and its battle against the adversary: night. Indeed, the solar king is at first
overtaken by night, as depicted by the superimposed image showing the
sleeping camp in which the penetrating enemy proceeds from east to
west.

A brief description of these scenes as well as of the nuances and
variations expressed according to the respective sites will make it clear
that this is distinctly a matter of symbolique, and will show the
importance of the orientations in interpretation.

Misled at first as to the importance of the armies he must combat
and as to their real position, the king realizes at the last moment that he
finds himself facing an immense coalition of thousands of chariots and
numberless warriors entrenched behind "Kadesh the Deceitful." The
king, isolated from his four army divisions (Amon, Ptah, Ra, Seth), finds
himself alone to battle an enemy who is preparing attack from all sides.
He addresses the following prayer to Amon:

Fig. 23b. *The Battle of Kadesh:* The King, alone, Conqueror of the
United Armies.
Pylon of the Temple of Luxor, east wing.

I invoke thee, O my father Amon! Here I am in the midst of great multitudes
of people whom I know not; all nations have joined themselves together against
me. My numerous soldiers have forsaken me, not one of my charioteers has looked
around for me, and when I call out to them, not one of them harkens to my voice.
But I believe that Amon is worth more to me than millions of soldiers, and
hundreds of thousands of chariots, more than a myriad of brethren or youths,
were they all united together! The work of many men is nothing. Amon surpasses
them all!

My voice reaches unto Hermonthis; Amon responds to my invocation, he
stretches forth his hand to me, and I rejoice; he calls out from behind me: "I am
rushing towards thee, to thee, Ramses Meriamon[14]! I am with thee. It is I, thy
father, my hand is with thee, and I am of more avail than a hundred thousand men.
I am the lord of strength, lover of valor." I have found a courageous heart and I am
content. All that I desire will come to pass.

I am like Month, I shoot my arrows from the right and wage battle on the left.
I am as Baal in his hour, before them. The two thousand five hundred chariots, in
whose midst I was, lie smashed into pieces before my steeds. Not one of them has
found his hand to fight; their hearts become faint and their limbs are become
powerless from fear. They are no longer able to shoot their arrows, and have no

[14]*Meriamon* = "Beloved of Amon."

more strength to hold their lances. I cause them to plunge into the waters, as
plunge the crocodiles; they are stretched out on the ground, one atop the other,
and I release arrows into their midst.[15]

It is midnight, indicated on the west side of the pylon by the
encounter of the royal armies with those of the Kheta and of the enemy
Sethians. The entire situation is reversed after the king's prayer. This
hour, the seventh of the night,[16] is called *"She who defeats the
accomplices of Seth"* and the following hour, *"Mistress of the Night,"* is
reached through the door called *"She who commands and does battle for
her Lord."* The guide for this hour is *Horus dwaty,* possibly one of the
names for the planet Mars,[17] and in the *Book of What is in the
Netherworld,*[18] the triumphant Osiris is borne by his vanquished
enemies.

After the prayer of Ramses on the east wing of the Luxor pylon, the
king is identified with Amon and all the enemy armies collapse before
him because the Eye of Ra emerges on the horizon. The king precipitates his enemies into the Orontes, while some of them seek
refuge behind the walls of "Kadesh the Deceitful."

The description of this battle clearly shows the symbolic nature of
the action by having Ramses, the Sun-king, single-handedly chase and
vanquish all the veils of the night with one gesture. "This battle of
Kadesh is the battle of the light against the shadows, but it is also the
fixation of this light in corporal form, which is the first great victory of
knowledge over ignorance, the becoming of *Tum* according to the
Heliopolitan mystery. It is impossible to enter the temple without it.
Atum (whence Adam) or *Tum,* is the product of this battle which the
tableaux of the pylon describe."[19]

To sum up, the first scene of the west wing represents the setting
sun and then the fronting about of the king; the scenes of the east wing
describing the battle underscore the nocturnal course and the awaiting
of sunrise. Hence all the action takes place in the darkness of night, the
sun being below the earth or within it. The reality of this symbolique is
confirmed by the representation of this same battle of Kadesh *inside* the
cave-temple of Abu-Simbel where it occupies the entire north wall of the
hypostyle hall.

[15]*Papyrus Sallier.* Tr. Emmanuel De Rougé.
[16]Night is considered to begin at 6:00 P.M.
[17]Mars is variously called *"Horus the Red," "Horus of the East," "Horus Hor-akhty."*
[18]See *Book of the Am-Dwat.*
[19]*Le Temple de l'Homme,* III, p. 342. It is evident that a sculptured work on such a scale would make no sense
at all were it meant to relate only the everyday fact of the rising sun. Even a cursory acquaintance with the texts
will confirm the Hermetic sense of the reliefs.

At Abu-Simbel, this representation is divided into two super-imposed horizontal bands. The lower register shows the Egyptian army proceeding from west to east in the sense of the nocturnal path of the sun, while the king, seated on the throne of the ligature of the Two-Lands, facing eastward, consults with the princes regarding the treason depicted beneath by the whipping of spies. Behind him, his camp is overrun, and the same moment that was called *midnight* at Luxor is indicated close to the middle of the wall, expressed by the clash of the two armies. At each end of the bottom register, the different divisions of the army, isolated and taken by surprise, attempt to defend themselves.

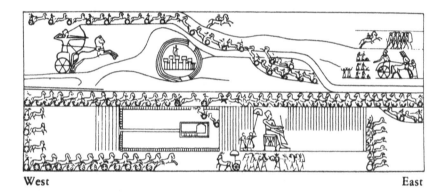

West   East

Fig. 24. *Diagram of the Battle of Kadesh.*
Abu-Simbel Temple, Hypostyle Hall, north wall.

The sequence of this story is taken up at the west end of the upper register where the fighting king, all alone in his chariot, charges from west to east, his arrows hurling the amassed enemy into the Orontes. The final victory, beyond the fortress of Kadesh, is represented at the east end of the scene where the hands of the vanquished are cut off while the Sun-king prepares his triumphant emergence thrugh the temple door, open eastward and guarded by four colossi, the four elements, pillars of the world.

To complete this ensemble, near the exit in the inner northeast corner of the hypostyle hall, there is a scene depicting the "ritual massacre of prisoners" with the white mace, in the presence of *Ra-Hor-akhty* (Ra, the Horus of the double horizon) (Fig. 27). This scene which usually indicates the *entrance* to the temple, here formally marks the

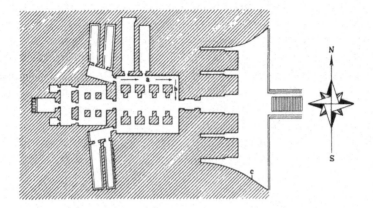

Fig. 25. *Schematic Map of the Cave-Temple of Abu-Simbel.*
(a) Battle of Kadesh.
(b) Ritual Massacre of the Captives.
(c) Marriage Stela.

triumphal *departure* of Ra from night's cavern toward the eastern horizon and *his entrance into the visible world.*[20]

It is precisely the characteristic of reversal, moreover, that underlies the deeper meaning of this rock-hewn temple. There is a double signification here: Eight Osirian columns lend this hall the feeling of a courtyard in front of the temple, and yet it never receives the light of day, no more than would an open courtyard at night.[21]

The king has vanquished the enemy and in the end has accepted peace conditions advantageous to the conquered; he has signed a treaty inscribed on a silver tablet by the Kheta chief.[22] Now, as we said, the king is going to marry his former enemy's daughter, offered by her father with numerous gifts. On the south rock near the facade of Abu-Simbel temple, Ramses II had the famous "marriage stela" carved to relate this event. On it is written that the new royal wife received the name of *She-who-sees-the-beauty-of-Ra,* the title of the last hour of the night.

With regard to this hour preceding daylight, the *Book of Hours* says:

[20]With regard to the nocturnal circumnavigation of the sun, the *Book of Caverns (Qererts)* confirms the entire symbolism of the battle, and this cavern-temple was chosen to house its description.

[21]The temple of Abu-Simbel is extremely rich in symbolic scenes and symbols, but we must confine ourselves to the battle of Kadesh alone.

[22]The moon is the luminary of the night. The fifteen years of combat can be likened to the fifteen days of the moon's waxing.

> The majesty of this Neter sails on and arrives at the eleventh door: "the one who rebuffs the allies of Seth" and at the twelfth hour: the one who sees the beauty of Ra.... [23]

In the *Book of What Is in the Dwat,* it is also said that the name of this "site" or hour is: *"the shadows which become the appearance of the births."*[24]

The Pharaonic name for this temple is *Per-mes-s,* that is, *"the house* (or temple) *that generated him* (or put him into the world)."[25]

In Thebes, the crossing over from the east bank of the Nile to the west bank where the kings are buried is marked in the symbolique of the battle of Kadish by a reversal of the images situated on the interior facades of the Ramesseum's first two pylons, exposed to the northwest. Here we are dealing with a funerary temple. The true orientation of the entrance is to the southeast, indicating the precise hour of the day, and the procession toward the sanctuary situated at the northwest brings to mind the sun's daily course and descent into *Amenti* (the western horizon).

On the inner facade of the right wing of the first pylon (hence to the left of the beholder), we find the king seated on his throne and, behind him, the camp. The battle of Kadesh is on the inner facade of the left wing (to the right of the beholder). Here, as at Luxor, there is a superposition of two successive compositions, but while at Luxor this superposition concerns the first phase (the seated king and the camp), the one of the Ramesseum treats of the second: that of the battle of Kadesh. The royal gesture of these two phases is directed from east to west, as in the first stage of the representation at Luxor.[26]

On the left wing, the first composition shows the king on the upper part of the scene, drawing his bow in the direction of the fortress of Kadesh and driving his enemies into the Orontes. Now covered over by the ranks of horses in the second composition, the older text surrounding the king's figure still shows through in several fragments

---

[23]A. Piankoff, *Le livre du jour et le livre de la nuit* (Cairo, 1942), p. 77. This is the phase of full moon and can be related to Greco-Roman myth: Semele wed by Jupiter in all his glory. The daughter of the king of the Kheta, King of the Night, can only be the Moon (Semele).

[24]G. Jéquier, *Le livre de ce qu'il y a dans l'Hadès* (Paris, 1894), p. 136.

[25]Another name for this temple consecrated to Ra-Hor-akhty, Amon, and Ptah is indicated in the scene of the massacre of prisoners in the presence of *"Ra-Hor-akhy who is at the heart of the dwelling of Ramses loving of Amon"* (*Ramses* = birth of Ra).

[26]To simplify the description of the scenes, we bring the axis of the temple to a theoretical north-south, which can be done in view of the fact that for the myth, north = west, and south = east. We must bear in mind that north = midnight, and south = noon. The hours of the day are counted starting at 6:00 A.M.

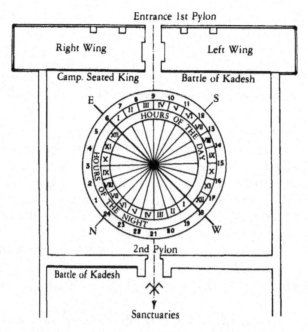

Fig. 26. Diagram showing the first two pylons of the Ramesseum
and position of the battle of Kadesh.

specifying that *"Ramses, loving of Amon, has taken up position south of
Kadesh,"* hence at noon.

At Luxor as well as at Abu-Simbel, the victory of the Sun-king is the
sunrise on the eastern horizon, while at the Ramesseum, the story of the
Sun-king conveys an entirely different teaching; here it is directly in
relation with the *Book of the Hours of Night and Day,* represented on
the ceilings of the royal tombs, and with the *Book of Caverns* in which it
is said:

> The majesty of this *Neter* is directed toward the hour called *arwt-ndjr,*[27]
> this hour being the sixth of the day. Arise, arise, so that the *Neters* who are in
> the barque may act in order to repulse Apopis, so that Seth may raise his hand
> in order to topple Apopis, says Isis in her incantations. It [the hour] arrives for
> Seth.[28]

It is the hour when the solar barque is arrested in its daily round by
a sand dune, and during which time three personages preceding the

---

[27]*Arwt-ndjr,* the name of the sixth hour of the day, can be understood as "door which takes" or "which seizes."
[28]Piankoff, op. cit., pp. 16 and 10.

barque force the serpent Apopis to disgorge the water he has swallowed, and cut his vertebrae.

The *"children of the serpent Apopis, the impious who haunt the wilderness and the desert,"* are also called the Settiu, that is, the Sethians, inasmuch as Asiatics. This appellation embraces the entire coalition, including the Kheta against whom Ramses directs his arrows. Noon here indicates the beginning of the battle against the powers of Seth. *Noon,* the sun's culminating moment of the day, marks the transition between rising and decline; it is a critical hour during which all of nature becomes silent. (In Chinese acupuncture, noon is the passage from solar *Yang* to lunar *Yin.*)

In the second and superimposed composition, the king is depicted on the bottom register and he is said to have taken up position to the northwest of Kadesh, meaning evening, the first hours following sunset. As night begins at six o'clock (the west), the specified orientation marks the time of the fourth hour of the night (nine to ten o'clock). Accordingly, it is said in the *Book of Hours of the Night:*

> The majesty of this Neter sails and arrives at the third door of cutting knives, regent of the Two-Lands, who punishes the enemies of "He whose heart is tired" [Osiris], who causes terror before "He who is sinless," "She who removes evil," and at the fourth hour, "She who is great in strength."[29]

This hour corresponds to the middle of the second *Qerert* or cavern, in which Ra, after a speech to the serpents who guard the entrance, addresses the rebels, the enemies of Osiris:

> O you decapitated ones in the Place of Terror.
> O you who have fallen, without soul, into the Place of Terror.
> O you who walk with hanging head, tied up, in the Place of Terror.
> O you upsidedown ones, the bloodstained ones, whose hearts have been torn out, in the Place of Terror.
> O enemies of Osiris, Lord of the beyond, chief of the Occidentals. Here, I have delivered you unto the Place of Terror, and now I deliver you to nothingness.[30]

Once again, on the inner facade of the second pylon, there is a description of this strange battle of Kadesh, but in an inverted position in relation to the scene to the left on the first pylon.[31]

---

[29]Ibid. p. 45.

[30]A. Piankoff, "La déscente aux enfers, dans les textes égyptiens," *Bulletin de la Société d'Archéologie Copte.* vol. VII (1941), p. 36.

[31]The wall bearing the right-hand scene of the second pylon no longer exists. It is not known when it was destroyed, but it could not have shown the image of the camp, which always comes before the battle scene and therefore, without apparent reason, would here follow it. Did this scene depict the mysteries of the night, of the netherworld, a theme always reserved for royal tombs?

Here we are dealing with the passage of the Sun-king through the "six caverns of the night" (the *Qererts*), and through the twelve gates, the twelve hours of the night referred to by the sages in the royal tombs. The teaching given by the *Qererts* (translated as "caverns" but more precisely referring to "that which is enveloped," or "that which is contained") is related to the vital organs of the anthropocosmos, hence to cosmic influences and human organs. This teaching is esoteric and of the nature of sacred science. Therefore it is comprehensible only in terms of the *Neters* of the *Book of Hours of Day and Night*, the *Book of Gates,* and the *Book of What Is in the Dwat*.

These succinct indications should demonstrate that the "battle of Kadesh" is pure symbolique; it speaks of something quite distinct from a profane dispute with Hittites or Syrians.

In the temple of Karnak, the representation of the battle of Kadesh on the outer south wall of the hypostyle hall was almost entirely obliterated by Ramses II himself, leaving a few fragments of the old image showing through the new series of scenes which depict his wars in Palestine and Syria. The dual character of this superposition is stressed by numerous subtleties found in all the newer scenes: surrender of *two* cities at a time, fortresses with *two* rows of battlements, each with *two* gates. The king tramples *two* captives, he ties up *two* enemy chieftains and, finally, he brings *two* lines of prisoners whom he presents to the enthroned Amon of Karnak. In this final scene, the older image shows through in such a way that the prisoners of the new composition are plunged to the waist in the Orontes waters of the first carving, while Amon's throne itself is poised on the water and surrounded by it.

We are here at one of the entrances to the great temple of Amon, where the image of water is always evoked. Accentuating this element, the composition goes so far as to use long lines of prisoners to symbolize undulating waves of water. In terms of the myth, Amon indeed manifests himself in the dew. The effect produced here by the superposition of two successive scenes is found clearly expressed in the interior of the great hypostyle hall at Karnak, by the representation of the Theban triad *in a naos poised on water* (Fig. 40).

To the right and left of the entrance door to this hypostyle hall, on the same south wall, the scene of the "ritual slaughter of prisoners" is represented; customarily, it indicates the entrance to the temple. The king, his white mace raised overhead, threatens a "bouquet" of prisoners that he holds together by their hair with a single hand. Facing him stands Amon, who holds out a sword to him. To the left of the entrance is the scene of "massacre," meant to convey the fixation or "terrifying" of the prisoners (gift of Amon). This tableau is superimposed on the first phase of the battle of Kadesh where the enthroned king is present at the beating of the spies. Amon, standing and holding out the sword, is here outlined against the threatened king. The invocations of Ramses II calling Amon to his aid are thus found realized: *it is Amon who acts on behalf of the king*. Here, in the temple of Amon, the principal aim of the superposition is precisely to concretize Amon, *evoked* in scenes of the battle of Kadesh but never actually appearing. It is obvious that in these images it is the Amonian principle that acts in place of the king.

The scene of the "ritual massacre of prisoners" represents entry toward the sanctuary, an essential phase of becoming, preparatory to animation; for if God breathed a soul into Adam, the latter must have been of a purity worthy of this divine breath. The prototype of this scene is found on the *Narmer* palette (First Dynasty) and on numerous stelas, particularly above the copper mines of the Sinai, about 300 kilometers south of the "route of the armies." It is therefore quite impossible to relate this "horrible massacre scene" to an act of war, as some historians rack their brains to do.

Among the numerous representations of the "massacre of the prisoners" in the temple of Karnak, there is one in the name of Thothmes III, carved on the outer facade of the sixth pylon in front of the sanctuary of the sacred boat. On the inner face of this same pylon, exactly on the reverse of the "massacre of the prisoners," inscriptions are found referring to the king's campaigns. They conclude with an exhortation to the temple officials:

> Be ye vigilant concerning your duty, be ye not careless concerning any of your rules, be ye pure, be ye clean concerning divine things, guard your heart. . . .

After the battles of Kadesh by Ramses ("birth of Ra"), let us again cite a symbolic gesture of Thothmes III, whose name means "birth of the moon," in order to show that it is actually a matter of symbolique involving the luminaries for which the personages are but sign-bearers.

Let us first of all recall that the "battle scenes" of Luxor, Karnak, and the Ramesseum, as well as those of Medinet-Habu by Ramses III, are all on the outer or inner surfaces of the pylons or of the walls, but always in *the open air*. Abu-Simbel, as a temple hewn out of living rock, constitutes an apparent anomaly, the meaning of which has been indicated earlier. The fact of encountering the "gesture" of Thothmes III inscribed in the sanctuary at Karnak thus makes for a very remarkable exception. Of his seventeen campaigns in Syria, Cyprus, and Nubia, moreover, the only detailed account related in his *Annals* is

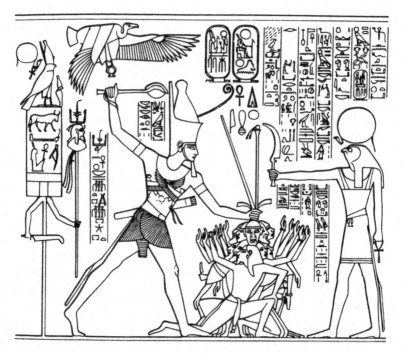

Fig. 27. *Ritual Massacre of the Captives* (Abu-Simbel Temple).
An analogous scene, where Ra-Hor-akhty is replaced by Amon, is
to be found at Karnak.

specifically the "battle of Megiddo." Without any image, the latter is
inscribed on the entire length of the north wall of the sanctuary of the
great temple of Karnak, a wall which is face to face with the granite *naos*
containing the sacred boat. Above this description is an immense scene
showing a rich offering of gold and silver vases as well as obelisks
surmounted by pyramidions covered with *electrum* (silver and gold
alloy) which the king offers to Amon-Ra, Master of Thebes. The king
specifies that all that he did during this first campaign was *written
every day on a leather scroll in the temple of Amon....*

   "At the time of these events, the Asiatics had fallen into discord"
and revolt rumbled against his majesty. Thus the king organized an
expedition to Palestine; upon reaching the town of Yehem, he held
council with his general staff. The leader of the Kheta had united all the
neighboring countries and was established in the fortress of Megiddo.
There were three different ways to reach this town: two circuitous roads
going through the mountains and a way that was direct but led through a
narrow path which made it necessary *to walk horse behind horse and
man behind man...* The generals evaluated the danger of engaging in

this cutthroat situation and begged Thothmes not to lead them through the *inaccessible roads (shta)*. But the king became very angry and swore that by the love of Ra and Amon's blessings, he would take the most direct route: Otherwise what would they think, these vile enemies whom Ra so detested? Let the officers who wanted to follow another road do so! Of course, the officers yielded and the king himself went to the head of the army, protecting his men one by one at the exit from the pass. The enemy awaited him on the two other routes *while the victorious army of his Majesty already overran the valley floor,* ready to combat the *barbarians.* But *the shadow had turned, measured by the sun* (it was thus after noon). Therefore camp was pitched and the men were warned that they must equip and prepare themselves to fight the loathsome enemy in the morning.

"Year 23, first month of the third season, 21st day, the day of the festival of the New Moon," the king appeared at daybreak and the order was given to deploy the entire army. Thothmes is at the center in his chariot of electrum like an avenging Horus, like Mentu of Thebes; with *Amon strengthening his arm,* he throws his miserable enemies into panic and they flee, abandoning their gold and silver chariots....

Thothmes III, at the beginning of his account, specifies the dates: He left the frontier of Zalu in the year 22, the fourth month of the winter season, the twenty-second day (the 22nd *Pharmuti*). He reached Gaza the day of the anniversary of his coronation, that is, in the year 23, in the first month of the harvest season, day 4 (the 4th day of *Pachons*). The battle of Magiddo having taken place on the 21st day of that same month, it follows that:

1. Between the departure for the frontier on the 22nd of *Pharmuti* and the day of the battle of Megiddo, the 21st of *Pachons,* there were twenty-nine days, that is, a lunar month contained *between two new moons.*

2. The date of the royal coronation, corresponding to the sojourn at Gaza, was thus found to be at *full moon.*[32]

The day of the battle corresponds to the dawn of the new moon, that is, to its birth or coming into the world *(Thoth-mes).* Furthermore the text specifies that the king's chariot was of electrum, that is, of silver and gold alloy, and that the vanquished army abandoned its gold and silver chariots.

---

[32]Transcribed into present-day notation, the sojourn at Gaza would have occurred on 29 February 1477 B.C. See A. Meyer, op. cit., p. 64.

Here gold and silver symbolize the morning of the new moon's birth, the appearance of the sun at the same time as the young moon.

With regard to the choice of a narrow and difficult road, qualified here as being inaccessible (*shta* also means "hidden," "mysterious"), I cite the same choice of a difficult route by Christian Rosenkreutz in the description of the *Chemical Wedding* by Andreae:

> . . . As soon as I had read this writing, all my joy flew from me. I who, before that, had been joyfully singing, I began to weep sadly, because I saw the three roads together before me and I knew, according to the time that was left for me, that I had the choice of but one alone. And I was worried that in choosing the stony road over the rocks, I would die miserably, or if I took the long roads I could lose myself in the by-ways and, because of this long voyage, I would never arrive on time. . . . [33]

And he chose the very difficult but direct road in order to arrive at the palace gate for the marriage of the King and the Queen just as *the guardian of the threshold* was about to close the doors. . . .

Side by side with these great narratives, there exist stories, often very long ones, written on papyrus. Some of these, such as the *Tale of the Two Brothers,* can also be compared to Hermetic texts. They transcribe more or less clearly the eternal conflict between Horus, the light, and Seth, the shadows. A good example is the tale of the *Contendings of Horus and Seth* or the story of *Truth and Falsehood.*

These tales have often been commented upon and compared with similar stories found in Homer, *The Thousand and One Nights,* and in Slavic or European tales.[34] *The Capture of Joppa,* for example, brings to mind *Ali-Baba and the Forty Thieves,* all the while insisting on the supernatural power of the royal mace, *hedj. The Story of the Shipwrecked Sailor* evokes the Fifth Book of the *Odyssey* and *the Adventures of Sinbad the Sailor,* but here the only one to have escaped from a terrible shipwreck has been cast by a wave of the sea onto the Island of the Ka where all kinds of food is found to grow in profusion. Its single inhabitant is a gigantic serpent thirty cubits long, his body encrusted with gold, his eyebrows of real lapis lazuli and his beard two cubits long. From this serpent, the shipwrecked sailor receives many

[33]Chymische Hochzeit, *Christian Rosenkreutz,* Anno 1456, Strasburg. In *Verlagung Lazart Zetzners,* Anno MDCXVI, p. 17. (Ed. note: Book in the author's possession.)

[34]G. Lefebvre, op. cit.

precious things such as incense with which the *Neters* are perfumed, as well as sacred unguents used in worship. These precious unguents are destined to repel the partisans of Seth and, with the Eye of Horus with which they are identified, to restore to the *Neter* a new life each day with the rising of Ra. Upon his return to Egypt, the shipwrecked sailor is made a "Companion" (Shems) by the king.

The translation of the word *Shemsu* (as it occurs in *Shemsu Hor* or *Shemsu Ra*) as "Followers" or "Companions" of Horus or of Ra is devoid of significance. A more realistic translation would be either "the emanations of" or "those knowing the secrets of" Horus or Ra, when it pertains, for example, to the first kings or Pharaohs of prehistory. Here, in this story, it is obvious that for this shipwrecked sailor, the situation is a matter of receiving the Light which indeed makes him a *"Shems of the King,"* of the true King.

The beginning of the *Tale of the Doomed Prince* resembles our *Tale of the Sleeping Beauty.* The Seven *Hathors,* like the seven fairies, fix the destiny of a young prince whose birth was due to divine intervention: he must die either by the crocodile, the serpent, or the dog, and his parents want to keep him sheltered from these risks. But the adult prince, fearless of his destiny, goes forth in quest of adventures and thus obtains the hand of a beautiful Syrian princess who was enclosed in a tower seventy cubits high and promised only to whoever should reach her window in one bound. In saving her husband from a snake, the young princess conjures his destiny for the first time. He is next menaced by a crocodile who offers to let him go if he succeeds in vanquishing and slaying the Spirit of the Waters against which he himself is in combat. . . and here the manuscript ends. The crocodile, be it noted, symbolizes the principle of *contraction.*

The famous prophetic story, *The Prophecy of Neferrohu,* from the Old Empire, has a different character: A sage predicts to the reigning king, Snefru, that a serious crisis will take place in the country, and that anarchy will soon hold sway, putting injustice in the place of justice until the coming of a king named Ameni. This pertains to the last decan of the sign of Taurus during which Egypt actually was disturbed by domestic problems and foreign invasions. Only the advent of Amenemhet, first king of the Twelfth Dynasty, opening the era of the astrological sign of Aries, the Ram (the animal sacred to Amon), was to bring about a return of splendor and peace.

In the *Adventures of Horus and Seth* who disputed the inheritance of Osiris for eighty years, the Ennead empowered to pronounce judgment declared itself incapable of so doing, and in desperation begged Thoth to refer the matter to Neith by writing her a letter soliciting her advice: Which of the two "young people" should inherit the throne? Thus all the *Neters,* as the Great Ennead, revealed themselves incapable of passing judgment. Only Neith, goddess of weaving, showed any discernment.

This is one of the teachings to be drawn from this long series of adventures rich in striking events of all kinds: *the Neters make no personal judgments; being principles, they are elements of cosmic harmony.* The Ennead symbolizes the male and female, active and passive, aspects of the four elements: Fire, Air, Water, and Earth commanded by the Quint-element, issue of Atum-Ra. It is a profound error, therefore, to consider these *Neters,* in imitation of our notion of God, as "gods" who judge and intervene arbitrarily as men might do.

In order to approach an understanding of ancient Egypt, it is necessary to eliminate the infantile notions which have been expressed with regard to Pharaonic thinking as a whole. The order of this thought-process was in reality formed by a knowledge of an elevated and estimable science. And it is but another manifestation of wisdom to transmit this highest of all teachings by means of narratives designed to be told to little children by their grandmothers, just as with our stories of *Little Red Riding Hood* or *Sleeping Beauty of the Forest.*

Symbols

Aside from these works of symbolique, we must examine the multitude of *symbols* which animate the entire Pharaonic Empire and form its treasure. The choice of these symbols is extremely strict. Never would the ancients have committed an error such as choosing, for example, a "Seed-sowing Woman" to allegedly "symbolize" a republican France. Logic alone should have guarded them from imagining such nonsense: The female waits, like the earth itself, to be inseminated; she hardly sows the seeds. In contrast, Pharaonic sages will depict a fly in order to speak of the *volatile,* a gold bee in order to speak of *honey*—that predigested product which Greek mythology seeks to find in Hymettus in order to make the hydromel of the gods. These are accurate symbols found in the titles of nobles (the fly) or of kings (the bee).

One of the most ancient known bas-reliefs, dating from the Third Dynasty and carved in wood, enumerates the titles of the great sage,

Hesy, whose profile shows admirable strength and beauty.[35] Hesy, whose name (written with the dual form of the purification-vase hs) means "twice-blessed," represents "he who has received the double benediction." This great personage bears the highest known titles, some of which are so ancient it is very difficult to determine their meaning.

> The great medicine man[36] (priest) hk of Mehyt the Ancient. Prophet of Min. Carpenter (of) royal Science, royal scribe. Grand Master of the Fly, Father of Min, Carpenter (of the) lioness.[37] Great of the city of Pe, Chief of the guides (?). Great of the Ten of Upper-Egypt. Priest of Horus of Mesen of the city of Pe, Hesy.

In the Edwin Smith surgical papyrus, every medicine man is a priest of Sekhmet, the lioness-goddess wife of Ptah, just as Hesy, here the great medicine man, is hk (unknown title) of the lioness-goddess Mehyt, wife of Onuris.[38]

The carpenter's symbol, the axe, inscribed beneath *royal science* (or, more exactly, "royal knowledge") and above *royal scribe,* is somewhat surprising: Given that Hesy is the first of the ten most important personages in the kingdom and that he combines several titles of priesthood, it is impossible to believe him a carpenter as well, unless a particular meaning is attached to this title. Indeed, already in the time of Horus Den, fifth king of the First Dynasty, there is a high functionary who bears the title of *Carpenter and Mason of the Golden Palace.* In the Middle Ages, the carpenter guilds had precedence in the processions and bore the raven on their banner as a symbol. This symbol is reminiscent of the Hermetic raven and the raven of Noah, support of the Light and of perfection when, for Noah, the dove no longer returns. The symbol of the raven, though akin to the black Bull-of-origin, is a volatile whose offspring are born white and according to legend are not recognized by their parents until they turn black. There is a relation in this conception of the raven with the carpenter who starts by making a framework and finishes with a covering superstructure. It may also be pertinent to recall that the father of Jesus was said to have been a carpenter.

---

[35] See Plate 1, photograph of wooden panel depicting Hesy. The inscription proves that the writing was completely developed before the Pyramid Texts, hence before the Fifth Dynasty, and that the "style" of the hieroglyphs had already attained a perfection that would never be surpassed. Note in particular the falcon, swallow, and lioness.

[36] For this reading, see Erman and Grapow, *Wörterbuch*, I, 319-320, the tooth as phonetic *un* confirms *sunu* as "medicine man," determined by the arrow, *Wörterbuch*, III, 427.

[37] The lioness-goddesses were, among others, Tefnut, Sekhmet, Mehyt, and Menhit.

[38] Cf. legends concerning Sekhmet and Mehyt.

When Hesy is next called "Grand Master of the Fly" and "Father of Min," and once again *carpenter* of the lioness bearing an unknown symbol on her back, the symbol of this title is to be compared to the *nekhakha* scepter which Min carries in his raised hand. This is to be understood as the *sublimation of Min*, analyzed first of all by the fly *(the volatile)* which here replaces the bee reserved for the king, then by the "father of Min" and the "carpenter of the lioness." This unknown symbol is found again on the back of the lioness and, curiously enough, in texts of the Middle Ages where it specifically carries the meaning of "sublimation."

Finally, the fourth column of titles mentions that Hesy is "Great in the City of Pe," double capital of the North (Dep and Pe); he is the most eminent and the greatest of the "Ten of Upper Egypt," that is, the first of the ten judges composing the supreme court sworn to the name of Maat, who is truth and justice. This title demands and implies well-tested moral qualities because it is to be remembered that *the Neter holds falsehood in abomination....* At all times in Egypt, justice and truth are what the accomplished man must bear in his heart, so that Maat is his sublime offering.

In the fifth column of the inscription, Hesy is called "priest of Horus of Mesen," the place where Horus will wage his final combat against Seth.[39]

The epitome of all these titles of nobility and priesthood is again reminiscent of the designation of *carpenter,* twice expressed by the symbol of the axe. The name of *mibt* is well known from woodworking scenes in the tombs of Fifth Dynasty nobility, and the usage of this symbol, as well as its name, are beyond discussion.[40] But variations in its spelling are puzzling, as for example in certain texts referring to works executed for the temple. There the axe *mibt* is replaced by a diadem *mdjhu* when designating a carpenter's work, as in this sentence of Ineni, high official of Thothmes I:

I "carpentered" [*mdjhu*] the august barge of 120 cubits in its length and of 40 cubits in its width in order to transport obelisks.[41]

Isn't the carpenter the one who crowns the house and executes the temple turrets which pierce the heavens? It is the function that must be sought when a tool is used as symbol, not the worker who uses it. Were the tool to designate the worker, it would cease to be a symbol.

[39]Geographically, the symbol of Mesen applies principally to Edfu and to the frontier city of Zalu, but as it is not determined here by the sign of the city, it very likely symbolizes the episode of conflict between Horus and Seth.

[40]Cf. Tomb of Tii, II, Pl. 129, the axe *mibt*.

[41]Breasted, *Ancient Records,* II, 105; Urk. IV, 56; and *Wörterbuch,* II, 190, for the carpenter *mdjhu*.

Hesy, the sage, is represented as carrying an inkstand on his right shoulder. In his left hand, across his chest, he holds the "scepter of prefect," *(aba* or *sekhm)* and the staff of a pilgrim. The symbolic meaning of the staff is found at all times, even in Wotan's staff of runes in the *Nibelungen* and that of the pilgrim seeking illumination at Saint-James of Compostella.

The very name of Hesy is written with *h.s.,* specified by the vase *hes,* and followed by the dual form which is indicated by two stalks of reeds. The vase *hes,* the coloring of which conveys that it is made of gold, silver, or lapis-lazuli, is used for purifications. This elegant oblong vase is used, for example, in the purifications of the king when he officiates as priest before entering the sanctuary. In the most typical of these rituals, (lunar) *Thoth* and (solar) *Horus,* with each one of these vases, pour "benediction" in two streams crisscrossing above the king's head. This purification is to be made four times, once toward each of the four cardinal points, and this ritual gesture is performed while declaring:

> Thy purification is my purification and my purification is thy purification....

There is identification between the one who makes the offering and the one who receives it. These offerings—or purifications—are made either with water (baptism during the name-giving by Amon), with the *ankhs* (key of life), or with the three symbols in succession: the *uas,* the *ankh,* and the *djed.* It is not a matter of actually pouring a liquid, be it water or any other fluid, but of a gesture of "influx" which can just as well be that of a celestial *Neter.*

Hesy himself, then, is the double vase of lunar silver or solar gold; he is identified with the Hermetic opus and, as *great medicine man of the* (Hermetic) *King,* he is master of sacred science.

uas   djed   ankh

uas   ankh   uas

Fig. 28.

The sideposts of the temple's great entrance doors are often ornamented with horizontal bands of bas-reliefs portraying the three symbols *uas, djed,* and *ankh* placed on a basket. The latter is reminiscent of the closed, secret basket of Dionysos. In Egypt, it represents the *all,* the totality, and in certain instances, mastery.

These three signs are generally read: prosperity for *uas,* life for *ankh,* and stability for *djed.*

The explanation of these symbols is really quite difficult. It is evident from their inscription on the doors and from the basket that supports them that they involve the three principles of beginning, the Magistery of origin incarnating the divine Word and causing the heterogeneity of a milieu which had previously been perfectly homogeneous *(Nun).*

They are the three principles *in puissance* but not yet manifested into existence. The nature of the objects which serve as symbols (inscribed in the stone) as well as the objects' attribution in various circumstances will therefore best uncover the reality these images are meant to evoke.

The *uas,* commonly called the "key of the Nile," is represented in Tut-Ankh-Amon's panoply of canes and scepters in its natural form: the branch of a tree entirely covered with gold. This symbol is indeed a tree branch, cut off along with a piece of the trunk or the larger branch from which it stems, and then again sectioned after having put forth two new young branches.

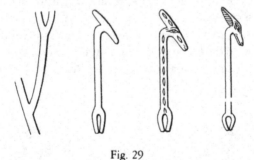

Fig. 29

We have already described the object's natural origin; seeing it in Tut-Ankh-Amon's treasure, carefully treated and entirely gilded, serves to confirm this choice as well as to show that the ancients knew how to compose their symbols. The *uas* scepter is placed in the hands of all the *Neters* and plays a very important role. In fact, it pertains to a living branch conducting the vivifying sap, but this sap only *ascends* without again *descending* as it must do in order to take on body beneath the bark. This is one of the reasons for choosing the object as symbol, and a particular regarding the intention: the flux of the Word—the nourishing sap, hyle of the philosophers—is not yet really manifested. It pertains to an activity, the creative function, which is not yet the created. We know that this creative function is the cessation of the unitary state, the fall of the absolute into the relative which the Jewish Kabbalah calls "the rebellious archangel"; in Pharaonic myth, it is Seth whose "evil" action is separation, the principle of dualization evoked by images of the cloven-hooved, forked-tongued devil of our Middle Ages, or the serpent of the Mosaic Genesis.

The *uas* is therefore at one and the same time the symbol of the marvelous act of creation, and of the evil in existence; the marvelous act of creation is simultaneously the origin of evil. The vitalizing sap divides (creates) oneness while generating opposites.

When the first aspect is to be represented, the piece of the large branch is left as is. When the maleficent act of division is to be shown, the stub of the large branch is transformed into a semblance of the head of an ass or of an anteater; the points of the ears are cut, ears which no longer know how to hear the divine utterance; thus an imaged expression is made of the evil Seth. The imagery of our Middle Ages gives the devil the head of a faun with pointed ears and the hooves of a goat, the animal symbolizing lubricity. The Pharaohs were more discreet and philosophical, yet they knew very well how to be direct and even crude in their descriptions without ever being immodest.[42]

The second symbol of this trinity is the *ankh*, which is said to be the symbol of life. Bas-reliefs show Amon or Isis, for example, giving life to the King, either through the neck or with breath through the nose. This *ankh* is presented as a loop crossed by a horizontal bar (a), but the two elements are not truly knotted. Sometimes the horizontal bar is girdled with a tie (b), sometimes it is hollowed out, containing another bar (c). This symbol is to be regarded as the potentiality of a ligature. This "crux ansata" is thus not really a *cross*, but a symbol of the intention to knot together two elements without having truly done so.

Although an actual mirror in the usual shape of the *ankh* has never been found, the latter is sometimes seen represented in the form of a mirror. This can be a guide to research, as can the fact that the

---

[42]A Blue ceramic *uas* scepter was found in the temple of *Seth* at Ombos, between Naqada and Ballas. Two meters 15 cm. in length, its stem, made of a single piece of clay without the slightest flaw, measures about 1 meter 53 cm. This is the greatest triumph of enamel work known from this epoch (Eighteenth Dynasty).

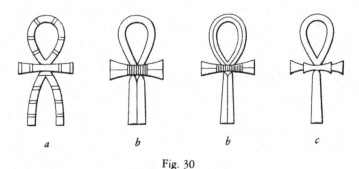

Fig. 30

casing containing the ordinary mirror is called *"house"* (or container) *of life (ankh).* Information such as this helps to discover the intention in the choice of the image. The mirror reflects an unreal image of the object while being the exact image in reverse. Basilius Valentinus, when speaking of *tincture* or *soul* in the "Greek Work," uses the symbol of the mirror as presenting an intangible appearance which the ancient sages called the *odor of the God.* It is said that the soul ties body to spirit and yet the soul, although visible, is not tangible: it is the Eye of Horus. Thus the knot of the *ankh,* indicated but not executed, is that which will give life to the spirit of the *uas* when linked to the third symbol, the *djed* column.

The *ankh* is not life, but it is the *ankh* that gives life once the two principles, spirit and body, exist.

Note that the basket, which contains or carries the whole as well as the three symbols, is itself an image, an explanation of the three principles, and not yet the "thing." Hence the *djed* or column of Osiris is the principle of stability bearing the four elements which make for formal existence: But the *djed* is not yet the *Ka. Djed* will be *Ka* as soon as there is corporeality, *through the distinction of spirit, of soul and of body,* which makes their interaction possible; and this will come about through either the direct way or the indirect way.

The column of Osiris is truly the symbol of stability, of continuity within life, but the principial *djed* next becomes the actual *Ka,* the fixed support, giving corporeal form to spirit and to soul, or specific tincture. When, in the course of these explanations, we see the basket bearing only the *ankh* framed by two *uas,* we obviously are not dealing with a bodily form but only with *the spiritual bearer of the soul.*

This image, represented in the door leading toward the temple—an image which was profusely reproduced during the Ptolemaic period—is a beautiful example of what is meant by "symbol," that is, *the writing evoking abstract states* difficult or impossible to describe in words, and which only the fact can render comprehensible.

The lesson to be drawn from this symbolic teaching is that there is a marvelous creation which puts the All into the world all at once: the Word of the beginning that is "in God," this "God" who is the Word. From it can result royal perfection, Christic or Horian, or contradictory existence with its rebirths, owing to the *djed* animated by the *uas* linked by the *ankh*.

Khonsu, the fruit portrayed in the Theban triad (Amon, Mut, and Khonsu), is the reunion of these three scepters in the final phase of the Pharaonic attainment. Khonsu also bears the *heq* and *nekhakha* scepters, attributes of royalty: hence he reunites all the scepters with the exception of the *wadj* (Figs. 40 and 48).

Khonsu as "dauphin," attested by the characteristic braid, is the reunion of all the powers, with the exception of *expansion, growth,* and *vegetation* which are symbolized by the *wadj,* a stalk of papyrus in full bloom. At this stage, Khonsu wears on his head a slender crescent supporting a disk: the new moon. In this manner, he represents the condition of growth or vegetation.

The Osirian column, the *djed,* as fixed support, here becomes the sheath containing the *ankh* and the *uas.* It is no longer the image of trinity borne by the *woven* basket, but the reunion of spirit, soul, and body within a new oneness and, as indicated by the *djed,* an incarnated unity capable of going toward resurrection; this is symbolized by the aquatic or "spiritual" character of the couple Amon-Mut reuniting under the *ankh* symbol of the soul all the attributes of all the phases, through the rounded and outspread horns of the ram of Amon.

The papyrus with the blooming corolla was chosen to symbolize expansion, the blossoming out in vegetative growth. This plant appears in the marshes of the Nile's waters like a first and intense explosion of vegetation. *Wadj* is also the sign of the color green, which is itself synonymous with vegetation and hence with growth. In adding another sign to a precise symbol like the *wadj,* such as an eye in a disk, the symbol is made to "speak"; in the manner of heraldic symbols, it becomes a speaking image. The disk is solar, the eye is light, and the *wadj* then represents vegetation; in this instance it will be tinted blue because the eye of Ra is *hidden* in or beneath the solar disk. The color blue pertains to the lunar light, the moon itself being white and reflecting solar light, like a mirror.

In order to complete the group of essential symbols pertaining to

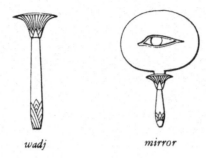

wadj   *mirror*

Fig. 31

the phases of genesis, we must cite the sign of the *ligature* represented by the tube of the tracheal artery ending at the heart and the lungs, the complex of the *haty*. This is the center of respiration, the ligature of "spirit" (here symbolized by air capable of animation) with the living and nourishing fluid of the blood. This symbol *sma* is often seen depicted on the base of the throne on which the King is seated; two Nile gods— one bearing the symbol of Upper Egypt belonging to the white crown, the other that of Lower Egypt belonging to the red crown—tie two flowers on the tracheal column: the bulrush of the South and the papyrus of the North.

This ligature can also be made by Horus, master of the North, and by Seth, master of the South, who is often replaced in this function by Thoth (Fig. 48).

Ra is the Sun absolute. The Eye of Ra is the visible sun, giver of vitalizing light and warmth, but also of burning fire. Aton is the solar disk, the sun's materialization. The Eye of Ra plays a very important role in the myth because it is the source of all life, this life which Horus

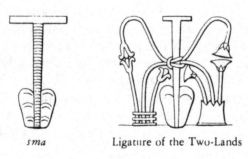

sma   Ligature of the Two-Lands

Fig. 32

represents in his function as subtle and sublimated fire. In legendary form it is said that one day "Ra had sent forth his Eye which did not return. So Ra sent Shu and Tefnut to bring it back. . . . *But the Eye was outraged when it returned because it found that another had grown in its stead."* And then Ra took the Eye and placed it on his brow in the likeness of a serpent. Since then, *the solar Eye governs the entire world* because this serpent became the symbol of Ra's puissance. It is since that day that Shu was called Onuris[43] which means *He-Who-Has-Brought-Back-the-Far-off-Distance.*

By this fact, the Eye of Ra which this *Neter* bears on his brow becomes the radiating Eye, the divine Word. It thus becomes the uraeus, the third eye of the King's forehead, powerful protector and destroyer of Ra's enemies. . . .

The uraeus is the *Naja* of Egypt, the dreaded though peaceful and timorous cobra, dangerous for its spit and deadly for its bite, but only if it believes itself attacked. The snake is the symbol of duality: It separates the right and left sides of the brain. Likewise, the nervous system is dual: sensory or motor, active-solar through the sympathetic, or passive-decontractile through the vagus or parasympathetic. This dual aspect is human; it is thus symbolized by two uraei, or one uraeus accompanied by a head of Mut, the vulture, symbol of hatching femininity.[44]

It must be understood that although the nervous, or physical, manifestation is provoked by the flux of the uraeus *(Kundalini),* the cause, the uraeus itself, is transcendent action. This cause can be influenced by certain practices of true yoga which are always withheld from general knowledge; on a vital level, they can be very dangerous.

Through sacred science, everything is ordered and related. When power is placed in the hands of men who are themselves not dominated by a superior force (which can be a moral force), its road will inevitably lead to evil. Where is the person who has never—absolutely never—abused his or her power, be it the power granted by fortune. . .or in the driving of an automobile?

---

[43]Onuris, worshipped at This, capital of the first kings of the historical empire, had the lioness-goddess, Mehit, for spouse.

[44]See Plate 4, the casing of fine linen covering the cranium of Tut-Ankh-Amon's mummy. Embroidered gold beads and semiprecious stones delineate the double uraeus, which indicates the scissure between the two hemispheres of the brain (Howard Carter, *The Tomb of Tut-Ankh-Amon,* II, PLXXXII). The single royal uraeus appears on the diadem and on the crown.

The only known instance on the monuments of the king wearing the double uraeus relates to the Ethiopian kings Chabaka, Chabatoka, and Taharqa.

6

Magic, Sorcery, Medicine

"Magician" is a word often associated with soothsayers, wise astrologers versed in the reading of prophecies which they have gleaned from the "stars"; with men, in other words, who contemplate an astronomy of harmonic constellations. *Magic,* therefore, in the broadest sense of the word, usually designates a "supernatural power." From the multiple definitions attempted of this word, we present but two examples: We shall look to Sigmund Freud for a general classification of the notion, and we shall consult Professor François Lexa on his specialty, as he is the author who collected the "magical" texts of Pharaonic times.

Freud says: "Magic introduces man to a technique which makes him master of spirits and souls, which allows him to dominate nature both animate and inanimate; it is the technique of animism."

Lexa objects that according to Freud's theory, "animism conceives the world under the influence of anthropomorphism, which is a way of seeing that is innate in man, just as zoomorphism is innate in animals. Primitive man is obsessed by such an opinion to the point of being unable to see the surrounding world from any point of view other than the anthropomorphic one. Every human action, then, according to Sigmund Freud, would be magical; it is obvious, therefore, that his definition of magic is too broad."[1]

This argument is fallacious: though it is evident that man cannot see in the universe anything else but himself, this does not imply that *animism,* as philosophy, logically qualifies all human action as magic.

Much can be said about these definitions, each one of which encompasses part of the problem, seen from different points of view: the perspectives of theology, history, science, psychology, etc. . . .

[1]Ph. Dr. François Lexa, *La magie dans l'Egypte antique* (Paris, 1925), I, p. 15.

Professor Lexa is quite right in saying that everyone would agree to call magical any act which would contradict the law of causality by producing an effect of different nature from the cause. He errs, however, when he cites as an example the simple citizen who for the first time sees a train pulled by a steam engine; according to Lexa, he would attribute the phenomenon to magical causes as he is unable to establish a connection between cause and effect. Perhaps our citizen will call it the devil's work, but this does not imply the idea of magic any more than does our calling the atomic bomb an infernal contraption. During the First World War, a German officer in Kenya, advised that the Germans were going to send an airplane overhead in order to "impress" the black populace, alerted the chieftain that his country would send *flying men*. The officer joined the chieftain at the scheduled time. But when the plane appeared, the black man, who knew nothing about aviation, said contemptuously, "Oh mechanics!"

This authentic anecdote confirms the rationalist's error in supposing that the unexpected, the apparently illogical, appears as magic to the simple mind. The latter may be terrified by the phenomenon, but will always search for its cause.

Actually, the law of causality is not missing from the magical phenomenon. *There exists a bond between cause and effect, and that bond is called the Neter.* It is this *Neter* which the believer hopes to spur into action through his appeal. Further, what this *Neter* represents as energetic and harmonic activity is consciously evoked by the sage. This conscious evocation must necessarily be a gesture or a word of the same nature as that of the *Neter* summoned, and by that fact the evocation becomes *the cause of the magical effect*.

Only the Creator can make something out of nothing. The connecting link between cause and effect is mysterious only for the ignoramus who is wont to consider the *Neter* in the form of a human being.

Even when sorcery is concerned, an action attempting to impress someone's wishes upon another person, for instance, or to produce phenomena by means of the "spirit" of the dead, such action is not in defiance of the law of causality: The higher animals, as well as the human animal, are totally bathed in a psychic atmosphere which establishes a bond between the individuals, a bond as explicit as the air which is breathed by all living things. In this psychic ambiance, every human can be compared to a radiating energetic source offering a kind of vibration of its own which is received by the other beings. Beings can be more or less aware of this, depending on the degree of their mental neutrality. In a psychic medium, these impulses are comparable to sounds in the physical medium of air. The psychic substance forms a body for the human as clearly defined as the physical body; this body subsists for a certain time after the death of the physical body's corporeal form.

When Freud speaks of animism as a technique through which man becomes master of spirits and souls and therefore capable of magical action, this excellent definition implies a science about which Freud says nothing. He is not aware of the *Neters,* and in default of *Neters* seems not to have understood the meaning of the Greek "daimon" and the "devas" of India.

Being the science which seeks to heal the physical and psychic ills of humanity by *natural* means instead of by the disastrous means of chemotherapy, true medicine actually is true magic: It consists first in placing the sick person under the favorable conditions of an energetic milieu, and then in combating his illness with natural products to be applied or absorbed; such a product could be a plant picked at the moment of its optimum vital activity, or it could be an animal product, judiciously chosen. The recipes in the Ebers medical papyrus recommending the use of goat excrement are laughable only to the superficial mind. Upon reflection, it will be realized that the goat, like all animals, nourishes itself in a manner peculiar to its species. What does it retain for its vital purposes? And what part of the nourishment does it reject?

Only omnivorous man takes his nourishment from any edible plant, root, leaf, or fruit, or from animal flesh; hence his waste lacks any *specific* character. A study on this topic could lead to some unexpected conclusions.

In India, healing powers are attributed to fresh cow dung when applied to a wound, which is akin to our use of chemical antibiotics. In the Coptic monasteries of Egypt, the remains of consecrated bread are carefully collected and left to mold, "to heal the brethren when they are sick," as they say. Penicillin-like substances and ferments have been a part of the medicine of Africa since antiquity. The fact bears underlining: *All that ferments has the gift of fixing the breath of the Neter.*

It must be remembered that sacred science in the sense defined above is founded on a true magical gesture. According to all authentic texts, knowledge of this gesture depends upon a revelation which no reasoning can substitute, but which reason, nevertheless, cannot call folly.

All Pharaonic texts bear witness to such a revelation of suprahuman origin; be it for the ritual of founding a temple or for a medical treatise, the divine origin of science is always recalled. The Ebers medical papyrus, for instance, mentions a very ancient *Treatise of the Heart* which dates back to the First Dynasty and begins thus:

> Beginning of the Book [of Healing] to expell the pains (which are) in all the limbs of a man, such as it was found among the writings of ancient times, under the feet of Anubis, in Khem [Letopolis]. It was then brought to His Majesty, the king of Upper and Lower Egypt, Semti [Udimu] true of voice.[2]

Anubis, the jackal, is the digester par excellence who keeps his prey until it decomposes before using it as nourishment. This decomposition is a fermentation. It is therefore Anubis the jackal which has been chosen in the symbolique to preside over all that concerns death and resurrection through mummifications, including the extraction of the viscera, their respectful preservation in the four Canopic jars, and the swaddling of the mummy. This throws some light on the allusion that the *Treatise of the Heart* was discovered "beneath the feet of Anubis."

The medicine man *(sunu)* is also priest of Sekhmet, the bloodthirsty lioness; he is often also said to be a magician. Oculists (like the scribes) placed themselves first of all under the protection of Thoth (the Greek Hermes) who, according to a very ancient myth, had reconstituted the Eye of Horus which Seth had shattered into sixty-four fragments. Medicine is not dissociated from theology. Thus the Ebers papyrus begins with an incantation to be pronounced—to be remembered, that is, whenever a remedy is to be applied to an ailing limb:

> I have come forth from Heliopolis with the great ones of the temples, those who possess protection, the Masters [ferments] of eternity. In the same way, I have come forth from Sais with the mother of the gods [Neith]. They have given me their protection; I possess formulas made by the universal Master [the one God] to drive back the pain caused by a male Neter, a female Neter, a dead male, a dead female, which is in this mine head, in this neck of mine. . . in order to put a stop to the *agent provocateur* which directs the penetration of disorder in this flesh of mine, of the disease in these limbs of mine. . . .
>
> I belong to Ra. He has said: "It is I who will protect him [the sick one] against his enemies. Thoth will be his guide, he who makes the writings speak and who is the author of the collection [of formulas], he gives ability to the savants and the

---

[2] G. Lefebvre, *Essai sur la médecine égyptienne de l'époque pharaonique* (Paris, 1956), p. 37, and note 1, Ebers Papyrus, no. 856a.

Udimu, "King Den," was the fifth king of the First Dynasty. A different version of this text specifies that the treatise was found "among the writings of ancient times *in a chest of books*, beneath the feet of Anubis." It can be concluded from this text that as far back as the First Dynasty, there existed books of science.

medicine men, his disciples, in order to deliver [from sickness] he whom God wishes to keep alive."[3]

Note that the medicine man-priest identifies with the sick person. This incantation, furthermore, recalls not only the divine origin of medicine and its teaching in the temples, but with the first sentence presents details on the character of the various teaching sites where instruction in medicine was given. When the medicine man says that he has come forth from *Heliopolis* with the Ancients, he implies that he obtained in that temple the philosophical grounding and the knowledge of metaphysical principles concerning the general laws of genesis. This is confirmed by the hieroglyphs which speak of the great divine temple and of the masters of protection symbolized by the *heq*, the ferment, or "staff of the *Neters*."

When further on the medicine man says that he has come forth from Sais with Neith, the mother of the *Neters*, he alludes to the site where the practical aspect of medicine is taught. Neith's symbol consists of two crossed arrows and she presides over weaving. Legends present her as endowed with the art of reasoning and the gift of discernment; it is indeed to her that Thoth comes for counsel on behalf of the Great Ennead. A science based on reasoning depends on recorded facts that have been observed through the senses. The faculty of reasoning stems from this dualization and from the comparing of any two notions. *Crossing* is what symbolizes this idea, and crossing represents a weaving. The intermeshing of threads forms a woven fabric, wherefore Neith (Net) is called the *Neter* of weaving. It is noteworthy that the hieroglyph for a notion allied to *science, knowledge, a savant,* or *comprehension* depicts a piece of woven material, and is read *sia*.

This incarnation well illustrates all that has previously been said concerning this *Neter,* which is not to be understood as a "god" but as a definite natural influence. The masculine or feminine *Neter* is specifically indicated as being an active or passive energetic puissance, either beneficial or harmful.

The Chinese, when confronted with disease, refer to a lack of equilibrium between *Yin* and *Yang;* the *"harm caused by a masculine Neter,"* for example, is comparable to an excess of *Yang,* meaning active nervous energy. It is a definition of this energy and of its character which is intended in the signs when they speak of "the formulas made by the universal Master." Knowledge of these formulas is what enables the medicine man to remedy any *agent provocateur*, any disseminator of disease-carrying disorder.

As has been said, Ra is not the sun itself, but rather the solar energy which, during the course of its daily cycle, animates all the organic functions of the human body, one after another, at each hour of the day and night. It is in this way that we are subject to it.

Thoth is the masterful intermediary in his relation with Time, with the hour. He guides his disciples through the knowledge of cosmic harmony. Thus he enables the medicine man to apply the efficacious remedy at the precise moment. The remedy is prepared according to instructions given by the temple as is shown, for example, by the order given in the case of a stomach ailment caused by a liver deficiency: *"You will resort to the secret medication of plants usually applied by a medicine man (in such cases)."*[4]

The secret refers to knowledge of certain vital laws in the plant world, of use in phytotherapy. Concerning the choice of time for the use of a remedy, the example can be given of the six paragraphs in the *Treatise of the Eyes*, where precise indications determine that period of the year when a specific remedy for *strengthening the vision* is to be administered:

> What must be done from the first winter month to the second winter month. . . .[5]

Another remedy will be efficacious from the *third to the fourth winter month*, and still another can be taken all year round, throughout the three seasons.

It should be borne in mind that each thirty-day month is subdivided into three periods of ten days called decans. Each one of these decans is subject to the influence of one particular *Neter*. Knowledge concerning these influences goes back at least to the Ancient Empire, seeing that certain decans are cited in the Pyramid Texts. Speaking of celestial influences, or astrology, an excerpt of *Maternus Firmicus* confirms the secret kept by the temple, the reality of sacred science and its Pharaonic origin:

> At the moment of my revealing the august secrets of this doctrine, secrets which the divine ancients communicated only with trepidation, and which they enveloped in profound darkness, fearful that the divine science, once brought to light of day, would become known to the profane, I beg you to heed me with your

[4]Ebers Papyrus, no. 188, in G. Lefebvre, op. cit., p. 23.
[5]G. Lefebvre, op. cit., pp. 87-88.

free and calm attention, empty of other pursuits so that all I shall tell you be instilled into your mind in the easiest manner. In the book of "Institution," I have said that every sign contains three decans. The decans are endowed with a great divine virtue and with a peculiar puissance: everything happens by their decree, all things fortunate or unfortunate. Wherefore the famed Neshepso, that perfectly just King of Egypt and excellent astrologer, has related to the decans all infirmities and all diseases, showing which decan causes which disease. And as every nature is vanquished by another nature (given that a god often triumphs over another god), from this opposition of natures and of celestial puissances he has drawn the remedy for all ailments, as he was so instructed by divine reason.[6]

This is the advice to his disciple from the text known as *Salomon:*

Here again are the plants of the seven planets, O very conscientious Roboam. When you wish to gather them, do so at the hour when the planet which is then active dominates time. Be certain to pronounce the nominal invocations and prayers, and you shall operate with these plants in a marvelous manner: but this is not to be revealed to anyone.[7]

And lastly, the recommendations of Apollonios of Tyana:

Book of wisdom and intelligence concerning the [astrological] accomplishments of Apollonios of Tyana, who is writing for the instruction of his disciple, Postumos Thalassos, and speaking in the following terms:

"Listen well to me, my son, and I will reveal to you the mystery of wisdom, a mystery unintelligible, unknown and hidden for many, concerning the seasons and the times, the hours of day and of night, concerning their denomination and their influence and concerning the true wisdom hidden therein. And I shall reveal to you the accomplishments of the science given to me by God and by which are taught the first elements of all that God has created on earth. I have indeed produced four books more precious than golden jewelry and stones of great value: one of astronomy, one of astrology, the third of "scholasticism" [?], and the fourth, noblest of all, contains powerful and terrible signs as well as marvels and mysteries. I am speaking of the book that teaches the first elements of the visible things created by God, so that he who reads this book may, if he chooses, be successful in realizing such wonders."

With great severity, he enjoins abstinence, and the text continues:

These recommendations, as I have said, are to be followed precisely if one desires to place under the yoke of necessity the beings of the earth "untying" the trees, "tying" the birds, the animals, the serpents, the breath of the winds and the course of the rivers. He who precisely practices this science speaks and

---

[6]R.P. Festugière, O.P., *La révélation d'Hermès Trismégiste*, I, p. 132, Book II of the *Mathésis of Firmicus Maternus.*

[7]Ibid., p. 152.

pronounces the names of the great and all-powerful God, names which pertain to each moment and to every season.

Apollonios of Tyana then enumerates:

—the zodiacal signs and the mystic name assigned to each season;
—the mystical name and the influence of every hour of the day;
—the mystical name and the influence of every hour of the night.

Then he adds:

> In each of the seven days, such are the hours blessed by God. If there be any operation that you wish to prepare, pay attention to these hours as one watches over buried treasure, for the sages have hidden these hours in their heart, like buried treasure, because within them resides the breath of wisdom. Be not disbelieving with regard to this book, for it is God himself who has established the progression of these hours of the day and of the night, and it is by means of his powerful and hidden name that everything is accomplished.[8]

Of the elements cited here, the decans, the hours of the day and the night, and the divine puissance connected with each one of them, all are purely Pharaonic in origin; such topics comprise the subject of "Books" well known in our day. This indicates that the wisest of Greeks, from their first contact with Egypt until the first centuries of our era, borrowed from the wisdom of the ancient Pharaohs.[9]

The classical authors frequently mention the many famous papyri. Searching for the true philosophy, Clement of Alexandria often affirms that the Greek philosophers borrowed a major part of their doctrines and their science from the Egyptians. To confirm his assertions, he provides a veritable library catalogue. The works to which he refers were kept in a chamber of the temple as a priceless treasure, the gift to the human race from Thoth, master of all science.[10] The famous *"Famine Stela"*, the original of which dates back to King Zoser (Third Dynasty), relates how the sage Imhotep, son of Ptah, wishing to determine the reason why the waters of the Nile were not flooding at their regular time, went to Hermopolis, to the chamber of books, where he unrolled the writings of Thoth.

Astrology depends upon long and patient observation of the rising and setting of heavenly bodies over thousands of years, and all evidence

---

[8]Ibid., I. pp. 341-342.

[9]See Appendix IV, "Excerpts from Clement of Alexandria."

[10]See Appendix V, Catalogue of Egyptian Books. Thoth having been called Hermes by the Greeks, the latter gave the name of *Hermetic Books* to these sacred writings.

points to the existence of such a science. Determining the character of
each hour of the day and night is a typically Pharaonic procedure fully
detailed in the "unrolled papyri" which decorate certain royal tombs.
These "Books" relate the transformations of the solar barque during its
daily round; each book develops a particular part of a teaching
understandable in all its import only through knowledge of each
symbol's true meaning, but most of these symbols are enigmatic.

Fig. 33. *Seventh Hour of the Day* (Tomb of Ramses VI,
Twentieth Dynasty).
This seventh hour (12 noon to 1:00 P.M.) is "that which rises for
Horus." Above the double rudder, the names of Hu and Sia.

The hours of the day are found only in the tomb of Ramses VI, given
with the name of the door preceding each hour, the name of the hour
itself, and the name of the *Neter* which acts as its protector and also as
guide of the solar barque. Certain details are given concerning the
different phases. Toward the middle of the day, for instance, Ra must
cross a sandbank and struggle against the serpent Apopis, the searing
fire that has dried out the river. With noon, however, there begins the
hour know as *expansion of the heart,* the hour which *rises for Horus.*
During the ninth hour of the day (2 P.M. to 3 P.M.), Ra's boat crosses the
Iaru fields where barley and wheat grow five cubits high and are
harvested by spirits. This hour bears the name *Mistress of Life,* the hour
when all nourishment is sublimated. This is an eloquent teaching on the
correspondence of the time of day with organic life in general. For
Chinese acupuncture, noon is the hour of the heart, and 2 P.M. the hour of
the small intestine.

It is in this fashion that texts and images are to be interpreted.
The Book of Hours of the Night is complemented by the *Book of*

Caverns (Qererts) and by the *Book of What Is in the Nether World* (the *Dwat*). Both of them describe Ra's entry into the "transposed world" by his crossing the mysterious horizon, and his glorious rebirth in the morning. But whereas one book gives the name of each door, of each hour and of the guiding *Neter,* the other emphasizes the serpents and the fire-spitting uraei which guard the entrances.

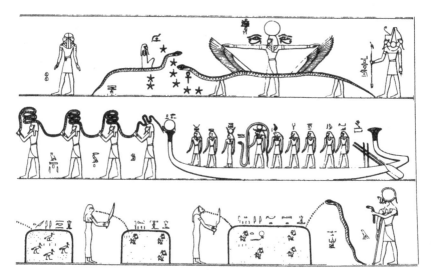

Fig. 34. *Eleventh Hour of the Night of the Book of What Is in the Nether World* (Tomb of Seti I, Nineteenth Dynasty).
This image, a fragment of a long series, shows clearly that this concerns an influence of cosmic, or stellar, character.

The *Book of Caverns* describes at length the punishments promised to the enemies of Osiris, and the *Book of the Dwat* stresses the specific character of each region or hour, of the numerous *Neters* that inhabit them. These *Neters,* for the most part, are not known from any other source. There is here the affirmation of a real science, but its meaning is not clarified for the profane beholder. Above all, recommendations are given to know the names of the regions of the *Dwat;* at the third hour of the night, for instance, it is said:

"Mysterious [or secret] souls" is the name given to the Neters that are in this region. As to the one who knows their names on Earth, he shall rise up as far as the site of Osiris. . . .

He who carries out these secret directives of the mysterious souls according to this form [that is, its characteristic quality] which is in the hidden writings of the Dwat. . . that will be beneficial for the man on Earth [and] in the other world, in truth. . . .

He who knows this, as soul and spirit, he will master his legs and will never enter into the place of destruction.

He will come forth in his forms, breathing the breaths toward his hour.

The third hour of the night (8 P.M. to 9 P.M.) is known to direct the respiratory action of the *haty,* the region of heart and lungs.

It is clearly asserted that knowledge of these things is useful on *earth* as well as in the *Dwat.* What is certain, however, is that every phrase needs a gloss of explanation, much like those in the surgical papyrus where every term is explained, or as in this New Empire commentary regarding a hymn of Atum-Ra:

I am the great *Neter* who has made himself, who creates his names, the master of the Divine Ennead.

What means this? It is Ra creating the names of his limbs, meaning: The Neters that are in his following came into existence.

The solar barque's procession through the hours confirms what was said concerning *Sia,* and thereby reveals a meaning of the boat: manning the *double* helm is *Sia,* knowledge, along with *Hu,* usually translated as *taste,* a meaning which should be broadened to *senses.* This symbol of the solar barque can be summarized as follows: Ra's energy, at this specific hour, must be perceived so that the vital teaching of this hour be put into practice.

Faith: The Neters

Olympiodoros, Zosimos, and Democritos the Philosopher, among others, never ceased to proclaim the existence of a sacred science in ancient Egypt, but because our own science knows nothing of it and does not believe in it, scholarly Egyptologists relegate such affirmations to the realm of fable. Consequently, this great ancient empire is rationalized, translated, and adjudged through the wrong mentality: through ours, and not through that of the sages of yore. As a result, allegorical and metaphorical writings concerned with matters beyond our ken are labeled as being conjuring spells. Texts implying the highest science given to man are called "magical," in the pejorative sense of "sorcery."

Nevertheless, many people are believers, including some who scorn any mention of the magic of the ancients. The Jew believes in the magic of the Torah, the Moslem believes in the magic of Allah's name. The rituals of Christian religion, be they Orthodox or Roman, are composed only of magical gestures; such are the rituals of the "holy water," Holy Saturday, prayers of exorcism, consecration of the priest, and, notwithstanding those who see in it a mere symbol, the sacred mystery of the Mass.

For a better understanding of what the ancients called "medicine," it suffices to clarify the true meaning of the word "magic" so as to distinguish it from "sorcery."

What must be understood is the existence of an essential power which plays a principal role in all instances: *faith*. What is this faith that is neither a belief, nor a conviction, nor any act of volition, and yet can move mountains? What is that state of the human being, that irrational puissance offering him this most powerful faith? It is true that whoever does not possess, or indeed, whose cerebration has stifled this curious faculty, *does not entertain this faith;* such people have *convictions,* they still hold to reasoning, being naive to the point of believing that an invincible argument is possible. Others, more serious, bestow their faith on the ultimate state of analysis: the mind's irreducible moment. They speak of *according their faith,* as if true faith depended upon our consent or on our will.

True faith is a certitude, but certitude has two faces: One results from observed and controlled experiment and is imposed by reason, the other is the certitude imposed by faith.

For example, when we accidentally injure ourselves, a state of hypnosis can be induced which eliminates this pain. When our mental or psychological consciousness is fascinated, effaced by an unknown will or by any other means, then the bodily sensation is muffled, and there remains only the order imposed either by another or by one's self. *Then absolute faith operates.*

"I have faith that such and such a phenomenon will occur." So be it! If I can eliminate all mental presence in myself, this phenomenon will take place. It will exist for me and be as real as any other phenomenon that exists only through mental projection. I project outside of myself a state of consciousness existing within me.

In reality, every living being is in contact with all the rhythms and harmonies of all the energies of his universe: The means of this contact is, of course, the self-same energy contained by this particular living being. Nothing separates this energetic state within an individual living being from the energy in which he is immersed, if not the cerebral presence, such as is the case with man. The animal does not lose this contact as it is not yet in possession of this mental "superiority." We speak of instinct but we fail to consider that this contact pertains to the true source of natural magic. Real power accrues to whoever can *consciously* regain this state known as "instinctive." This power is rare, because we neglect to do what is necessary to acquire it. Yet it can respond to the call—in other words, to prayer, the summons which incites us to strike a harmony with the energy of Nature; and when this energy has a known "functional" name, one can say as in ancient Egypt: *to summon the Neter.* Rather foolishly, we treat this as superstition.

It is essential to understand thoroughly what the word *Neter* means. We have seen that in every month of each seasonal period of the year, every hour of the day has its *Neter,* because each one of these hours has its own character. It is known that the blue morning-glory blooms at sunrise and closes at midday like the lotus flower. This is observed but not understood. More easily understood is the fact that certain fruits require the afternoon sun in order to ripen and to color. Here observation can bear on the living phenomenon. A young pepper plant, for example, leans toward the *burning* sun of the morning, which differs from the *cooking* sun of the afternoon. In these instances, there is a visible and tangible product, with sunlight as the visible and perceptible cause: These facts are therefore "rational."

As far as the vital phenomenon in Nature is concerned, we will draw the conclusion that a relationship exists between the fruit, for example, its taste, and the sun of its ripening, and, for the pepper plant, between the fire of the pepper and the fire of the sun. There is a harmony in their "nature."

If a good gardener plants his cauliflower on the day of full moon, and a bad gardener plants them at new moon, the former will have rich, white cauliflower and the latter will harvest nothing but stunted plants. It is sufficient to try this in order to prove it. *So it is for everything that grows and lives.* Why these effects? Direct rays of sunlight or indirect rays reflected by the moon? Certainly, but for quite another, less material reason as well: *cosmic harmony.* Purely material reasons no longer explain why the season, even the month and precise date, must be taken into account for the best results: Invisible cosmic influences come into play. After many experiments, we can affirm that these influences play a predominant role.

We cannot here enter into the detail which goes so far as to label the influence of each hour. It is enough to realize that every essential moment can actually be designated *by a name:* the name of a *Neter.* In the history of all of sacred science, the name has always played a preponderant role, and *knowledge of this name* (says the Egyptian *Book of the Dead*) is indispensable for crossing the gates of the *Dwat*, the world of the transposed sky, the netherworld. To know the name of the *Neter* means to know its particular activity, because the *Neter* is a *functional principle* and not a "god," as popular custom would have it, be it Jewish, Greek, or Christian.

In Genesis, Moses makes the still androgynous Adam walk through earthly, or manifest, Paradise, so that he may give a *name* to each thing. Indeed, this Adam, created in the image of God, knows all the functions, all the harmonies of the universe.

That these principles have been humanized for and by the popular mind is understandable, but here we must clarify the deeper significance of these problems. The symbolique of the Isenheim altarpiece[11] provides an example of how ideas can be reversed: this symbolique, embodying certain virtues in Saint Anthony, supposedly represents an episode in his life when his sanctity was revealed by prodigious powers. Actually, these images symbolize certain natural functions, certain influences, that is, *a certain Neter* given human form.... How else, save through these personifications would it be possible for ignorant people to transmit essential truths metaphysical in character? One must know how to disregard the vehicle of the idea in order to consider its motivation alone. *The true name of the Neter is the function it incarnates.* Subconsciously, moreover, this is how a people's instinct grasps it and this leads them to imagine the *Neter* of a mountain, a valley, a river, or of any other object—or phenomenon—which strikes their emotional nature.

The *Neter* is necessarily linked to the milieu in which it acts: Coincidence, contradiction, or interference can occur in its evocation with reference to this milieu. In what manner can this "invocation" or "prayer" act on the *Neter,* how can it affect a specific well-defined function? *Who* invokes? *Who* prays? Isn't it the human being, guided by his desire, his desperation, his fear or greed? If, for example, one who suffers greatly, such as the man in the throes of "Saint Anthony's Fire" evoked by the above-mentioned symbolique, prays to Saint Anthony for recovery, there is only one condition under which the "miracle" will take place: it demands *real faith,* provided the suppliant is capable of experiencing it, because spirit is all-powerful over body. I say "real faith" for were it a question of *belief* (no matter how firm), subconscious doubt would always be more powerful than that false faith. What is called belief is mental and therefore it is a false

[11]See Chapter 5, "Symbolique and Symbol."

faith. The healing power of Saint Anthony, depicted in this symbolique, is of another kind. It consists in applying the meaning of this *Neter,* its signification as an activity in cosmic harmony, and this the disciples of Anthony—the Antonins of Isenheim—knew how to achieve.

When one speaks of harmony, it is always music that first comes to mind. Through the sense of hearing, music is certainly the most tangible manifestation of this mysterious phenomenon, but there is also harmony in any material, energetic, or functional complex in general. For example, there is a possibility of harmony between the typical disease of a country and the flora and fauna of that same country. The vital milieu produces plants or animal life of a similar nature. Consequently, as in the instance of a vital disorder being caused by the vital milieu, the latter will offer substances able to cause as well as to cure this malady because every action contains its reaction. Here the *dates of vitalization* must be known, as they influence the active or reactive effects.

These dates are but cosmic dispositions, planetary and stellar arrangements in relation to the movements of our earth, and this is the juncture of the greatest harmonic activity. But if there are harmonious moments, there are necessarily disharmonies as well. It is the great marvel of human understanding that it can ascertain directly the effect of these laws which make for what is known in music as perfect chords and of dispositions according to different keys.

It is an erroneous interpretation of astrology to opine that special forces emanate from the planets and the stars. The sun and moon are sources of direct emanation, but the planets transmit nothing to us in this manner. Everything in the universe moves and, for that reason, there is constant modification in the arrangement of celestial bodies and in their reciprocal relation. The forces which control these movements create these relations through harmonious or disharmonious arrangements; these forces are the primitive powers known to our physical science in their material manifestation. Anyone who has observed the Brownian movement of corpuscles in a colloidal medium knows that no particle (star or planet) ever falls upon another, no matter what its speed, as long as the viscous medium subsists. Every particle, by virtue of its constitution, has a polarity, and when drawing near one another, the particles repel each other. This is a primitive, energetic "life" which, with natural chemical affinity, *compels* cosmic order, be it of a drop of colloidal liquid or of nebulae in the starry heavens.

"Harmony" is a puissance we can define geometrically, yet we cannot *understand* the reason for its logical existence; I say "geometrically" in the mathematical acceptation, though our senses are capable of selecting what is harmonious or disharmonious: through the ear, the most purely direct sense, through the eye which demands mental judgment; also through the sense of smell and through taste combined with smell.

Accordingly, by means of the power of the true faith, through the true meaning of the *Neter* and its evocation, and through the true harmonic situation, magic and medicine become accessible and cease to be the superstitions and phantasms that superficial judgment would have them be.

Clarification of the use of "magic words" and "magic formulas" will round out our reflections in this domain.

The literal sense of the words can have no magic efficacy unless it be by the power of suggestion. Related to this problem is the frequently formulated question: Is there such a thing as a sacred language?

The *Logos* of the Gospel according to John is a term which has many meanings: Word, Intellect, Reason, and others. It is generally (and especially in literature) taken to mean "word" *(verbum)*, but it would be more exact to relate it to the term "weaving" in its traditional symbolic sense. It stands for the intersection of complementary notions, as in the craft of weaving where intersection gives form to two threads which by themselves cannot be situated. Taken in this acceptation of "weaving," the term *Logos* in the Gospel of John actually contains in itself the significance of that "circuit-phrase": "the manifestation or divine work of creation as well as the immanence of the Creator of this work." The word is not to be considered as magical, but the action it implies is magical action par excellence.

Sacred or magical language is not to be understood as a succession of terms with definite meanings. Actually, the pronouncement of each sound of the language puts very precise nerves and breathings into action. The excitation of certain nervous centers as well as the breath-action upon the chakras, such physiological effects are evoked by the utterance of certain letters or words which make no sense in themselves.

The Pharaonic texts are rich in examples of litanies playing a magical role through the repetition of sounds in words and through word play. The hieroglyphic writings allow us to confirm this, although their transcription into our language is impossible since the pronunciation of this language is unknown. Nevertheless, it was still a living language until the first centuries of our era; Asklepios among others, in a cruel evaluation of the Greek idiom, affirms the existence of this magical effect of the words of the Pharaohs' language. A letter from Asklepios to King Ammon opens with the formal recommendation that an important writing not be translated into Greek "for fear that the arrogant elocution of the Greeks, with its lack of nerve and what can be called its false graces, might pale and eradicate the profundity, the solidity, and the efficacious virtue of the vocable of our [Egyptian] language. Because the Greeks, O King, have but empty discourses good for producing demonstrations, and therein lies all the philosophy of the Greeks, a clamor of words. As for us, we do not use simple words, but sounds all filled with power."[12]

[12]*Corpus Hermeticum*, XVI, 2, in R. P. Festugière, op. cit., p. 236.

7

Cosmic Ambiance

"Egypt is made in the image of heaven." The expression is well known, although its meaning is rather difficult to explain. It is obviously not meant to imply a copy of the starry sky, but rather a reflection upon earth of cosmic harmony: in the image of a harmonic coincidence with influences of a celestial order. The facts, the astronomical observations, can be ascertained: only life, however, only the vital effect in relation with these facts, can demonstrate the influence, which is here the topic at hand.

There is nothing scientific in speaking about such "influences." Astrologers observe certain planetary harmonies in the zodiacal cycle, and how they coincide with events in the life of an individual whose "birth theme" is known. Is this a matter of *influence* or *harmony?* Though the term is difficult to replace, "influence" is actually not correct. The term "harmony" is preferable, though no more explicit. The fact is ascertained beyond doubt, but its cause is defined with a word of musical meaning, its value difficult to understand when a planetary grouping of the sky's annual or diurnal circuit is concerned.

But the emotional effects of music, equally well ascertained, also remain unexplained. The harmonic phenomenon is supranatural, a result of inborn consciousness in all things, causing affinities in material elements and sympathy or antipathy among living creatures. Thus cosmic harmony is in direct relation with all that exists, be this cycle indefinitely long for the worlds in the sky, or indefinitely short for the beings living on a planet or on a speck of dust.

This is the true *music of the spheres.*

It is relevant here to recall a very ancient text that epitomizes a wisdom founded on knowledge of the laws of harmony and genesis:

The Emerald Tablet, where emerald is the color that chiefly symbolizes vegetation and life:

> True it is, without falsehood, certain, and very real:
>
> What is below is as that which is above, and what is above is as that which is below, in order to perform the Miracle of one thing only.
>
> And just as all things have been and have come forth from One, so all things have been born of this sole-singular thing, by adaptation.
>
> The Sun is its Father, the Moon is its Mother and the Wind has carried it in its belly; the Earth is its nurse. The Father of the entire Teleme of the whole world is here. Its force or puissance is entire if it be converted into Earth.
>
> Thou shalt separate the Earth from the Fire, the Subtile from the Dense, gently, with great ingenuity. It rises from Earth to Heaven, and again descends into Earth, and it receives the strength of things above and below. By this means thou shalt have the glory of all the World, and through it, all obscurity will flee from thee.
>
> This is the strong Strength of all strength, for it will vanquish any subtile thing and penetrate any solid thing.
>
> Thus has the world been created.
>
> From this there shall be and there will come forth marvelous adaptations, the means of which is here.
>
> Therefore, I have been called Hermes Trismegistos, possessing the three parts of the Philosophy of the entire world.
>
> What I have said concerning the operation of the Sun is accomplished and perfected.[1]

The Calendar

Because "Egypt is made in the image of heaven," we must consider what the ancients knew about astronomy; their knowledge in that domain is revelatory of the true workings of their minds, seeing that the land is organized in this image, in the sense expressed by The Emerald Tablet.

The day was divided into twenty-four hours, twelve hours of light and twelve hours of darkness; each hour bore a name specifying its influence. The hours of the day were determined by means of sundials, and the hours of the night by clepsydras. In addition, mechanical clocks are known to have existed.

In royal tombs of the Twentieth Dynasty, star tables have been found which indicate, hour by hour, the positions of the principal stars by two week periods. These are observations akin to our observations of

---

[1] "The Emerald Tablet" from the *Commentaries de l'Hortulain,* in *Bibliotèque des philosophes alchymiques ou hermétiques* (Paris, 1756).

a star's crossing the meridian. Classical texts assert, moreover, that the rising and setting of stars had been observed in Egypt for an incredible number of years and had been recorded on special tablets.[2]

The ancients never strove for a concordance of the absolutely incompatible solar and lunar cycles which have always confounded astronomers. The months were of two kinds. There was the *lunar month* of 29 and 30 days alternately; each day had its name and certain religious ceremonies corresponded to the phases of the moon, the celebration of *Min's coming forth,* for instance, which took place on the day of new moon. There was also a division of the solar cycle with twelve months of thirty days each, or 360 days to which were added *the five days preceding the year;* it was said that the *Neters* were born on these days. They are consecrated consecutively to Osiris, Horus, Seth, Isis, and Nephthys; transliterated from the hieroglyphs, the names read: *Osir, Her, Seth, Aset,* and *Nebt-het.* The totality of 365 days formed the *vague year* according to which all civil acts were dated.

The five *Neters* of these intercalary (epagomenal) days are the natural puissances immanent to the year. Osiris is cut into pieces (distributed throughout the year) by Seth, who holds back the Fire fallen into earth, carrying off the divine Light that is Lucifer, or Horus. At a particular moment, Isis conceives Horus from the phallus of Osiris, principle of fecundity; Nephthys, in turn revives Osiris.

There are three seasons in Pharaonic Egypt, each of four months, commanded by the Nile: the dry season, inundation, and germination, or life. Seth is implied in the dry season as is Isis in the flood season. According to the myth, it is a teardrop of Isis, falling from the heavens, which makes the Nile waters swell at the moment of the heliacal rising of Sirius, star of Isis. Osiris is the principle of constant, cyclical renewal, and Nephthys, that of the return of life. On this occasion, Isis and Nephthys are symbolized by two kites (two volatiles); sometimes, in their anthropomorphized aspect, Isis is shown dressed in white on red and Nephthys in red on white.

By means of astronomical observations of the sun, the moon, the stars, and their movements in relation to the earth, the Pharaonic sages had to establish a calendar allowing facts to be accurately situated in time. Their calendar achieved a degree of perfection not surpassed by any other, and this wonder merits our admiration.

All is movement in the universe. It can even be said that the universe is nothing but movement. This movement is physical in its

---

[2]See Appendix VI, "The Egyptians' Knowledge of Astronomy."

spatial relativity, but from a vital point of view, movement is a sequence of phases progressing in time from an origin or seed toward its accomplishment or fruit. Of these two points of view, one is mechanical, the other is vital. This is a mental dissociation of a natural phenomenon in which spatial and temporal movements are actually inseparable.

But wisdom rejects the call for dissociation through the mental faculties, of use only to give us a consciousness of "outside of us" and "inside of us." This is of aid in ascertaining facts, but does not further our knowing Being. The life phenomenon is the effect of this identification between the harmony of physical movements in space and the phases of any and all genesis.

Our earth, with all that lives on it, is a part of a living whole, and its movements in space are submitted to a "celestial respiration" just as every cell in our body is submitted to the vital effect of our own respiration. This latter function is exercised by our *haty*, comprised of *lungs* and *heart*, by the living organs which measure our space and time.

Instead of attempting the formulation of a rigid calendar, the ancients knew how to take into account all celestial movements and to relate them to life on earth. We have seen that these sages gave consideration to both the lunar and the solar cycle, while keeping them separate one from the other. The solar cycle is complex in itself; in our day, use is made of both the *tropical year*, which is the time span between two consecutive returns of the globe to the spring equinox, and of the *sidereal year*, which is the time span elapsed between two conjunctions of the earth with the same star.[3] But both of these periods involve fractions of days, minutes, and seconds, and cannot be used as a fixed temporal unit because they need constant adjustments. Accordingly, the ancients adopted neither one nor the other, but rather based themselves on the *Sothic year* of 365¼ days exactly, the year determined by the periodic return of the heliacal rising of *Sirius*. It is a fact that among the extremely slow movements of the stars called "fixed" in relation to one another, Sirius is the only one that allows the compensation of irrational discrepancy of time: therefore, it permits establishment of a *fixed year—or year of God—* which serves as a measure of reference to keep track of all celestial movements. The heliacal rising of Sirius determined New Year's Day, called "opening of the year."

---

[3]The *tropical year*, on which our Gregorian calendar is based, is 365.24219879...days long. The *sidereal year* is 365.256361...days long. The first is shorter, the second longer than the *Julian year* of 365¼ days still employed in astronomy and which corresponds exactly to the Pharaonic *fixed year*.

An exceptional feature of the Pharaonic calendar was the establishment of the civil calendar on the very basis of the shift of the *vague year* of 365 days in relation to the *fixed year* of 365¼ days. It is this difference of one day every four years[4] which in fact allows for precise dating whenever the documents furnish a *double date,* for in the course of a 1,460-year *Sothic cycle,* New Year's Day falls successively on each day of the vague year. As the heliacal rising of Sirius takes place one day earlier for each degree of latitude going from north to south, according to the official date of the New Year corresponding to July 19 of our Julian calendar, it has been possible to determine with exactitude that the heliacal rising of Sirius was calculated in Heliopolis. In those days, as the texts show, it was announced ahead of time from this temple to all the other cities of Egypt on what day of what month of the current vague year that New Year's Day was to be celebrated.

This system of dating is like a *vernier,* or sliding gauge, *in time.*[5] Here is an example:

> Year 9, under the majesty of the King of Upper and Lower Egypt, Zeser-Ka-Re [Amenophis I, second king of the Eighteenth Dynasty],
> Festival of the New Year, third month of the season of Shmu, day 9, rising of Sirius.[6]

This date is easily interpreted by the chronologist: Year 9 of Amenophis I was one of the four years from 1550 to 1547 B.C., and if the length of the reign of the other kings is known, this information makes it possible to reconstruct the order of the entire dynasty.

Another example is found in a text of Thothmes III where the date of the new year is also given in relation to the civil year but the year of the reign is lost:

> . . . the third month of the season of Shmu, day 28, festival of the rising of Sirius.

This inscription can be dated exactly between the years 1474 and 1471 B.C. To complete this information, however, and to recover the date

---

[4]This interval of one day every four years was adopted by the Greeks in order to determine the period of the Olympiads, celebrated every four years by the Olympic games.

[5]The principle of the vernier is based on the recurrent coincidence of the divisions of two differently graduated scales, one of which is mobile.

A decimal vernier, for instance, consists of ten divisions equal to nine divisions of the fixed scale for the same length, thus allowing a decimal reading.

Parallelly, there are 1,461 vague years in the Sothic cycle of 1,460 fixed years.

[6]E. Meyer, *Chronologie égyptienne,* pp. 58-61.

of the beginning of Thothmes III's reign, mention is made of a lunar date which can be found in a text relating the foundation of this monarch's *Sed festival* temple:

> My Majesty ordered that the ceremony of stretching the cord be prepared at the approach of the day of the New Moon festival in order that the cord be stretched for this monument, in the year 24, second month of the Pert season, last day. . . .[7]

This foundation ceremony is thus dated 23 February 1477 B.C., and the beginning of the reign of Thothmes III from 1501.

In contrast with these demonstrative examples, our calendar will never enable future archeologists to situate an event in time because our year one is determined by a theological datum and not an astronomical date.

The "double dates" provided by the documents have made it possible, moreover, to define the precise dates at which the *fixed year* and the *vague year* coincided once more, i.e., in the year A.D. 140 and in the years 1320, 2780, and 4240 B.C. Hence the foundation of the calendar must necessarily go back to one of those dates. As the Pyramid Texts, judging from their archaic style, must in part precede Menes, and as Sothis (Sirius) already figures in these texts as presiding over the year, the Sothic period 2780 must be excluded as too recent and the conclusion can be reached that the Pharonic calendar was introduced in 4240 B.C.[8]

In order to establish the fixed year, it is a fact that the ancient Egyptians deliberately chose *the heliacal rising of Sirus,* the only star to return periodically every 365¼ days, during the entire Empire. This fact implies exceptional astronomical knowledge as well as a very long period of observation preceding the introduction of the calendar. There is much controversy concerning their knowledge of the heavens, which is admired by some and contested by others with arguments worthy of derision.

There is a further particularity to the Pharaonic calendar. In contrast with our division of the Gregorian year, the ancients made no attempt to arrive at a rigorous concurrence with the seasons, notwithstanding the fact that the latter command the whole of agricultural life. This constitutes another "vernier in time." Indeed, while for us the summer solstice returns each year on June 21-22, thus determining a fixed reference point, *for the Pharaonic Sothic cycle of*

---

[7] Ibid., pp. 61-64.
[8] This date, demonstrated by E. Meyer, op. cit., p. 51, is elsewhere disputed. See Appendix VIII.

1,460 years, the summer solstice advanced 11.5 days in relation to the rising of Sirius. That this fact was perfectly well known to the ancients is shown by the temporal correction brought to the celebration of the summer solstice or "Birth of Ra."

The essential facts are as follows:

1. The first day of the first month of the fixed year, or *festival of the New Year,* has always been determined by *the heliacal rising of Sirius.*

2. In the year 4240 B.C., the *summer solstice* fell six to nine days *after* the New Year, and was consequently celebrated under the name of *Birth of Ra* during the first month of the fixed year. But as the solstice advanced from five to six days in each Sothic half-cycle, it happened that the *Birth of Ra* coincided with the *New Year* around the year 3400. In the year 2780, the solstice fell during the "five days of the birth of the *Neters"* (the "epagomenae"). This remained in keeping with the calendar of celebrations as these days were considered "the five days over the year." After two Sothic cycles, however, in the year 1320 under Seti I, the Birth of Ra or summer solstice no longer took place either during the first month or during the five intercalary days, but between the nineteenth and the twenty-second day of the twelfth month of the Sirian year, in other words, *thirteen days before* the rising of Sirius or *New Year's Day.*[9]

At that stage, a reform seemed in order, not as far as concerned the calendar, which remained immutable, but for the reckoning of religious festivities: The *Birth of Ra* was celebrated during the twelfth month instead of the first; this conformed to the true displacement of the solsticial point among the constellations. This reform resulted in the shifting of one month for all other religious festivities and these events in the end gave their names to the months of the Late Empire, names that were transmitted as such in Coptic.

If we keep in mind that the solstices *gain* approximately eleven days per Sothic cycle with respect to the rising of Sirius, it may be observed that the periodic return of a star to a particular meridian *loses* approximately nine days during the same cycle, so that *the vernal point* is displaced by approximately twenty days in 1460 years among the constellations of the zodiac. This is the precession of the equinoxes; its discovery was hitherto attributed to Hipparchos. On the one hand, however, considering that tables of the star risings are known to have existed, as well as lists of the thirty-six decans, each corresponding to one third of a theoretical zodiacal sign, and that on the other hand

---

[9]See *Cf.* E. Meyer, op cit., pp. 16 and 312; details on this problem and dates by Professors Ginzel and Förster.

evidence exists of the shifting of the calendar's monthly festivities, *it is incontestable that the ancient Egyptians ascertained the phenomenon of the precession of the equinoxes; this is attested to by the modifications brought to the festival calendar of the tropic year* (hence to the seasons) *with respect to the Sirian cycle.*

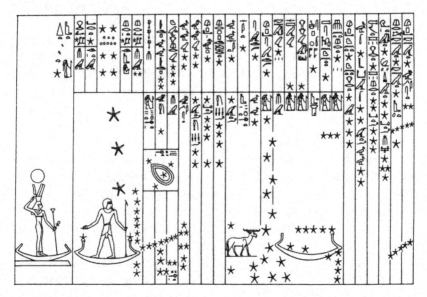

Fig. 35. *List of the Decans followed by Orion and Sirius.*
Ceiling of the tomb of Senmut. Deir el-Bahari, Eighteenth
Dynasty.

    It is significant also that tradition has already related the heliacal rising of Sirius with the beginning of the Nile's flooding and with the zodiacal sign of Leo; indeed, since the foundation of the calendar to the beginning of our era, *in Egypt the sun was always situated in the constellation Leo at the date of the heliacal rising of Sirius.* This is the reason why, since the Ancient Empire, the temple gargoyles were carved in the shape of lion heads.[10] In the zodiacal cycle, the sign of Leo is opposed and complemented by Aquarius, a sign represented on the Dendera zodiac by two vases from which water pours; this symbol is placed in the hands of the Nile god, Hapi. In the fifth millennium B.C., the heliacal rising of Sirius took place in the constellation Virgo; this could have motivated the attribution of Sirius to Isis, along with the mythical

[10] J.-B. Biot, *Recherche sur plusieurs points de l'astronomie égyptienne:* Horapollon, no. 21, and Borchardt, *Pyramide de Sah-ou-Re.*

and vital significance of the character of Isis' star, Sothis (Sirius) which was also called "the great provider."[11]

The summer solstice, which during the Ancient Empire occurred when the sun was in the constellation Leo, shifted into Cancer from the beginning of the Middle Empire onward, and there with the vernal point passed from Taurus to Aries.

The precessional cycle, therefore, is in theory that span of 26,000 years during which the vernal point travels through the twelve sites of the sky designated by their dominant constellations.[12] This cycle is composed of twelve months, each with a duration of about 2,160 years; each month is subdivided into three decans of 720 years.[13] These precessional months designate *the great Neter of the cult* whose influence colors all the other principles.

Yet it is always *Nun*, the primordial, indeterminate state (or ocean) which receives the characteristic impulse of the celestial influence, and this impulse varies according to the precessional month.

Thus it is that Pharaonic prehistory was dominated by the Twins *Shu* and *Tefnut*, whose nature consists in separating Heaven from Earth. This has been interpreted as representing the two crowns of the Empire, as yet dualized. At that time there existed the kingdom of the South with its double capital, *Nekhen* and *Nekheb*, and the kingdom of the North with its dual capital, *Dep* and *Pe*. The vestiges of this period show a pronounced double character and it is certainly at this time that the Heliopolitan mystery of primordial dualization was revealed.

At Memphis, under the Ancient Empire, there was the domination of Hap the Bull, who precipitated celestial fire into terrestrial form. The Bull, the great *Neter* of the historical period extending from 4380 to 2200 B.C., commands the Cretan civilization as well.

From the Middle Empire to the beginning of the Christian era, we see the domination of Amon the Ram. It is in Thebes, under the predominance of Amon, that the generating fire is "extracted," so to speak, from its terrestrial gangue-matrix, Khonsu, by the grace of Djehuti (Thoth), master of Hermopolis.

Nun is invariable, while the receptive milieux, or environments, are generative, and hence feminine. They are successively: *Nut* in Heliopolis, *Sekhmet-Hathor* in Memphis, and then *Mut* in Thebes.

[11]See, Chapter 2, "The Deviation."

[12]The division of the zodiacal band into twelve equal regions is purely theoretical.

[13]According to the 1953 *Annuaire de Flammarion*, the precessional period diminished by 11.4 years per century. It was 25,783 years long by the year 1942 and 26,000 years long in the year A.D. 50. But in 3,000 B.C., it corresponded to approximately 18 Sothic cycles, or 26,280 years. Each decan lasted 730 years, that is, half of a Sothic cycle

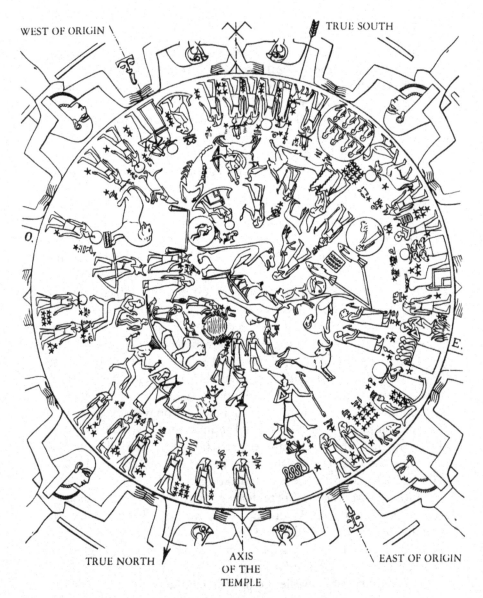

WEST OF ORIGIN   TRUE SOUTH

TRUE NORTH   AXIS   EAST OF ORIGIN
                    OF THE
                    TEMPLE

Fig. 36. *The circular Zodiac of Dendera.*
(See Appendix VII, part 2.)

What was elaborated at Heliopolis was Shu and Tefnut as creation; in Memphis it becomes Nefertum, issue of the couple Ptah-Sekhmet, while at Thebes, the product of Amon and Mut is Khonsu.

But succession means generation and not juxtaposition, although the philosophical legend must situate the principles as if coexisting personages were involved.

Finally, toward the year 60 B.C., with the end of the political empire of Egypt under Cleopatra, our Christian era of Pisces begins.

Thus there are cosmic seasons defined by the precession of the equinoxes, stellar seasons with Sothis, planetary seasons through the circuit and particular movements of the planets on the ecliptic, and lastly, the seasons of the luminaries through the sun and the moon.

Sun and moon give the essential primary complements. The planets, called the *Wanderers,* give the qualitative *orientations* through their situations in different sites of the starry heavens. The groupings of fixed stars tinge the celestial sites and delimit them; through Sothis in coincidence with the sun, they modify the sun's intensities (the eye of Ra), because Sothis is the *great purveyor* of energy.

The displacement of the vernal point from one zodiacal region to another transposes the entire system on which our earth depends across the stellar cosmic zones, thereby coloring the seasons. Around 2200 B.C., the precessional entry into the *constellation* Aries coincided with the annual terrestrial spring astrologically always situated in the *sign* of Aries.

The myth is directly related to the cosmic movements, to cosmic harmony. Because of its calendar, it is possible to situate the essential phases of Pharaonic Egypt's history, and by means of it, we are able to understand the modifications brought to the essential cult.

It has by now been fully documented that the basis of the religious cult changed coincidentally with the astronomical phases of the precession of the equinoxes. The possibility that the ancient Egyptians might have possessed knowledge concerning precessional cycles had been hitherto excluded. Herewith the reasons for the change of the cult of Hap the Bull into that of Amon the Ram stand clarified, as does the profound significance to be attached to what is represented by Amon.

Amon is at once the lunar Amon—inasmuch as primordial Water (such as the fetal amniotic and the cerebral spinal fluids)—and the solar Amon-Ra, the animating, fecundating seminal Fire. Amon is not what we take to mean by "a god": Amon is the *cosmic milieu,* source of all present life, as was Hap before him, as Pisces still is today, as Aquarius already begins to be for tomorrow.

During the long period of a precessional month, the dominant constellation influences life on earth on a universal scale, just as spring or another season does for our short annual cycles.

By what means did these influences and their specificities become known? This is a long and fascinating story which does not enter into the framework of this book. It suffices to know that there exists a cosmic *functional prototype* for each organic specificity, the totality of which makes for the human body. From this there stems, inversely, the doctrine of anthropocosmos which takes man as model in the study of the All.

Fig. 36a. *Ivory Tablet from the beginning of the First Dynasty* (circa 3,300 B.C.)
Inscribed: "Sothis. Opener of the Year's Flood."
(Petrie, *Royal Tombs*, vol. II, Pls. V, 1, VIa, 2.)

The Amonian principle dominates the best-known period of Pharaonic Egypt. Once its true meaning has been clarified, the myth takes on a living meaning. Images and "stories" of all times concerning the *Neters* are to be understood as one and the same expression, only colored by the sky which determines the characteristic influence of the period. Let us suppose that the fact of having entered into the constellation Aries situates us in a yellow light; in that case, solar red will be orange, lunar blue will be green, and violet will be annulled. Such would be the domination of *Amon-whose-name-is-hidden.*

Indeed, who can give a name to this influence?

A perennial concern for remaining in harmony with the heavens amply justifies events such as the displacement of cult centers or the accentuation of the dominant character of the epoch as well as many modifications in the monuments and figurations for which there is no other explanation.

8

Myth

The myth which we have been discussing here is neither fiction nor legend in the ordinary sense, but a hieroglyphic writing composed of anthropomorphized functions and abstractions. It is a writing, because myth must be read like an ideogram, according to the language and understanding of each reader. This writing is hieroglyphic since it is concerned only with divine and sacred principles of Nature. These are functions in their universal meaning, abstractions which require symbols for their expression. These ideas are anthropomorphized (not humanized) because man, in the cosmic sense, as Nature's ultimate product, bears within himself—or better, *has* within himself—all the principles and all the functions.

It is not in this sense, however, that myth is generally considered by those who write about it. It has been seen as a primitive expression of thought, or as being pantheistic in character, or again, as idolatry. At best, as with Pharaonic myth, it is treated as a syncretism of sign-symbols, tribal customs, and various "theological systems."

In our definition, myth is the means of expression employed by sages who teach the esoterism of natural facts inexpressible in words.

To be achieved is a historical transcription of natural philosophy: It involves neither a systematized teaching nor the recital, in a rational sequence, of the becoming of things. The world-opus has as many aspects as there are "embryonic types" for the fetal birth of the world-king, the preconceived aim. No single road can be followed: All paths must be integrated into the myth, whence its seeming disjointedness. One foundation nevertheless underlies the whole. The latter includes what Pharaonic Egypt called the three mysteries: that of Heliopolis, of Memphis, and of Thebes, about which we will speak later.

The teaching of myth is necessarily "functional." It relates facts: Facts and concrete objects perceptible through the senses and through human intelligence serve as basis, but it is not these *things* which are described. They only serve as fulcrums in the evocation of functions universal in character. This is the true meaning of symbolique. The aim is the teaching of a science which is a knowledge revealed, a gnosis never transmitted by direct transcription, an impossible task: Though no mystery remains unknown, still sacerdotal science includes in its application numerous rites whose effective realization depends on the spiritual preparation of the celebrant.

Sacred science as taught through myth concerns the human being and it is addressed only to this being, Nature's *final, actual* issue, because the human being logically recapitulates all the aspects of gestation preceding his birth as a human creature. Pharaonic myth therefore anthropomorphizes the functions rather than humanizing them as did Greece and Rome. The human body, specified by a characteristic sign (scepters, crown, gesture, attribute) will be the support of the symbol because it epitomizes all the functions.

For example, a woman's body with the head of a cow signifies the femininity of the animal as well as the maternal character of the woman, but the animal itself takes on a sacred character because it is the *incarnation* of a specific quality and function.

Only our misguided mentality could venture to speak of zoolatry, taking the representation of the animal as the image of an idol. In the Pharaonic spirit, *the animal is not adored but revered as the incarnation of a specific function of which it is the symbol. It is the function which is the Neter, and not the animal.* Thus Anubis as a black jackal is portrayed lying on a closed treasure chest under the title of *guardian of the secret.* Treated as *Neter,* however, Anubis is simply depicted by a jackal's head on a human body, because the *function* characterizing the jackal is the *Neter* of digestion, an essential function of life. That is why a jackal's head is placed as lid on the Canopic jar containing the stomach and sometimes the small intestine.

The Egyptian sages thus searched the different realms for creatures typifying a particular quality, be it a functional character in the gestation of the universe, even in the realm of metals and minerals (iron and copper, for example), or the organic incarnation of an essential vital function among plants (for instance the lotus and the papyrus), or in the animal kingdom (such as certain vultures, the falcon, the cow, etc.). This choice was so strict that it can almost be inferred that animals not chosen for the symbolique, although part of Egyptian fauna, were considered as "incomplete types," or types more or less bastardized or deformed.

Fig. 37. The jackal *Anubis* as Ap-uat, the "Opener of the ways," lying on the chest as "guardian of the secret." The King offers him white bread, that is, white nourishment (chyle). Abydos, Nineteenth Dynasty.

Certain symbols chosen from among animals make their appearance as early as prehistory. Seeing that from the Middle Empire on, no new additions from the animal realm were introduced into the hieroglyphs, such symbolism must go back to the very origins.

For the symbolique, man becomes the support of the vital functions which were realized in the animal state. This much is comprehensible, and constitutes the guiding principle of what is called anthropocosmos. Being universe himself, man can know of that universe on which he "rests" nothing but what is *functionally* incarnated in him. Quite another matter is the reasoned explanation man gives of the phenomena which his senses register and which he perceives as being *outside of himself;* this strange *return reflection of our interiority projected outside of us* results in the phenomenon of mind. Note that we are constantly tempted to complete the phenomenon with a rational explanation, when such a complement does not really exist outside of us. Thus, for example, we complete a musical scale by rational means when no more than two tones, only a basic proportion, are given. The musical example is typical of such complementation, but can be appreciated only by the correct placement of the principles of harmony.

Harmony

The principle of harmony is cosmic law, the voice of God. Whatever the disorder caused by man or natural accident, Nature, if left to her own devices, will reestablish order by means of affinity, the consciouness innate in all things. Harmony is *law a priori,* expressed in Nature through and through; and though the existence of harmony is ever present to intelligence, it remains incomprehensible in itself. Whenever a proportion is given, be it metaphysically in the initial scission of oneness or in the splitting of a living cell, there is always a consequence which we call the scale of seven. This scale can pertain to energy, to sound, and with colors, to light.

What is specific in an activity—its function—is ordered by an energetic ensemble upon which the physical surroundings have left their mark. Activity does not *make* the organ: An abstract harmony, energetic in nature, summons the organ, creates it. The environment of a tropical swamp will be inhabited by a variety of animals, fowl, amphibians, mammals, and so forth, to all of which this environment is suited: *They are not adapted to the milieu, they are born from it.* Successful adaptation of certain other living beings to the milieu, should it be necessary, is possible only if the organic entity as a whole is already *harmonically* oriented in this direction.

The idea of *form* antecedes physical definition. *The golden mean* is the original separative function, though in its physical realization it needs first a division into two equal parts.[1] The proportions of a new born human, for instance, are as 1 is to 2, for its height is divided into two equal parts by the navel. This same person as an adult is divided by the

---

[1]This also applies to the geometric figuration of the *golden mean;* first a separation into two equal parts must be obtained.

navel according to the *golden mean*. The adult age actually being the finality of man whose proportions are preconceived, it appears that his growth obeys the function Φ, present from origin. In this sense, the very first embryonic cell contains virtually the entire future form. As to the specified organic cells of fetal becoming, their actual image lives in the entire animal genesis, the phases of which have responded to ambient energies for their development. These specifications follow the preconceived Idea for the characteristics of the cell such as it appears in the organic genesis of the fetus. Each element that enters the constitution of the ambiance has thus been conceived energetically (one might say spiritually) before its physical formation. Moses' terrestrial paradise, the legends of giants and "sons of Heaven" consorting with the "daughters of Earth," the divine prehistory of Egypt, all these are but examples of a symbolique concerning an ideal or metaphysical preformation of terrestrial life. But they are the symbols as well of a spiritual activity which causes the physical appearing of corporeal form. This cabala expresses the Heliopolitan mystery, as it does, in general, the spiritual prefiguration of incarnation.

The becoming of form is subject to numbers in the sense of a simple and initial proportion necessarily calling in response—in reaction—a harmonic scale. The functional nature of number is what orders this harmonic scale.

The number two is the expression of sexuality, of division, of opposition, of complementation, and this is how the true vital sense of number is to be understood.

Harmony is expressed geometrically in the figures which we have called "syntheses."[2] These figures schematize in a natural way and without calculation the *a priori* function which orders harmony; they show harmonic development based on and beginning with any simple proportion whatsoever.

Our rational thinking always applies itself to the sensory appearance to the effect, but this effect is immanent in the cause. It appears *in obedience to a harmonic law* which is order divine. We nevertheless approach this order by reasoning, basing ourselves on appearances which we can evidently not help noticing. But we must concede that no reasoning explains the harmonic function: *Without reasoning,* we experience the equilibrium lent to the human body, to a surface, to a division, by the function of the golden mean; and so our ear experiences consonance or dissonance in musical sounds, and our eye possesses an exquisite sense for the chords of color.

[2]*Le Temple de l'Homme, I,* pp. 288-289, 493-497, 502.

These principles, or Ideas, which preside over forms and functions, were called *Neters* in Pharaonic Egypt. It is unfortunate that Egyptology interprets these glyphs as meaning "gods." There are no "gods" in existence: *God is*. Only in created Nature do the divine qualities show themselves, and then they exist. And the *Neters* exist.

The Neters

Among *Neters*, three categories are to be distinguished:

The *metaphysical Neters*, such as Atum, Ra, Ptah. These are the vital principles. In terms of harmony, they represent harmonic *summons*.

The *cosmic Neters*, which are seasonal. Variable as is all of creation, they obey the laws of life and of genesis in general. Typical among them are the ram-headed Amon-Aries and the five *Neters* attributed to the epagomenal or intercalary days: Osiris, Seth, Isis, Nephthys, and Horus. They depend directly on astronomical and astrological harmony: They are the harmonic reply to the summons.

The *natural Neters*, which are the functional life of natural objects, such as Renenutet for harvests, Hapi for the Nile, Selkit for childbearing, Apet for gestation, the vulture Nekhebit for incubation, and so forth. They preside over all reproduction and regeneration, from mineral to man, for the metal is live in its lode.

The metaphysical *Neters* are principles of the universe. They are a direct creation, are not engendered by Nature, and are represented as having no navel (as with Atum, for example). The *Neters* in general are considered to be *without cranial skullcaps*, which means they are devoid of their own or arbitrary judgment. They are powers acting in a set way, the determination of which is made clear by a crown, by a symbol, or by an animal head. They cannot of themselves modify the orientation of their activity.

The principle does not act, the principle merely betokens the *mode of action*. Yet for ancient Egypt, there exists a principle of principles, *Neter of Neters (Neter-Neteru)*, nameless, and truly the concept of a supreme deity: the one and only inconceivable Oneness, sole-singular Cause. Actions pleasing to the *Neter of Neters* remain in a state of harmony with the divine order; actions displeasing thereto go against that harmony: evil consequences naturally result from such actions.

The aim of the superior man, the desired goal, is to enter consciously into that harmony. In no way is harmony a human endeavor: It is a supranatural state of being presiding over all vital phenomena, a state that prescribes and not one that obeys. *The Neters are the expression of this harmony.* They order affinities command concordances, give rise to forms and signatures, and exercise authority over the phases of becoming and of the return to the source. They manifest life.

Furthermore, the philosophy of the *Neters'* character is transmitted by legends which vary with every man center or temple. This must be so because the same mode of action, or principle, changes aspect according to the milieu where it obtains. The action of fire is different upon fire, for instance, than it is upon water, air, or solid bodies.

The Mysteries of Heliopolis, Memphis, and Thebes

Revealed at Heliopolis is the creative act and the appearance of Tum (or Atum) as well as of the Ogdoad, which is the analysis of that creative act.

Taught at Memphis is the work of Ptah, which is the giving of form and the animation of these forms.

At Thebes, the fruit of this genesis is *defined* through Amon, Mut, and Khonsu.

At Hermopolis, the milieu of generation is found *described* through Tehuti, or Thoth, connecting the three mysteries.

The teaching of these centers constitutes a whole that cannot be segmented; yet, through the universality of their respective mysteries, the myth of each temple retains an aspect of totality.

The texts which speak of the mysteries pertaining to a particular center are concerned with the phases of the *Neters'* becoming. This theogony, as it may well be called, has given rise to strange interpretations and assumptions, such as the belief, for instance, in theological rivalries. As far as the principles (or *Neters*) are concerned, they have been regarded as personalities that act with the free will of humans. In general, there has been a refusal to consider the differences characterizing these texts as being descriptive of the genesis which leads the principle of origin toward its manifestation, its animation in Nature.

Here is how the nature of the Theban Amon is defined in a papyrus of the Ramessid period (the Leyden papyrus):

> All the gods are three: Amon, Ra, and Ptah, who have no equals. He whose nature [literally, whose name] is mysterious, being Amon; Ra is the head, Ptah is the body. Their cities on earth, established forever, are Thebes, Heliopolis, and Memphis (stable) for eternity. When a message comes from heaven, it is heard at

Heliopolis, it is repeated at Memphis to Ptah and it is made into a letter, written in the letters of Thoth, for the city of Amon (Thebes). The answer and decision are given at Thebes, and addressed to the divine Ennead, all that issues from its mouth, the mouth of Amon. The gods are established for him, according to his commandments. The message, it is to slay or to let live. Life and death depend on it for all beings, except for Him, Amon, for Ra [and for Ptah] unity-trinity.[3]

Such mysteries are not to be grasped by the reasoning process of the mind's intelligence. In practice, the ternary is found as the end of all analysis. Incarnation is the natural effect of complementation, and consequently the third term of the ternary; a triangular unity is formed by the whole. Redemption is extracorporeal, it is an abstract reality to be circumscribed but not to be understood: It is the return of spirit to spirit, having lived as body all aspects latently immanent in spirit.

As the mystery teaching of Memphis speaks of a cosmic *Neter, celestial* or *ectypal* (the living sky being its intermediary), so the Heliopolitan mystery teaching speaks of the metaphysical—the supra*celestial* or archetypal—*Neter*.

The Heliopolitan Mystery

In the Pyramid Texts concerned with the King's life in the netherworld, he is sometimes compared to Atum and to the entire work of genesis; elsewhere, the King is treated as Atum's son. The King is considered as being the preconceived final issue, existing virtually from the beginning. Accordingly, in the Pyramid Texts of Pepi I, expressions such as the following are encountered: *"Pepi was born in the Nu...."* Or again, in the Pyramid Texts of Pepi II, this passage relating to the appearance of Atum (or *Tum*) in the context of the Heliopolitan mystery.

> He who was born in the Nu,
> before the sky came into being,
> before the earth came into being,
> before the two supports [Shu-Tefnut] came into being,
> before the Quarrel [between Horus and Seth] took place,
> before that Fear which arose on account of the Eye of Horus existed,
> King Pepi is the One of this great "company" who was born aforetime in Heliopolis.[4]

Details are given in the papyrus of Nesiamsu, dating from the early

[3]A. Moret, *Mystères égyptiens* (Paris, 1913), p. 127.
[4]*Pyr.* 1040-1041.

Ptolemaic epoch, the text of which, however, goes back at least to the Theban New Empire:

> When Atum emerged from Nun, the primordial waters, before sky and earth were born and before the creation of worm or reptile, he found no place on which to stand....[5]

Nun[6] is the abstract and primordial milieu *symbolized* by the waters, the cosmic ocean; it recalls the fact that all life, including the human fetal gestation, begins in water. Then again, the first effect of the creative act is liquid, an animated water; this means that it necessarily contains a styptic fire capable of coagulating it in the same manner as the female albuminoid liquid is coagulated by heat. Thus *Tum* (or Atum) is first an invisible coagulating fire and next becomes water coagulated into fire-containing earth. Therefore *Tum* is simultaneously the impulse to life in its material appearance, and the negation of the sole-singular Being of origin (Adamic *Tum,* the *tem* of negation).[7]

> Tum became: you became high like the primordial hillock, you rose up like the bird of the [*ben-ben*] stone in the mansion of the Phoenix at Heliopolis.
> You spat out Shu [*ishsh-n-k m Shu*],
> You expectorated Tefnut [*tfn-k m Tfnt*][8]

Thus did Atum arise, but there was no site where he could stand and he "arose" like a hillock. Can there be any doubt that in fact Atum himself became that hillock? The mysterious and divine action of the primordial scission of oneness occurs in *Nun.* This milieu is likened to the primordial ocean which will coagulate into the first earth, thus incarcerating Fire. The latter, in Memphis, is called Ptah when this metaphysical fire produces its effects in Nature, in the perceptible universe.

In an incomprehensible manner, the Heliopolitan mystery realizes a living *water* as well as an equally living black and red *earth.* The black earth is accursed, the Sethian jailer of divine light; the red earth is Horian. As Philolaos says: "...*what the artist can see with his own eyes*..." These are two substances from which the world and,

---

[5] A. Erman, op. cit., p. 116.

[6] See pp. 191-192 for the distinction between *Nu* and *Nun.*

[7] *Tum* designates Atum, *Neter* of creation; *tm* is the totality of created things and beings, and *tm* stands for negation par excellence, nonbeing, negation of all activity

[8] *Pyr.* 1652.

philosophically, the perfect King, come forth.[9] In Hermetic art as well, the two substances "of identical origin" generate the solid triangular *stone* which is the foundation of all truth.

Another Pyramid Text to be cited here evokes the creation of the "King" by his father, Atum, and his genesis in the lower world *before* the existence of all things.

> The mother of Pepi who is in the world of the transposed sky, formed him,
> when this Pepi was put into the world by his father Atum,
>> before the sky came into being,
>> before the earth came into being,
>> before humanity came into being,
>> before the *Neters* were born [put into the world],
>> before death existed.[10]

The creation myth is also evoked in another passage from the Pyramid Texts:

> Tum is he who came into being [from himself] through his autogenesis in Heliopolis.[11]
>> He took his phallus in his grasp that he might create joy in himself,
>> bringing about the twins, Shu and Tefnut,
>> they placed this King between them. . . .[12]

Without visible or tangible form, the seed is the model, the Idea of what it engenders: It is a transcendent puissance. Around a bodyless model, a formless substance coagulates into a living being, complete and complex, a being thought by the puissance.

From the esoteric action of the Idea to the form which is its finality, esoteric and transitory "finalities" result as so many apparent stages of form.

It is the marvel of the world, and all that is, all that exists bears seed; thus for mental creation, will and thought are seeds.

---

[9]It could be objected that the desert, a synonym for redness, pertains to Seth; in the Pyramid Texts, however, there is a call to Seth toward the *Mountains of Blackness*, and in that passage, there is a play on words between *dju*, mountains, and *dju*, evil. In the parallel text. Horus is called *toward the divine city (Pyr. 1268-1269).*

As to the divine, red Horian light, the following words are found in *Pyramid Texts* 252-253: "*May the red-eyed Horus protect you.*" This is said after the King has been called the *black sr*, son of the *black srt*, following two horns and two bulls. Thus the King is here assimilated with the black ram, then with the bull, and he is protected by Horus of the red eyes (appearances).

[10]*Pyr.* 1466.

[11]*Pyr.* 1248. Literally, the hieroglyphic group translates as "masturbation," *iw-saw*, meaning "to make come the seed from his loins."

[12]Ibid.

One thought in the transcendent puissance compels *one* substance of the passive universal substance to become such and such a product, such and such an heir, a world succeeding to a world; *one single Puissance in one single Substance* throughout all transitory finalities toward a foreseen finality: Man. . . .

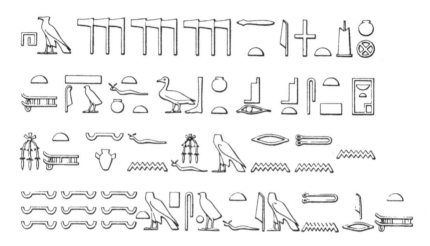

Fig. 38. *Hieroglyphic Text of the Great Ennead.*

There is a mystery which renders visible the invisible and which makes ponderable the imponderable; the Word of wisdom is the reality of that mysterious evidence. What is invariable in the law of genesis forms the basis of traditional philosophy. To quest without these guides leads to an impasse or to nothingness.

The appearance of *Tum* implies the beginning of all the elements which make visible the invisible. Philosophically speaking, they are called constitutional elements of matter, and are defined by four essential qualities: hot and cold, humid and dry, in other words, essentially Fire and Water, as one cannot exist without the other.

O great Ennead [*psdj.t*] of *Neters* which is in Heliopolis: Tum, Shu, Tefnut, Geb, Nut, Osiris, Isis, Seth, and Nephthys, which Tum put into the world through projection [*pdj*] of his heart, as his own birth, in your name of "Nine Bows" [*psdj pdj.t*], none of you is separate from Tum. . . . [13]

[13] *Pyr.* 1655.

Tum, by the power or by the fire of his heart, projects his own self into *Nun* for his own nativity into the world. By this same projection, he makes the great Ennead appear in *Nu.* "Projecting," here written with the hieroglyph of the bow, in this text signifies "to make appear in the distance" (or "to appear above"), in the milieu of the primordial water *Nu.* This latter concept is to be distinguished from the primordial ocean, *Nun.*[14]

The bow symbolizes the repulsing force and signifies the act of projecting out of oneself; it is to be understood in the same sense as the puissance in *Tum,* who projects himself as a hillock emerging from *Nun.*

The *Neters* of the Ennead *(psdj.t)* present the *fait accompli,* projected light *(psdj),* while the act of projecting *(pdj)* is represented by the bow.

What in Heliopolis (*On* of the north) is situated philosophically at the absolute origin of things is also the primitive function presiding at every manifestation of life, be it mineral, vegetal, or animal. In other words, the mystery is limited neither spatially to Heliopolis nor temporally to the life work.

The Memphite Mystery

What Heliopolis affirms, Memphis explains in the temple of Ptah, who materializes the metaphysical principles. Here the *Neters* have their perceptible image: no longer is Atum the first hillock issued from *Nun,* but he takes his *great name,* meaning his functional title of *Tatenen,* which signifies "earth fettering the two energies":

> *This is the Ptah who is called by the great name.... He who brought himself into being, says Atum. He who gave birth to the company of the nine Neters....*
> *He is the unifier of this earth, named with the great name Tatenen. He who is at the south of his wall, the Lord of eternity....*
> The bulrush and papyrus were placed at the double door to the temple of Ptah: this signifies the reconciled and unified Horus and Seth.[15]

This Ancient Empire text, taken up again by Shabaka in the Twenty-fifth Dynasty, next enumerates the eight names of the eight *Neters* who have their form in Ptah, the primordial, active, corporified Fire. It is the heart of Ptah-Tatenen which makes all that exists and, like Adam in Genesis, his tongue names each thing:

> It arises as heart, it arises as tongue, in the form of Atum....
> The heart and the tongue have power over all the limbs; it is taught that he

---

[14]*Nu,* written with the symbol of a vase, and *Nun* with the three lines of water, are implied in this text.
[15]Maj. Sandman Holmberg, *The God Ptah* (Lund, 1946).

[Ptah] is found [as heart] within each body and [as tongue] in the mouth of each Neter, of all men. . . of whatever lives. And that it is he who thinks [as heart] and who commands [as tongue] anything that he desires. . . .

Yet, the nine *Neters* are the teeth and lips of [Ptah's] mouth which utters the names of all things. . . .

What the eyes see, what the ears hear, what the nose breathes, all that is communicated to the heart. It is this [heart] which makes all knowledge manifest, and it is the tongue which repeats what has been thought by the heart. Thus were born all the *Neters* and the Ennead came into being. Every divine utterance manifested itself through the thought of the heart and commandment of the tongue.[16]

This text of Shabaka epitomizes the entire Memphite teaching; it concerns the work of Ptah, whose reality is the active primordial fire incarcerated within *Tum.* The latter is the effect of the creative act described in the Heliopolitan mystery texts.

Ptah himself is the Ennead. *The tongue of Ptah* has named everything through his utterance, expressing what the heart (Atum's fixed center) has manifested:

Thus Ptah was satisfied after having made all things and all the words of the *Neters.* In truth he caused the *Neters* to be born, created the cities, established the nomes and installed the *Neters* in their places of adoration. He determined their offerings and established their sanctuaries; he made likenesses of their bodies according to their desire. Thus the *Neters* entered into their bodies of every variety of wood, every type of mineral, every type of clay, and all kinds of other things which grow thereupon, in which they have taken shape.[17]

As inseminator of all that will vegetate, Ptah is *ithyphallic Min.* There remains the need for a womblike milieu to receive the seed after the living—or animated—water of Isis has delivered it from the prison (coagulation) where Seth keeps it jealously bound to earth.

In this phase of dissolution and vegetation, *Nun,* by the fact of creating Tefnut, makes a living water which the Hebrew Kabbalah calls *Eshmajin,* whence the Arab *Ashmounein,* which designates the ancient city of Hermopolis. The theme taught there was consecrated to the aquatic and lunar aspect epitomized by Thoth-Djhuti.

At Memphis, the principles *Nun, Atum,* and *Shu-Tefnut* become the triad *Ptah, Sekhmet-Hathor,* and *Nefertum.* Hathor is the aspect of the female matrix in Sekhmet, the animated water of Khmunu (Hermopolis); Nefertum is the lotus, the seed-bearing vegetal which brings forth Fire from Water. This mysterious Hermetic water is the

[16]Tr. after Holmberg and Alexandre Piankoff.

[17]Holmberg, op. cit., p. 22. This entire passage describes terrestrial Paradise.

bond between the beginning and the ending of the cosmic opus. Thus Khmunu forms the bond between Memphis and Heliopolis and later with the completion of the work in Thebes. The light comes forth from Khmunu first as sun, as physical light. As a result of genesis and subtilization, this light becomes Horus, the Eye, held back in Ptah by the terrestrial and ardent Seth. It is an eye because it is visible Fire, but not yet tangible; before appearing, it demands first a death of the physical sun.

Hermopolis

Hermopolis, accordingly, takes up again the themes of Heliopolis and Memphis, but this time in their "aquatic" or—according to Hermetic symbolism—mercurial aspect.

Fig. 39. *The King Kneeling before Ptah and Sekhmet.*
Ptah holds the three principles, *djed, ankh,* and *uas.* The King offers him the royal scepters *heq* and *nekhakha,* with the *uas* and the bracelets, that is, the ligatures, that which is made possible by *Sekhmet* who holds the *wadj,* female sublimation. Bas-relief, Abydos, Nineteenth Dynasty.

The Water which appeared with creation, carrying the dark hillock Tum, becomes the object of the Hermopolitan teaching. The sacred name of Hermopolis, fifteenth nome of Upper Egypt, was Khemenu, the city of the Eight, meaning the eight Primordials; its civil name was *Un,* meaning "existence."

What is involved here is the generation of a primordial water that is to become a living water. Out of the living water comes the sun: The theme in its entirety always reappears in each of its parts.

The eight principles then change names as they are born from the mud formed by Water and Earth. They become serpents and frogs under the names of *Night, Obscurity, Secret,* and *Eternity,* four males and four females, all living together in the mud. The crawling serpent and the frog, Batrachia emerging from the waters to become terrestrial, together formed the egg from which a *goose* was born. This cackling goose took wing and flew off, appearing as *Sun.*[18]

From Theban temples of a later period, it is known that before the eight Primordials, there existed a snake, *Kem-atef, "the one who has fulfilled his time."* As the name indicates, this *Neter,* having fulfilled his time, ceased to exist. His son, the snake *Ir-ta,* "creator of earth," brought forth the eight Primordials.

Kem-atef of Hermopolis becomes Amon of Karnak, whose name means "the hidden," and Ir-ta becomes assimilated into the ithyphallic Amon of Luxor.[19]

As for Thoth himself, this is how he is designated at Dendera:

> Thoth, twice great, the most ancient of all, master of the city of Hermopolis the great, the great *Neter* of Tentyris, the sovereign God creator of Good, heart of Ra, tongue of Atum, throat of the god whose name is hidden [Amon], Lord of Time, king of the years, scribe annals of the Ennead.
>
> Revelation of the god of light, Ra, he who existed since the beginning, Thoth, he who rests on truth. What issues from his heart immediately comes into existence; his utterances subsist for eternity.[20]

The only clarification of what is meant by the theme of the city of Khemenu, i.e., the work of Tehuti (Thoth), comes from the relationship which the Hermopolitan Thoth entertains with the city of Thebes.

---

[18]The goose is a terrestrial volatile which is partial to muddy ground. Basilius Valentinus, among others, takes up again this symbol of the goose, leaving the ducks to those who are content to remain in the waters, but recommending geese to the others, roasted geese in particular, an image constantly encountered in ancient Egypt among the offerings to the *Neters.*

[19]See A. Erman, op. cit., p. 121.

[20]R. P. Restugière, op. cit., p. 69.

The Theban Mystery

Intriguing, in Thebes, is the development of the Ogdoad which multiplies to the extent of becoming fifteen. The fact must not be overlooked that the number fifteen is no longer in relation with the primordial principles but with the monthly and lunar character of Tehuti (Saturn as Lead).

Thebes represents the ultimate phase of the first royal becoming. Whereas the temple of Luxor is the fulfillment, the human epitome of the cosmic opus, the temple of conception and birth of Royal Man, at Thebes the cosmic triad dominates. Under the names of Amon, Mut, and their son, Khonsu, its history constitutes the principle subject of the temple of Karnak.

At Thebes, we are thus concerned with a stage where the milieu Nut-Sekhmet, by means of Tehuti (Thoth), becomes the principle Mut. A living, maternal milieu, rich in active Fire lent by Ptah, Mut receives the Amonian seed by means of which Atum-Nefertum, at this phase, will become Khonsu. This Khonsu is somehow a new, spiritualized Atum, and this one will make Horus reappear in all his glory, this Horus-Lucifer whom Seth held bound in Ptah, for Seth is the one who shackles and incarcerates.

The mysterious Khonsu plays a preponderant role in Thebes; his symbols comprise all the scepters tied together, with the exception of the *wadj*, the sign of opening, an expansion that only Thoth of Khemenu can bring about. As crown, Khonsu wears a disk on a crescent, the representation of both New Moon and of eclipse, Moon and Sun united. Khonsu is functionally not to be dissociated from Osiris when the latter principle is in its renascent phase; Apet, the female hippopotamus, symbolizes the matrix that carries what is reborn.

Nefertum prefigures the realization which Khonsu definitively allows. That is the difference between them. Thoth of Khemenu, animated by Isis, creates Mut. Once animated by the soul of Horus which is offered by Khonsu, Mut-Isis is called Hathor, the lunisolar aspect of Sekhmet. Sekhmet "precipitates" what Hathor sublimates and carries off, namely, the soul of Horus which can then incorporate, once again reuniting Seth and Horus, this time in beauty. This was announced by the two bulrushes in front of the temple of Ptah in Memphis.

To set free the divine Word, to deliver the living Fire from its terrestrial prison where it is incarnated and corporified, such is the aim proposed by all spiritual revelations; myth illustrates the initiation to this end. This aim is offered to mankind in general, yet the means to its attainment is knowledge of the world of causes, the key to all power for the human being. Understandably, then, the absolute conditions for unlocking this door lie in purity, selflessness, and the mastery of instincts. This explains the enigmatic character of these teachings. Our own day already manifests the disaster of ignoring such moral preparation. And yet only "intellectual" secrets are involved today, not the secret of divine spirituality.

The very important story of the liberation of the Eye of Horus and of Horus, son of Isis and Osiris, is repeated in different ways. Likewise, the texts of the Prophets, assembled in the Old Testament, treat the same theme in a variety of forms.

The three Pharaonic Mysteries give the general directives. Though only the concluding moments of each phase are revealed in the legends, the entire genetic sequence and its transformations form the subject of the Mysteries of initiation in the temples. Prepared and privileged men alone were allowed in the presence of these Mysteries, among them certain Roman emperors during the closing stages of the Pharaonic temple: Trajan at Medamud and at Philae, and Domitian at Karnak.

The five principles or *Neters* which form the five intercalary days of the year—Osiris, Horus, Seth, Isis, and Nephthys—represent the functions of the yearly cycle. Among the five "epagomenal" *Neters*, Osiris, Isis, Seth, and Nephthys represent immanent *functions* characteristic of the four elements. Horus finally joins this quaternary as quintessence, an active and immaterial Fire. Later, become perceptible, he is delivered from the evil represented by Seth, the earthy jailor from the beginning of time.

It is in this manner that these stories are to be understood; they do, after all, conform to all revelatory texts. "Evil" will stand for all that reduces the spiritual to the corporeal, and this corporeal must die to allow the return to its source of the spiritual. But the *fall* of the divine into perishable Matter has tarnished it, and these blemishes must be eliminated for the return to be complete: This requires the Passion. Indeed, the divine Word of the beginning is All; what we call "spiritual" as well as *what caused it to fall into the mortal.* This is the cause of the work and struggle indispensable to the attainment of final deliverance.

This is the Pharaonic *Opus Magnum.* It ends in the Christic revelation which is founded on the human incarnation of the divine, revealing the ultimate phase. In the Pharaonic Mysteries, this phase was called *"the reconciliation of Seth and Horus," but it was not actually realized in Egypt's own historic gestation.* This explains why the Pharaonic sages considered the precessional transition from Aries to Pisces a natural genesis—foreseen by the temple—toward Christianity.

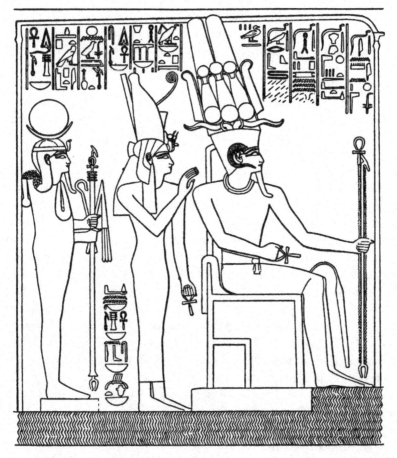

Fig. 40. *The Theban Triad.*
Amon, seated on his throne, which is placed in water, wears the
triple crown of Atef poised above the horns of Khnum. The ram's
horns of Amon curve around his ears. Mut wears the white crown
in front of the red crown on her headdress of vulture. Khonsu
wears the braid of the heir apparent and the lunar crescent. In his
hands he holds the three principles, the *ankh* and *uas* emerging
from the *djed,* and the *heq* and *nekhakha* scepters. Karnak,
Nineteenth Dynasty.

The first Christians in Egypt had no hesitations about adopting
Pharaonic symbolism to the new revelation: the crossing through the
cross, for instance, and the basic concepts of the suprahuman history of
royal becoming such as it is represented in the temple of Luxor: the
annunciation of spiritual conception, the divine birth, humanization,

baptism and the gift of name, and appearance in public at the age of twelve. . . .

Allegories must always be sought in the teaching evoked by their imagery. So for the legend of Ra, or Isis' struggle to save her son Horus from the domination of the scorpion, symbol of Seth (as related in the Chester Beatty papyrus), and many other such "allegorical tales."

It is never by arbitrary whim that one same *Neter* is given different names. Sekhmet, for instance, the child-devouring lioness, becomes Hathor, house of Horus: Seth becomes scorpion of the contractile poison, and so forth. These are so many luminaries proffered *to whoever wants to see them.*

Through its figurations, the teachings of Pharaonic Egypt become a marvelous history which speaks of what has always been, what always shall be the essential knowledge concerning origin, aim, and finality of life.

Imhotep and Amenhotep

According to tradition, all the puissance and possibilities of Ptah were incarnated in the sage Imhotep, called son of Ptah (son of the celestial fire), as later, in Thebes, all the wisdom of the epoch of Amon became incarnated in Amenhotep, son of Hapu (son of the Nile, the celestial water).

Imhotep is above all a medicine man in the broadest sense of the term, but he is architect as well, Master of Works, quite in the nature of Ptah.

Amenhotep, son of Hapu, is primarily an architect, a builder, and his supreme *oeuvre* is the realization of Man, which is indeed the Theban *oeuvre:* giving life to Royal Man.

Philosophy of Myth

Pharaonic myth and its teaching, as well as the nature and aim of the temple inscriptions, are here considered in the light of a sacerdotal science. It becomes imperative, therefore, to clarify the broad outlines of such a science on the basis of what is known through Hermetic tradition.

As is the case in India, for example, architecture, writing, statuary, and bas-reliefs become symbols of a genesis where historical facts are used as mere pretexts. This is confirmed by the obvious tendency of these accounts to turn into fable what is non-sense in terms of time and space (geographical sites, etc.).

The facts that serve as pretexts are important because they stress a play of circumstances beyond human volition. The will, to the contrary, is evoked and facilitated by the cosmic ambiance that makes the *fact* possible, the action "willed" by man. Hence there is a relation between these facts and the esoteric meaning the myth aims to reveal. But when wisdom speaks, the historicity of the fact itself loses all importance.

Obviously, there is a history of the Pharaonic Empire but it is not transcribed as such in the temples, and the figurations of the kings are certainly not "portraits," even if there might have been some resemblance in the features.

The mystic names of the kings adapting the basis of the cult to cosmic time, the styles, the typical character of the temples, all conform too closely to the traditional knowledge-teachings for any doubt to remain regarding the intention. It is a deliberate transcription of thinking humanity's highest goal and the most exalted promise made to mortal beings: *to bear proof of divine reality and to demonstrate experimentally the reality of the supranatural.*

What value would there be in these descriptions of supranatural life and of the avatars of the being after the body's death, were there no tangible proof? What explanation would there be for the similarities between what is recounted, for example, in the Tibetan *Bardo Thödol,* in the Vedas and Upanishads of India, and in the collection of texts designated as the Pharaonic *Book of the Dead?*

These royal tombs, with their paintings depicting life beyond Nature, can they really be dismissed as fantasy and sham?

The perfection and richness of the objects surrounding the royal mummies indisputably indicate a high civilization, and each of these objects obviously has a symbolic meaning connected to the teaching of a superior way of knowing that escapes our rationalism.

Can it really be said that before the day of our pretentious science, humanity was composed solely of imbeciles and of the superstitious?

At all times, from the remotest known antiquity, religious traditions, including the rites of the Catholic mass, have proclaimed the selfsame truth. This truth is translated through knowledge of the divine boon granted to humanity: recognition of its origin and its aim, and the possibility of conscious return to its source.

Sacred science provides proof; adepts, the apostles of wisdom, know and affirm. We must grant them our faith, for unless we attain to the same illumination, our endeavors will never transcend the natural, hence never surpass the mortal.

On Becoming

Here are the broad outlines of the teaching:

In order for undefined Being to become a definite being, a seed is necessary.

The seed, or impulse determining the undetermined, can effectuate either a universal determination or a particular determination.

The ordinary natural effect is a determination in particular by the seed.

From the first impulse, there starts a genesis toward the realization of the aim, or fruit, and this genesis obeys immutable phases: The same process will rule in everything that is similarly determined.

Every time any seed whatsoever gives the impulse to a determination of absolute Being, whatever is thus called into existence is indestructible: This being—no matter what form it may take, and notwithstanding the decompositions or deaths the form undergoes— this being will be indestructible and can only return to original Being through gestation. The gestation consists of acquiring, through the coagulating seed-power, "a nature alike to the nature of Being" which was coagulated into transient form.

For example, if a moving ball (the activity of undetermined Being) encounters another ball in repose (the seed-obstacle), an exchange of energy will occur. But if, as a result of the many shocks received (shocks of deaths and rebirths), the inert ball is put into motion and this motion becomes alike to the motion of the active ball, then there is an equality; there is no further exchange of energy, there is identity: existence ceases as phenomenon.

This image conveys: first the effect of the determining seed (through its resistance to the infinite activity of undetermined Being); then existence through the exchange of energy; and then deaths and rebirths, that is, real becoming, in order to end with liberation from particular existence.

Existence in particular and the phases of the genesis of the particular form serve as general symbol to describe a becoming which involves three essential aspects:

First of all, the seed produces a scission of the undefined into definition. This is what is called corruption (corrupt: Latin *com*, together, + *rumpere*, to break into pieces), the "philosophical putrefaction." In this phase, the seed loses its initial aspect. It now fixes undefined Being and begins its corporification. The seed rots in the earth, the spermatozoon apparently dies; this is metaphorically called the *black phase*. This original scission produces at one and the same time the root, black in nature (chorion, placenta) and the germ (the embryo in the amnion), *white* in nature.

The second aspect is *white*. This is the vegetative phase giving form and body to the undefined. Nourishment and respiration give life to the being now determined; the black impurity has been cast away "below."

The third aspect is *red*. It is animation, the completion of the fruit, the concretizing of the original and abstract impulse into a particular form which can give forth a new seed and then die again.

These are the three great *phases* of genesis which are constantly evoked in ancient Egypt and which can be found at the basis of all its symbolism. For example, the sacred scarab is the hieroglyph designating all transformation or evolution; the life of this insect presents the following characteristics:

—The scarab lays its egg in a pellet of dung which it buries underground in absolute darkness: *the black phase* which will last for about one month until the egg reaches maturity.

—From this egg, a white larva is born, which during the second month, *the white phase,* feeds on the substance of the egg and digests.

—Next there comes the nymphal phase during which the immobile mummy works its transformation: From this mummy emerges the new scarab, "the head and thorax of *dark red,* the abdomen of opaque white, and the wing-sheaths of translucent white. . . ."[21] The scarab itself, the final fruit, will again be *black.*

Can the three phases and even the three colors be better symbolized?

The Symbols of the Phases

Black, white, and *red* bring to mind the three colors constantly evoked in the Pharaonic symbolique.

Black is one of the names of Egypt because of its black soil (black is called *km* and the Black *kmt* or *Kemit*).

White (hdj) is the homonym for light and also designates the *white mace* that strikes the impure in order to evoke the pure; it also designates

---

[21] J.-H. Fabre, *Souvenirs entomologiques* (1879), V, pp. 84-85.

the *white crown* of the South. In the temple of Luxor, south corresponds to east through the arrangement of the crowns, so that south = east, the sunrise = the left = white, and consequently corresponds to our spring.

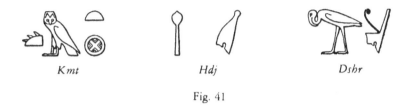

Kmt   Hdj   Dshr

Fig. 41

Red (dshr) qualifies the desert (dryness), and the Sethian animals of the blazing land. It is also the crown of the north, Horus, who at Luxor takes his place in the west so that north = west, sunset = the right = red, and corresponds to our autumn.

South   East   North   West

Fig. 42

This equating of north, west, and red, and of south, east, and white, is already specified in one of the Pyramid Texts, and many instances of it are found in the temples of Karnak, among others.

In the *ritual of the divine daily cult,* one again encounters the four white vases and the four red vases used in purifications.

The three aspects of genesis can also be approached from the three seasons of the Pharaonic year:

The *pert* season, winter (mid-November to mid-March): *Pert* means "seed," "to emerge"; the meaning of this denomination is *the emergence of the black earth* when the flood-waters recede, an annual repetition of the Creation myth: "when from the primordial waters the first earth emerges." This earth is *kmt, the Black.*

The *shmw* season, spring-summer (mid-March to mid-July): *shmw* is written with the basin and three lines of water, which intrigues philologists, for it would sooner seem to be the symbol of inundation. Nevertheless, one can attribute to it the *white,* luminous *hedj* character of spring and of summer's beginning (Cancer-Moon).

The *akh.t* season, the inundation (mid-July to mid-November), begins with the heliacal rising of Sirius around July 19 of the Julian calendar (actually the 4th of August), the sun entering into the constellation Leo.

Pert

Shmw

Akh.t

Fig. 43

Akh.t has numerous homonyms including horizon, fire, glory, splendor, the blaze of solar rays. But in order to designate the flood season, which is a culmination and opens the time of renewal, this word is written with a papyrus clump: the first appearance of life. This is certainly an allusion to the heliacal rising of Sirius, Sothis, the great provider.[22]

Taking the gestation of the human fetus as an example, we can conclude that there are "times" for the phases of genesis: three black months, four white months (making seven) ending in a first viable being, and then two months more (making nine) for completing the perfect gestation of the prefigured fruit.

The colors are to be considered as qualitative aspects and the months as temporal succession (the scarab reunites the two).

The Colors and Centers of the Myth

The tangible phenomenon of the works of Nature serves as symbol for the principles of a supranatural opus This work bestows upon absolute undetermined Being an existence which is no longer particular, but which has become universal, adaptable to every form: the King.

This is the great mystery, a secret never unveiled save through the enigmas of myth, first of all through the three centers: Heliopolis, Memphis, and Thebes.

The Heliopolitan Mystery speaks of *Tum*'s self-creation emerging from the waters of *Nun* (undetermined Being): the *black* aspect. It

---

[22]See Chapter 7, "Cosmic Ambiance."

corresponds, in the chronology of the Pharaonic Empire, to the three "prehistoric" months consecrated to the Twins, Shu and Tefnut.

The Memphite Mystery is revealed in the city of the White Wall (Memphis), where Fire fallen into Earth (Ptah, who unites Seth and Horus) calls forth vegetation which gives form to all things and summons the *white* body, realized at Hermopolis.

The *red* Horian animation is presented at Thebes. And the symbol of Thebes is the *uas* (called "key of the Nile"), the principle that makes for reuniting the Horian flux issued from the Ptah of origin (Horus the Elder) with the completed work of gestation (Horus, son of Isis).

The analysis of these aspects and phases is given at Abydos for the white, at Dendera and at Edfu for the red, but all the functions are explained in that basilica known as Karnak, while the cosmic meaning is specified in the *Temple of Man*, the temple of Luxor.

Indeed, all the moments of this genesis are consecrated by different temples. It is therefore impossible to untangle this maze without knowing its aim and general guiding principles. These sanctuaries are always located on sites corresponding geologically and biologically to the theme represented by their architecture and inscriptions. This corresponds to the fact that natural plant and animal life is always adapted to the vital influence and the flux of specific regions. The work of supranatural genesis must obey cosmic imperatives that are specified, meaning particularly defined in natural life.

This succinct and general image of the supranatural opus includes a multitude of details for each aspect and for each part of each phase. Thus, for example, the black aspect specifies the general principles of what is or becomes fixed; the foundation, the seat.

The *active, living principle* of the first fixation which is *Tum*, the black, is symbolized by the hieroglyph *men*, foundation, *men.t* the thigh, *Mentu* the sacred bull. But the *principle of fixity* is found in all of nature through the four elements, and can equally well be white, red, or "mottled" (white speckled with red). Inasmuch as function, the *principle of fixity* is therefore not to be confused with a state or an aspect; this is why *Apis*, the sacred bull of Memphis, is black; but the four *Mentus* (of Karnak, Medamud, Erman, and Tod, surrounding Thebes), which symbolize the four *qualities* of fixity (earth, water, air, and fire), are respectively *black, white, red,* and *mottled.*

Another example of the four aspects is given by the offering of the four calves (lunar, nourishing milk): *black, white, red,* and *mottled;* or again by the four white and the four red vases; and for the mottled, the white crown in the red crown or in front of the red crown.

Here the vision of Zechariah 6:1-5 comes to mind:

And I turned, and lifted up mine eyes, and looked, and, behold, there came four chariots out from between two mountains.... In the first chariot were red horses; and in the second chariot black horses; and in the third chariot white horses; and in the fourth chariot grizzled and bay horses. Then I answered and said unto the angel that talked with me, What are these, my lord? And the angel answered and said unto me, These are the four spirits of the heavens, which go forth from standing before the Lord of all the earth.

But we also find these principles as *Neters* or as cosmic functional principles. In that case, they are represented by ithyphallic *Amon,* bound as a mummy, standing and provoking emission of the white seed. The latter is represented by the *nekhakha* scepter placed above his raised right hand.

One must learn to reduce the multiple aspects of the same idea into a simple synthesis principle; otherwise the multiplicity of symbols will only confuse all understanding. This multiplication of the symbols of one singular principle also has its reasons: As the effect is general, analysis shows its aspects in the multiple applications and in the various moments of its genesis or manifestation.

Myth is the exhaustive study of the multiple effects of simple causes.

Correspondence of Numbers

A general correspondence is given by numbers and can serve as guide:

Oneness is always origin, either metaphysical or as final accomplishment.

The number *two* always indicates complementaries, oppositions, sexuality.

The number *three* always speaks of the original ternary, be it the Trinity of the divine Word or the basic ternary in the ultimate reduction of all understanding.

The number *four* always speaks of the four elements, the quadruplet of all physico-corporeal foundation.

The number *five* pertains to the quintessence, the surevolution going beyond the four elements.

The number *six* is that of equilibrium, the complementation of opposites and their annihilation, the fruit of their work.

The number *seven* is that of terrestrial Nature, manifestation of the *nine* archangelic puissances.

The number *eight* is the number of death for resurrection.

The number *ten* is the synthesis, the origin of phenomenal Nature and its aim.

The number *twelve* echoes the Zodiac and relates to it.

When myth makes use of number in its images, therefore, the meaning must be linked to the symbolic value of numbers.

9

The Two Paths Of Liberation

The scientific orientation of present-day thinking undermines churches and impairs faith, all to the benefit of a rational science. Human problems are neglected and give way to the Moloch-Machine which already compels individuals to submit their lives to its demands. The Machine imposes the limits of its possibilities, after having falsely promised to place itself at the service of man. But a time will come when human problems will again be raised, as they cannot forever be avoided. These fluctuations in humanity's psychological history are cyclical, but the present crisis is particularly severe because the cult of intellectuality is in the process of reversing all traditions, obscuring and negating all the symbols of a metaphysics transmitted through theologies and mores.[1]

Dialectics and reasoning are replacing the vital quest for the *Neters,* the principles of Nature, to which the sages of all times have given meaningful names. The principle of "conservation of energy" in thermodynamics, for example, is rationally more satisfying than the principle of the universe's cycle of "becoming and return." The first leads to mechanics, the second poses the problem of abstract cause. Nevertheless the fact remains that seasons and astronomical cycles influence the earth's vital phenomena, but it is impossible to understand what mechanism is involved; rationalism, on the other hand, would like to detect a mechanical reason in everything. Yet when the particular ceases to identify with the whole, humanity gives up hope of finding answers. When the time comes that reason despairs, it will no longer be possible to identify with the "All," animator of transitory

[1] Europe, Asia, and Africa, the only places still struggling to maintain some traditions, are examples of this dissolution.

form: the elements which allow this identification to occur will have been forgotten.

The "elevated spheres of abstract mathematical thought" paradoxically end up in technique, and technique creates fragmentation through specialization, a dispersion into the inextricable jungle of possibilities, without any guiding synthesis. The danger of such a mental orientation does not appear to those who tread these multiple scattered paths, because they necessarily believe they are on the right track: each builder of the Tower of Babel believed himself capable of ending up at the summit which plunged into the heavens, but the elements of his masonry never dovetailed that of the other builders.

And yet the human aspect of our science is seductive. A kind of international understanding is created among scientists, a scientific liberalism among researchers. The rigor of study creates what is nowadays the most honest, the most righteous of human categories, compared, for example, with that of politicians. We are not speaking here of the struggle of jealousies, the competition arising in applied science with the multiplication of its inventions. But left to our mentality, isn't pure science itself destined eventually to lapse into "technique"?

The impure can become pure through the process of elimination, but error can never be transformed into truth. A radical change is absolutely essential; through the natural law of reaction, our thought orientation will itself create the instrument of its reversal. After the disappearance of the builders of Babel, the great questions will once again be raised: What is man? Where does he come from? Where is he going? What is it that animates him? Has he a soul? What becomes of it after the body's death? Is there such a thing as "Good and Evil" which affects eventual survival? And what is the nature of this survival?

But is any mortal capable of answering these questions other than by philosophical speculation or with a simple affirmation granted as an article of faith? The Vedic texts, the Buddhist doctrine, the enigmatic Jewish Bible, Christianity based on the Gospels—are they anything other than affirmations without proof, as far as today's rationalistic mentality is concerned?

The formulation of these questions lacks precision, inspired as they are by an unconscious opposition: rational physical man as opposed to some abstract state. One believes in the tangible body and doubts the possibility of a different state. One says that man has a soul, *which is false:* It is the soul that has man. From the most primitive cell to man, Being animates the form. The latter is but the totality of "passible" and variable elements, each one of which is an open door for consciousness: the manifestation of the qualities of Being.[2]

There is a truth which is everywhere confirmed: When the dualization of sole-singular Being has given *existence to being,* this existence can no longer retrogress; it must undergo the entire genesis. This genesis may be directed toward a preconceived aim (Jesus Christ, the finite anthropocosmos), or it may be indirect, but it may also be arrested or "blocked," kept in abeyance for a new cosmic cycle.[3]

The present human being is the vital end-term of a long lineage beginning with the first living cell, seed-synthesis of prefigured man. Therefore, bodily man is transitory, a form animated by Being which has its fixation in the corporeal essence, an indestructible salt. These facts can only be affirmed in the light of a revealed science which can actually demonstrate them. Without this science, there remains but hypothesis or opinion. It was proclaimed as such by the Greek atomists who, unlike Pythagoras, were ignorant of the teachings of the temple.

By virtue of its origin, Being, passing into bodily form has three aspects:

The first is existence, namely, its indestructible corporeal point which, as an *end of genesis,* demands to be brought to its resurrection within the oneness of its origin: This is precisely what the Pharaonic myth expresses by qualifying Osiris, principle of the cycle of deaths and rebirths, as *Osiris-Un-nefer:* accomplished existence.

A further aspect is its *animating effect,* which is the soul of all forms and of their own experiences, experiences that make for the successive unveiling of consciousness.

The third aspect is Being's *essence of origin,* the spirit of oneness which solicits return into this unity and so to speak forces or compels this genesis.

It is this existence aspect of Being that imposes a surviving, a continuity in a new form after destruction of the present form. The *end of genesis,* resurrection in oneness, can come about only through the acquisition in the body of all the life experiences. This can happen *all at once in the course of the direct path,* be it Horian or Christic, or else *it demands numerous incarnations* on the Osirian or indirect path.

Such is the reason for the two paths.

It is this complexity of all the phases and avatars of Being which the myth describes. Here the symbolique is indispensable because of the (physical, mental, and spiritual) universality of the various aspects of

---

[2]"Passible" = susceptible to suffering.

[3]These are the "Rejects of the Light" during Ra's passage through the caverns of the *Dwat.*

genesis as well as for evoking the *intuition* capable of leading to a sacred science no logic can reveal.

Indeed, a grace of inspiration is involved in this moment: The actual state of Being finds itself in perfect accord and in resonance exactly concordant with an instant of cosmic harmony. What is meant by "God-given grace" should be understood along these lines and not as a "dear god" who busies himself with us personally. The harmony equilibrating the universe is always ready to respond to the harmonic call of Being incarnate, whatever its actual form, from mineral to man. His pyschological consciousness awakened by the faculty of negation, man has the power of contributing to the realization of this propitious moment. The possibility arises here of *a summons to the Neter,* Egypt's constant prayer, whose meaning we have attempted to demonstrate elsewhere.

It can be objected that these are the themes of common religious teaching, although differently expressed. Certainly! But it is worthwhile here to clarify the reasons for such statements and to show the supporting points of these assertions.

Just as there is a neutron at the heart of the energetic atoms which preoccupy today's science, so in every form of Nature there is a *salt* (read: *neutron*) nothing can destroy and which fixes the character of each *incarnation,* that is, of each changing form. The sequence which makes us speak of evolution exists owing to this "fixed point." It is a succession of living forms extending from amoeba to man without any visible transition between genus and species. This evolutive "granulation" of Being is the tangible appearance of a continuous *genesis of energy.* It takes its image from an assertion made by Hermetic texts according to which metals, each one a typical individual, are evolutionary phases *arrested* in a genesis toward silver or gold; the initial metallic state, had it remained in its matrix, could have become silver or gold.

A famous text[4] says that the direct path has two roads and that the indirect path has five. In certain tombs of the Eleventh Dynasty, the deceased is depicted as entering the domain of *Sokaris* where he is offered two paths, both capable of conducting him into the *Abode of the Blessed (akhu):* one by the (dry) path of earth, the other by the (humid) path of water; but there is no passing from one to the other because a fiery sea stretches between them. The earth road leads to the land of *Ro-Setau* and it is guarded by a flaming gate; the watery road leads to the lake of *Ro-Setau* and is guarded by a ram-headed crocodile armed with a knife.[5]

[4] *Geheime Figuren der Rosenkreutzer,* aus dem 16 und 17 Jahrhundert (Altona, 1785).

[5] Ro-Setau is the name of the metropolis of Gizeh. The knife signifies separation.

"Many are the ways for realizing one sole-singular thing."
Certainly man's aim is uniquely one: to go beyond mortal man in order to
enter into cosmic man, Man of the four cardinal directions, so as to
resuscitate *what is untouchable for women.*[6]

The path of reincarnations is the Osirian or karmic path, in the
sense that every cause provokes its consequence or effect. For the human
being, the reasons for the necessity of reincarnations are voluntary acts
contrary to his purification or liberation; therefore he must exhaust the
consequences of those acts for which he was responsible.

According to the texts, the deceased must appear before the
tribunal of Osiris and his forty-two assessors. For example, King *Meri-
ka-Rê (Beloved-of-the-Ka-of-Ra)* teaches his son the importance of
actions in this life because one day he will be judged and, says he, in
speaking of his judges:

> "You know that they are not merciful the day when they judge the miserable
> one. . . . Do not count on the passage of the years; they consider a lifetime as but
> an hour. After death, man remains in existence and his acts accumulate beside
> him." Life in the other world is eternal, "but he who arrives without sin before the
> Judge of the Dead, he will be there as a *Neter* and he will walk freely as do the
> masters of eternity."

Here is the prayer uttered by all those who consider themselves to
be pure on the day of the great judgment:

> Homage to you, O *Neters!* I know you and I know your names. Cast me not
> down before your sword of justice. Bring not my wickedness into the presence of
> the god whom you follow: I pray you, declare me right and true before the great
> God of All. For I have done that which is just in Egypt; I have not outraged the
> *Neters* and the reigning king had nothing for which to reproach me.
>
> Homage to you, O *Neters*, who live in the hall of the two Maats and who
> have no evil in your bodies and who feed upon truth . . . in the presence of Horus
> who lives in his sun. Deliver ye me from Baabi[7] who feeds on the entrails of the
> mighty ones, on the day of the great settling of accounts. Behold, I have come
> unto you without sin, without fault. . . .
>
> I live in truth, and I feed upon the truth of my heart. That which men have
> bidden I have done, and the *Neters* are satisfied therewith. I have pacified the
> god for I have done his will. I have given bread unto the hungry and water unto
> the thirsty, clothing unto the naked, and a boat unto the shipwrecked. I have
> made holy offerings unto the *Neters*, and I have made funerary gifts to the great
> departed ones.

---

[6]See John 20:17; and p. 222 on the text of Unas, *Pyr.* 369.

[7]Baabi is the monster who stands between Osiris and Thoth on Judgment Day.

Oh, then, deliver me and protect me! Accuse me not before the great god. I am pure of mouth, and I am pure of hands. May those who see me say: "Come in peace, come in peace."[8]

At another moment, the deceased addresses his heart:

Heart of my mother, heart of my birth, heart of my life upon earth, rise not in witness against me; be not my adversary in the presence of the divine powers; weigh not against me. . . . Let it not be said, "Look at what he has done; of a truth he has done it"; . . . Make not complaints against me in the presence of the great *Neter* of the West [Osiris]?[9]

This is a magnificent image of subconscious remorse contradicting uttered words.

Fig. 44. *Psychostasia Scene, or the Weighing of the Soul.*
On the left, the deceased between the two *Maats*. On one of the pans of the scale, his heart, on the other, the soul. On the right, in front of Osiris, Master of the West, an animal hide rolled up on a post, and the four Sons of Horus standing on the flower of a full-blown lotus. Deir el-Medina.

Usir, or Osiris, signifies renewal in general, renewal of Nature as well as of the human individual, and this is why Osiris, in the presence of the deceased King, is often designated as being the *Ka* of the latter; for it is through renewals that the *Ka* is presented with the means of spiritualization.

Accordingly, the deceased sovereign is also called an Osiris, since whatever can die is still condemned to renewal. Through a final death,

[8]*Book of the Dead*, Chap. CXXV, tr. after E. A. W. Budge. See A. Erman, *La religion égyptienne*, p. 265.
[9]Ibid., Chap. XXX. Cf. A. Moret, *The Nile and Egyptian Civilization* (New York, 1918), p. 467. Tr. after Dobie.

however, the being can be summoned to more subtle cycles and then symbolic reference will be made to the passage of the King into celestial constellations.

The King is always conceived as King of divine essence, the ferment of perfection; the ferment is symbolized by the *heq,* his scepter in the form of a hook which brings to mind the crozier of bishops, the shepherd's crook. The *heq*'s intention is to gather together what is represented by the other scepter, called *nekhakha,* in the form of a staff from which the three aspects of Being stream in three waves. The *heq* and the *nekhakha* are also carried by Osiris in his aspect of "destiny." In this symbolique, the position of the scepter-bearing hands must be carefully observed: They may be crossed at the wrists, which signifies death, or opposed by the two fists, which signifies judgment. The double crossing, of the hands and then of the scepters, always indicates resurrection, either for this life or for a higher life following earthly existence.

As principle of renewal par excellence, *Osiris* is said *to be born in his months as the moon . . . to appear at the monthly festival, to be pure for the festival of the New Moon.*[10] Barley is threshed for him, wheat (spelt) is reaped for him, and offerings of it are made at his monthly festivals and again at his semimonthly festivals, as his father, Geb, commanded. He is told: *"Arise, O King, for thou hast not died!"*[11]

Osiris is also the annual renewal of all vegetation, symbolized by an effigy upon which seed is sown and made to germinate. Osiris is likewise the *new-water,* the fertilizing Nile, the flood after the soil's dessication. At the same time, he is the *Ka* of Horus, his son:

Horus has come, he has counted [recognized] thee.[12]
He has smitten Seth for thee, he has (bound) him.
Thou art his Ka. Horus has driven off (Seth) from thee.
Thou art great, greater than thine enemy who swims bearing thee,
Who supports one greater than he who is in thee. . . .
Horus has come, he "counts" [recognizes] his father in thee.
Thou art the renewed one in thy name of [annual] "Fresh Water."[13]

Osiris himself is reborn as germ, symbolized by the seed emerging from the base of his throne and blooming into a lotus flower which supports the four *sons of Horus, the four protectors of man's four essential organic functions.*

[10]*Pyr.* 733, 1711.
[11]*Pyr.* 657.
[12]*Ip,* "to count," means "to discern" as well as "to gestate."
[13]*Pyr.* 587-589.

Fig. 45. In front of Isis and Nephthys, Osiris, bearing the *heq* and the *nekhakha,* is seated on a throne poised on a pond from which germinated the seed that has bloomed into a lotus flower bearing the four Sons of Horus. The vulture's body is replaced by an eye. Hunefer Papyrus.

The Eight Principles of Incarnation

1. The polarization of the One (absolute consciousness, the Pharaonic *Nun*) makes for the appearance (in existence) of a relation between the positive and the negative, i.e., between two absolute complements; this defines the corporeal. Pharaonic concept: *Nun* and *Tum.*

2. This principle of polarization (division) continues; everything that exists, meaning everything that appears as body and that can be perceived by the senses, everything is a relation between two complements. For example: acid and alkaline = salt; positive and negative = energetic effect or neutral body. *Yang* and *Yin* make for objective life.

3. Existence includes: (a) a corporeal genesis going from the origin to man; (b) a psychospiritual genesis starting with man (the final corporeal term, and with the vital reversal which is the beginning of return).

4. In the work of genesis, the end of corporealizations (deaths and reincarnations) corresponds to the *subtilization* of the corporeal (the fixed salt of the earth). One text phrases it: "that which has communicated its fixity to the volatile."[14] This state represents a dissolving fixity and becomes energetically radiant. It brings to mind the marrow in the vegetal. This "fixed volatile," being *oriented* (which means that it is borne by a specified seed), reincarnates specifically.

5. Consciousness has two aspects: One is its innateness in form, the other its self-recognition due to the cerebral cortex; these two aspects are complementary to each other and, reunited *at the end of genesis,* they again make for absolute and immortal consciousness.

6. Consciousness of form is personal consciousness, specifically characteristic of the form; it is transmitted by means of personal reincarnation with the aid of the generic seed, but not *through* this seed. Mental consciousness is the means of choice and makes psychospiritual genesis possible.

7. Death is the separation of the subtile from the corporeal. Each of these carries one of the complements which together make for absolute consciousness, *similar* to the consciousness of origin before the original separation.

8. Definitive rebirth or resurrection is absolute complementation. *Ba* is the volatile, the subtile, and *Ka* is the energetic fixity which is the magnet for *Ba*. The text says that *the Ba must recover its Ka.*

Some of these principles demand clarification.

The *consciousness* here discussed must be distinguished from psychological consciousness, which is essentially mental and of the moment. Retained by the two permanent aspects of the individual, consciousness such as we understand it here is an inscription left by profoundly experienced events in the course of earthly life. That consciousness is inscribed in what is most permanent; it also determines the particular affinity for the new specification, and it is owing to such affinity that the new juncture can be made between states which had become separated and can be rejoined beyond time and space.[15]

---

[14]Jâbir Ibn-Hayyân (Geber), eighth century.

[15]See Isha Schwaller de Lubicz, *The Opening of the Light* (Inner Traditions, 1982), Chap. VI, *The two aspects of soul and consciousness.*

It is also necessary to bear in mind what is said concerning mutations: as the constituent elements separate to form a new conjunction, there is a moment when the *Neters*, the cosmic emanations, conforming to the laws of harmony, can intervene in order to create a new being. "Creation" is here merely a manner of speaking, but at least this intervention offers the opportunity for a surevolution.

This is what is symbolized by Seth's dismemberment of Osiris, and by the long litanies uttered in order to beseech the *Neters* to reconstitute him. Every evening, when Ra settles into Amenti, the particular *Neter* of each temple is considered to undergo the passion of Osiris. Then, during the rising of Ra, the celebrant—the king—performs the rite of the daily divine cult. He offers incense, purifications with four red vases and four white vases (once toward each cardinal point), sacred unguents, etc., which serve to recall the *renewal*, the reconstitution of the dismembered body and its resurrection by day. This can occur only by the grace of the mysterious Eye of Horus which is "counted down" (analyzed) by the offerings of oil, incense, water, or food. The sacrifice of this Eye of Horus serves as a daily reminder of rebirth, the Eye of Horus wrested by Seth and recovered through the sacrifice of Sethian animals whose nature is specified by the offerings. The strange identification of the Eye of Horus with specific offerings that have many shades of meaning signifies nothing other than the phases of the soul's return to existence. The Pyramid Texts express this in the following way:

> Horus has come, he embraces thee [Osiris] Teti. . . .
> Thy son Horus has smitten Seth, he has wrested his Eye from his hand, he has given it to thee; thou hast thy soul by means of it, thou hast power by means of it.[16]

The subtle part which separates from the individual at death naturally seeks its supporting point in order to take form again, but if it has retained a regret or a violent desire, this will cause it to seek any substance whatsoever, psychic in particular, borrowed from a living being, in order to return to a ghostlike shadow-existence. Real personal reincarnation can only be achieved by the reunion of the *Ba* with its *Ka*,[17] as the texts confirm.

For this reason, the tomb is called "house of the *Ka*" and the priests in charge of it, "priests of the *Ka*." All food offerings and purifications

---

[16]*Pyr.* 575-578.

[17]This pertains to the *Ba* as animating spirit and to the Osirian *Ka* called "*Ka* of transformations."

are made "to the *Ka*" of the deceased. It is also said that the *Kas* are the forces of life, the nutriments, and that it is *the Ka which engenders the son*. At the same time that Khnemu models the royal infant on his potter's wheel, he also fashions his *Ka*, and the *Ka* awaits birth during the parturition from *Mut-m-uia* (*Mut-in-the-boat*, mother of Amenophis III). The *Ka* follows the officiating king in the temple and during the Sed festival of renewal. Here it is the divine *Ka*, bearer of the king's Horus-name, held between two upraised arms (symbol of the *Ka* and also the name of the bull *Ka*). It is said that as long as a man is *master of a Ka* and *goes with his Ka*, he is alive. In order to summon his rebirth, therefore, it is said to the dead Osiris:

> Purify thyself, Unas! Open thy mouth by means of the Eye of Horus. Invoke thy Ka, Osir, that he may protect thee from all wrath of the dead![18]

The "*Ka* of transformations" has an evolutionary character; it is more corporeal with human beings close to the earth and becomes more spiritual (one might say energetic) in proportion to the individual's exhaustion of his earthly attachments.

The organic seed (human sperm and ovule) is evidently necessary for the return to human form. It is here that the specific affinity comes into play in the choice of genre and milieu. This is different from the generic continuity of the same bloodline and from a proliferation through conception and birth which transmits only physical, mental, and emotional qualities characteristic of a certain family. And yet it is within such a lineage that the *personal, individual reincarnation* inserts itself. This is why, according to tradition, ancient peoples always sought burial in their own native land, the (organic) seminal lineage being considered most favorable to the reincarnation of the same individual. This is also the reason for the ancestor cult in China, for example, as well as in Egypt.

On the east wall of the entrance corridor to the pyramid of Pepi II Nefer-ka-Rê, it is said:

> Do not travel on those Western waterways!
> Those who travel thereon do not come [toward Ra].
> Walk, O thou Pepi Nefer-ka-Rê, upon these Eastern waterways among the Followers of Ra of the sublime arm, who is in the East.[19]

[18]*Pyr.* 63.
[19]*Pyr.* 393-394.

These words open the door to the royal path, also called the direct way.

It is the mysterious story of the resurrection of Being without passing through lives and reincarnations; mysterious because its genesis is invisible although spiritually commanded by the same laws.

Being is created as *Tum*, it is liberated from earth as Horus, it is purified by spirit and animated with the Horian fire; it has assimilated all the qualities within an hour, whereas on the Western path, it is necessary to pass through all earthly sufferings: Osirian Passion.

The inscriptions covering the walls of the pyramid chambers are concerned with the enumeration of these phases, accidents, or acquisitions. Only their qualities and not their "forms" are specified. Here are several excerpts from the texts on the *east* wall of the antechamber leading to the *Serdab*. The latter contains the statue of the king, the king's double, gazing toward the sarcophagus chamber. The orientation of the walls on which the texts are inscribed has its importance; these east-wall inscriptions thus face the direction of the sun's rising for terrestrial man. Here we find enumerated what Unas has undergone and acquired during his human lifetime up to the hour of culmination at mid-day:

> The sky is overcast, the stars are darkened [are eclipsed].
> The celestial expanses quiver, the bones of Aker (the earth-god) tremble,
> The *gnmw* are stilled,
> [When] they have seen Unas appearing as a soul [*Ba*],
> as a *Neter* who lives upon[within, with] his fathers and feeds upon [within, with] his mothers.
> It is Unas, Master of wisdom (*sabut*).[20]

Several correlations are to be drawn: the allusion, for instance, to the darkness and earth tremors that mark the apparition of the deceased king "as soul," is reminiscent of the account in the Gospel of Matthew relating to Christ's death.[21] Indeed, this does not refer to an ordinary man but to the "King," meaning the Horian or direct path. Though not suffering the avatars of the body, human nature must be within Unas in order to give him existence, and it is useful to stress here that this allegedly human king *is himself called Unas,* a glyph which means existence.[22]

---

[20] *Pyr.* 393-394.

[21] Matthew 27: 45-51.

[22] *Un-is,* name of the last king of the Fifth Dynasty (Unas), is formed from the root *un,* existence, and from the enclitic particle *is,* employed to strengthen an assertion or to place value on a substantive. *Un-is* thus signifies: "(Yes, it is) Existence" or again, "(It is) Existence, certainly." See G. Lefebvre, *Grammaire de l'égyptien classique* (Cairo, 1955), no. 550.

The King is compared to a *Neter,* or principle. He is thought *to have expanded his consciousness* through his fathers and mothers by means of which he nourished himself for his spiritual genesis. Then he becomes Master of wisdom *(sabut).*

> *The glory of Unas is in the sky. His power is in the horizon like* [that of] his father Tum who begat him. . . .
> The *Kas* of Unas are behind him, his virtues are before him, his *Neters* are upon him, his Uraei are on the crown of his head. . . . [23]

The King is identified with Atum, which is to say he is virtually Atum and is going to enter directly into the path of regeneration. It is then said: Unas has his *Kas* behind him, his *virtues* in front of him. The virtues *(hemsut)* are determined by three symbols of Neith *(Net),* the goddess of weaving and of intelligence acquired during the course of existence.[24] The *Neters* are above him and his uraei protect him. His *Ba* and his *Ka* are with him but not as yet unified.

> Unas is the wild-hearted Bull of the Sky who lives in [with] the becoming of every *Neter,*[25] existing on their works [when] they come with their bodies full of magic "through the action of [celestial] fire."[26]

Unas is the Bull of Heaven, the fecundating fire of heaven. Once enriched with "each *Neter's* raison d'être" and hence with their supernatural power, Unas can reunite his spirits *(akhu);* this signifies transfiguration, light, splendor, all of which is comparable to the "light emerging from the shadows."[27]

> Unas is the well-provided one who assembles his spirits. Unas has appeared as this Great One, Master of those who exercise their functions. Unas sits with his back [turned] to Geb [the earth]. It is Unas who will give judgment together with He-Whose-Name-Is-Hidden, on that day of sacrificing the Elder One . . . [that is, the former Unas].[28]

"To sacrifice the Elder One" means to slay the form of that *Unas* who has lived, "elder" here referring to the king's *former state.*
After having judged himself with *He-Whose-Name-Is-'Hidden* or

---

[23]*Pyr.* 395-396.
[24]With regard to *hemsut* and *Neith,* see Isha Schwaller de Lubicz, *Her-Bak Initiate* (New York, 1978).
[25]"To live in, or with, the becoming of every *Neter"* means "to be in communion with every *Neter."*
[26]*Pyr.* 397.
[27]See Isha Schwaller de Lubicz, op. cit.
[28]*Pyr.* 398-399.

the Unknowable One, Unas sacrifices himself in order to tie off the *Ka* which bears all the qualities "previous lives on the indirect path have given it."

There follows a long passage where words are used without determinatives, leaving the door open to several interpretations. Each expression demands detailed analysis and contains a cabalistic meaning. Actually, Unas goes directly from his origin to his perfection, but there is a *passage* involved, namely a unique, one-time action that brings together everything an earthly King Unas "would humanly have undergone and transcended," and this is what is enumerated. In other words, the king must sacrifice all his previous attachments so that his *Ba* is no longer attracted toward a terrestrial *Ka* demanding his reincarnation.

Unas is here said to be the *master of messages* gathered for him by the *chief of writings,* messages which are in truth the accounts and inscriptions made during the course of the previous life. But it is only after the integral destruction of all tangible forms that Unas will be identified with the great scepter *Sekhem* (of the Power) which will assure him the mastery of the *skhemu* (the powers). At that time he will receive the parchment or divine (secret) scroll from Orion and then:

> Unas has appeared again in the heavens. He is crowned as Lord of the Horizon. He has reckoned up [*hesb*] the dorsal vertebrae of the spinal cord [column of fire and of life]. He has seized possession of the *"hatys"* of the *Neters.* He has sustained [*un*] himself on the Red Crown, he has swallowed the Green One [meaning all that is vegetal]. Unas feeds himself on the union [*sma,* the conjunction that makes-for] of the Sages. He is satisfied [*htp,* more exactly, sublimated] with living on the *"hatys"* and their magic power.

The conclusion of this enigmatic text is summarized by the following phrase:

> The "signatures" of Unas do not weaken in his hand [that is, they are in his possession] for he has swallowed the wisdom [or knowledge] of every *Neter.*[29]

In some way, it is the humanity of *Horus* that is evoked here, and accordingly, it can be said that the King is *sustained* (nourished) on human nature and that he lives on the principles *(Neters)* thanks to which he will become an "Accomplished One" and return to his source of origin.

[29]*Pyr.* 409-411.

After the description on the *east* wall expressing in its entirety the principles of man's becoming and his sacrifices, the sun's culmination is reached: this is the hour of justice, of equilibrium and of the passage toward the other world (the transition of *Yang* to *Yin,* as the Chinese phrase it).[30] This critical moment can be put in parallel with the judgment of the crucified Lord Christ when he separates the thief who confesses his faults and his faith from the other thief who blasphemes.

Thus on the *south* wall of this same chamber, Unas appears as Horus, heir of his father (written with the sign of a femur).[31] He is the fourth of these offering-bearers *who through the thighbone descend from their fathers,* and he hopes that he will be justified.

> "Unas has been judged by Tefen and Tefnut," and Shu was a witness for his limbs to be reunited.
> Unas comes out on this day in the true form of a living spirit [*akhu*]. . . .
> Unas interrupts the fight and quells the revolt. Unas goes forth with Maat [his truth or conscience], he leads her away in front of him.[32]

Then one after the other, the *Neters* are entreated not to ignore the King so that he may recognize each one of them; next he ascends to the heights of heaven where he is raised up by Ra.

> Unas is accomplished with his *Ka.* Unas lives together with his *Ka.*

Lastly, the King, rising to heaven, leaves the earth, *"far from wife and rank."*[33]

> This Unas washes himself when Ra appears. The divine Great Ennead shines forth. Seth of Ombos [the separator] is high at the head of the Sanctuary of the South.
> Unas is liberated from the humanity that is in his limbs. This Unas seizes the great white crown from the hand of the two divine Enneads. Isis nurses him, Nephthys suckles him.
> Horus takes him in his fingers, eternally living. He purifies this Unas in the Jackal Lake,[34] he delivers the *Ka* of Unas in the lake of the Netherworld [*Daty*], he destroys the [human] flesh of the *Ka* of this Unas for his body of resurrection, by means of what is on Ra's arms. . . .

---

[31] Regarding the word "heir" written with a femur, see *Le Temple de l'Homme,* I, p. 67, and III, pp. 178-79.

[30] In the *Book of the Hours of the Day,* the *two hours* on either side of noon are consecrated to Seth and Horus.

[32] *Pyr.* 317, 318, 338.

[33] *Pyr.* 369. Cf. John 20: 17.

[34] The jackal is synonymous with "judge"; it is the digester par excellence. The Lake of the Jackal is that of the divine *Ka's* purification. Cf. this purification in reference to the descent of Jesus into hell before his resurrection.

The Two-Lands shine forth.[35] and the face of the *Neters* radiates while he [Horus] leads the *Ka* of this Unas and his own body of resurrection toward the great mansion.

And then Unas is in heaven, and he conducts *those who are imperishable,* symbolized by the circumpolar stars.

Perfect is this Unas in his perfection, he is no longer corruptible. Foremost is this Unas in his pre-eminence, for his *Ka* has reached him. . . .
May Unas be with you, O *Neters!*
May you exist with Unas, O *Neters!*
May Unas live with you, O *Neters!*
May you live together with Unas, O *Neters!*
May Unas love you, O *Neters!*
You love him. . . .

The father of Unas is Atum, and the King is delivered to these Perfect, Wise, Imperishable *Neters.* . . .

In this country to which Unas is going, he will know neither hunger nor thirst, throughout eternity.
God appeared to Unas and Unas is seated upon the great throne at the side of the Great God.[36]

Next, on the *west* wall, facing the setting sun, all is accomplished, and terrestrial life has been survived. Here *Un* (existence) is glorified:

Hail to thee, O Wise One! Geb has created thee, the Divine Ennead has borne thee. Hor is sublimated [*htp*] through his father. Atum is spiritualized [*htp*] through his years [cycles of the times].
The Neters of the East and of the West are sublimated [*htp*][37] through the great interior transformation [produced] by this divine birth.[38]

Then, in the image of the resurrection of Osiris, Unas "raises himself up on his side,"[39] and then "he is shining like a star," and "he sets Truth in the place of Error."[40]

---

[35] Allusion to the two crowns.

[36] *Pyr.* 369-391.

[37] *htp*, reversal of *pth* or *Ptah*, signifies a *sublimation* in terms of action, and a *spiritualization* in terms of effect.

[38] *Pyr.* 258.

[39] Reference to the "side" is found in the *Eleventh Key* of Basilius Valentinus because before the last great glorification, the left (lunar) side of the (aquatic) female is distinguished from the right (solar) and sanguine side of the (Hermetic) King On the cross of the great Passion, *water and blood intermingled* flow from *the right side of the crucified Christ.*

[40] *Pyr.* 265.

Then there follows the apotheosis of the King:

> It is Unas who is at the head of the *Kas,* who united hearts in the face of the
> supreme Sage [*saa*], bearer of the divine scroll [the secret], the Knower of wisdom
> [*si..*] at the right hand of Ra.
> Unas comes toward his throne which dominates the *Kas.* Unas unites the
> hearts in the face of supreme wisdom. Unas becomes like the Knower of wisdom
> [*sia*], bearer of the divine scroll, who is at the right of Ra.
> Unas is liberated "by and within himself."
> Unas says what is in the heart of the Great One at the feast of weaving [that is,
> at creation].
> It is Unas! It is Unas! the Knower of wisdom who is at the right of Ra.[41]

One time Unas is before the divine throne, one time he goes
toward the divine throne, and one time he is definitely *at the right of
Ra,* the One.

There is here a remarkable similarity to the words of the Christic
Passion when after definitive unification, the Lord Christ, purely
spiritual and become untouchable for woman,[42] is then said to be risen
and *seated at the right of the Father.*[43]

Two paths, two ways to a single goal. Two ways that distinguish
those who have renounced from those who remain subject to desire or
must still taste the joys and sorrows of this life.

Is this religion? No, it is more than faith: for some it is knowledge
of the divine world-ordering word, and this knowledge is also the
sacred science. For others it is an inevitable order: Believers or doubters,
they suffer the consequences of all the causes generated by their actions.
This is the indirect road, the most logical, sure, and comforting of laws; it
leaves each one to judge for himself what he is, what he understands, and
what are his hopes.

The path of Osiris is not imposed by anyone; it is the reality of
Nature that dictates. From the moment a man is born on earth, he enters
a cycle he cannot escape until the causes of disharmony, which he himself
created, have been exhausted.

To believe or not to believe is one and the same for the natural
course of the Osirian way. Be good, be just, be charitable, and the sooner
you will reap illumination. Be evil, be cruel, be egotistical, whether you

---

[41]*Pyr.* 267-268.

[42]John 20: 17. Christ's words to Mary Magdalene after his resurrection: "Touch me not; for I am not yet
ascended to my Father."

[43]Mark 16:19: "So then, after the Lord had spoken unto them, he was received up into heaven, and sat on
the right hand of God."

believe or not, you will pay. You say: "I don't remember my past lives." Your illumination, if you have opened to it, your sufferings, if you have generated them—are these not recollections?

Every human life is necessarily a *consequence* involving either compensation or payment, but it is also cause for its sequence: cause of the continuation of slavery, or cause of liberation by consciously breaking the chains. This breakthrough is a joyous renunciation which is neither flight nor fear, but an irresistible summons toward the Light. And when this call makes itself heard, the temple doors open of their own accord: Horus, Christ—divine unction, in fine—begins to do its work.

This is what has been said by the sages of all times, those who have beheld the certainty of the simplest of truths.

Egypt maintained itself for millenia because the way of renewal held its people on a righteous track, certain that death is but change in life's continuity.

The temple reserved the direct path for the illuminated, the path which was later, and with all the consequences this entailed, openly taught by Christianity.

10

The King

The royal principle on which ancient Egypt was founded has nothing in common with our usual concept of "king."[1]

It is never a human being that is involved, a particular man, such as France's Louis, Charles, or François. The reigning king is a symbol, a guise embodying the mythical and the mystical as well as the Hermetic sense of a ray of original Light's corporification, the Horian Logos. Through its fall into Nature the "creative Word" is imprisoned in earth by Seth. As *Neter,* this "fire in earth" is Ptah, the Greek Hephaestos. The King is animated by the Horian or Luciferian aspect of the fallen archangel.

The temple ritual explains the royal fulfillment of the Horian light through the phases it must undergo on the way to its corporeal exaltation, "the philosopher's stone," as it was called in medieval times. This is the King of divine origin, almighty in things of created Nature.

Titles and qualities are attributed to the reigning king. They describe what he symbolizes in the phases of becoming. Through this symbolization of the object of sacred science, a bond is maintained that ties the esoteric meaning of the myth—basis of religion—to science in general as well as to the king as head of the social organization. This is the true meaning of a theocratic order, not to be confused with a royalty directed by a religious organism.

The royal progression in the succession of its stages—from its origin to the formal accomplishment, namely the work of its realization as described by the ritual—is reproduced in the table of mystic names showing the genealogy of the kings of this Empire: a gestation of the incarnate spirit for which the king symbolizes the end to be attained by all mortals: Anthropocosmos fulfilled. The course of this aim is charted

[1]The King of the theocracy should be conceived as a synthesis of everything heretofore treated in this book

by religious teaching and sustained by ever-present example. This is the positive way to travel the most abstract of paths.

What this reigning king represents as a man is almost secondary. Yet history shows that a severe distinction is always drawn at the time of inhumation, between the worthy king and the king of lesser worth.

But it is always *the royal principle* which officiates in the daily ritual of the temple: the king as priest and the priest as king.

A parallelism appears to exist between the Pharaonic royal principle and the "King" of Hermetic tradition as he is described in all serious texts concerning these questions. On both sides, the same qualifications and identical enigmas are found.

A distinction is of course to be made between the historical and the purely hieratic-symbolic aspect. It is to the latter that the temple is dedicated, with all that it comprises: architecture, colonnades, obelisks, bas-reliefs, statuary, colors, and materials.

As we are conditioned and imprisoned in material form, in the corporeal universe, we are unable to envision the problem of beginning other than by positing as the source of all things a state which lies outside of this universe. That would be the "One in all through One." Two essential lines stem from this initial proposition: either spontaneous generation, or an ordered becoming in time, an ordinance which will necessarily be *the law* applicable to everything. Each phase in this case is a final stage, contributing to the realization of a faculty virtually implied in the nature of the cause.

Each final stage is an end in itself in the realms of the mineral, the plant, the animal, and the human-animal. These stages are symbols, formal "words" of the law which participate in the latter's total expression. This can only be the fulfillment of all virtualities immanent in the cause.

Cosmic man is this fulfillment, the *anthropocosmos* whose image is the King; the stages in time are the hieroglyphs, whereas the symbolization of *functional definitions* yields the elements of myth.

In the course of incarnation or corporeal becoming, there are two lineages whose replica is found in human gestation: One is the white lunar (the viable infant of seven months' terms); the other is the red solar (the completed embryo of nine months' term). These two finalities are represented by the white and the red crowns.

The white crown signifies corporification, the first great finality of becoming; the second finality, the red crown, begins the return of the corporeal to its energetic source. One phase needs the other, as they define one another.

In the symbolic history of the Pharaonic Empire as well as in the history of the myth, we find the analysis of this becoming in every nuance of each phase.

Only by seeing ancient Egypt in this light can the formidable maze of its history be cleared: the social organization, the myth, the so-called religious crises, the dynastic chronology, the picture writing, and the teachings of the monuments.

This is not a matter of "philosophy"; in very general lines, such consideration needs no explanation for its acceptance. It finds proof in the natural fact of every procreation and becomes a science if this becoming can be experimentally proved, starting from a beginning, starting, that is, from a universal genesis. This would mean capturing energy in its pure and unpolarized state (an irrational endeavor), and corporifying it in order to use it as universal source of a first generation, its specification depending upon the coincidences of cosmic harmony. This proposition poses spontaneous (albeit mastered) generation as starting point for an ordered genesis.

The "temple" professes to possess this knowledge of causes. This excludes "philosophy," as the latter pertains only to a search for knowledge. In Egypt, thinking remains "technical" and not "academic"; the source of origin is the only abstraction, whereas all that follows is linked by a logic which is not syllogistic, but vital. Everything that we now know concerning the Pharaonic Empire confirms such a position.

The variations and varieties of species and genera are the effects of harmonic coordinates explained and ordered by number. Conditions such as these rule a mentality no longer sharing common ground with ours. The myth situates the moments of harmonic activity which are purely functional. Judgment and thought are no longer concerned with facts that are concretely linked, but with *types of functions* that produce effects. This can be expressed in a popularized fashion as: The *Neter* "so-and-so" does such-and-such, produces this or that phenomenon. The sage knows what is meant; for the people in general, there are symbolic figurations of these powers, such as: Amon and Mentu (periods of the sidereal precession), Ptah (Promethean Fire and animating seed), Osiris (the cyclic principle of seasonal or cosmic rebirth), Seth (the destructive Fire), Horus (generating and animating Fire), Sekhmet (the devouring Aphrodite which, through desire, can become regenerative as Hathor), Khnemu (the specifying form-giver), and so on, each *function* having its name.

In order to complete the symbolism, those types are chosen from living Nature in which functions are most specifically incarnated.

In the social order, the incarnate king stands for corporification of the universal source which will clothe itself in all the aspects of his activity, thereby justifying his "mystic name." Indeed, for a full understanding, the *meaning* of the name must be read. It is not sufficient merely to enunciate the name as is usually done. For example, we have said that Amon is the energetic (stellar) milieu for the period when the sun rises in the constellation of Aries at the moment of the vernal equinox. Ptah signifies "Fire fallen into earth," the "fall" into earth of the Kabbalah's faithless archangel. The reversal of *pth* into *htp*, *Ptah* into *hotep*, clarifies the meaning of Amen-hotep," the reversal into Amon of the Fire fallen into earth," a spiritualization of that Fire.

Akh-n-Aton means "glorification of the sun" (the physical disk); *Tut-ankh-Amon*, "the corporification or stabilization of Amon's life"; *Thoth-mes*, "the corporeal birth of Thoth (Hermes)"; *Sen-nefer*, "the two energies"; *Iah-mes*, "birth of the moon."

There are different royal genealogies, and knowledge of the analyzed genetic sequence of the whole amounts to knowing the dynastic chronology. The Thothmes are part of the Amenhotep dynasty; later comes Hor-m-heb, "annunciation or feast of Horus," the solar Saint John, the herald who will prepare the coming of the Ramses (or *Ra-mes-s*), "birth of Ra."

These are the mythic names of the Kings.

The Royal Names

To name means calling into existence and knowing.

Pharaonic tradition seems to indicate that the mother's first words upon the birth of the child form the name to be given to this incarnate being.

As far as the king is concerned, it must be well understood that the heavens are the *mother*, figured by the conjunction of the starry sky. Today this would be called the synthetic character of the child's astrological theme.

The king is in any case a symbol of the cosmic King; he is always first of all a *Horus* in one of the specific astrological aspects: this is his *Horus-name*, supported by the *Ka* symbol.

His second name situates him as an incarnation of the *two initial principles:* it is the name of the *Two Goddesses*, the cobra *Uatchet* of the North and the vulture *Nekhebit* of the South.

The third name lends the king the aspect of *Golden Horus*, the perfected Horus, and no longer the *Universal Horus*.

He is next called *Master of the Two-Lands,* and symbolized by the bulrush of the South and the bee of the North; lastly, he is designated as *Son of Ra,* the solar principle incarnate.

Those are the five titles of the royal protocol.

The first designation of N. as *Horus* must have a horoscopic meaning. The three names that follow define the king's development. The second brings to mind the *Tum* of origin; as primordial Earth, it spells out the two perfections which generate the Golden Horus. Only the latter can have dominion over the two realizations: the high white crown and the low red crown.

This second name is dominated by the two principles of origin; they can be Seth and Horus, which would accentuate duality; or else the two puissances of the magical fire adorning the king's forehead, the vulture and the cobra represented on two baskets; the vulture's tail is placed on the cobra's basket to evoke the idea of *junction.*

Egyptologists express astonishment at the terms in which the title and praises of the king of Upper and Lower Egypt are couched. The enumeration of the qualities in such exaggerated terms and in this dithyrambic form seem inadmissible for a mere mortal king.

When the king is *compared* to the sun and to Horian perfection, such flattery might be ascribed to Oriental custom. An example of this can be seen in the poem addressed to King Seti II on the occasion of his accession, by an official of the Treasury:

> Turn thy face toward me, thou rising Sun who lights the Two-Lands with [thy] beauty.[2]
> Thou Sun of men, who drives the darkness from Egypt.
> Thou dost appear as thy father, Ra, who rises in the sky.
> Thy rays penetrate down into the caverns, and there is no place devoid of thy beauty.
> All that happens in every land is told thee, when thou art resting in the palace.
> Thou dost hear the words of all the lands, for thou hast millions of ears.
> Thine eye is clearer than the stars of heaven.
> Thy vision is superior to the sun's.
> Whatever is said, even by one whose mouth be in the cavern [?], it reaches thine ear, and if something hidden is done, thine eye will nevertheless behold it.
> O Seti, thou the master of beauty, thou who creates the breath.[3]

[2]The true sense of the word *nefer,* "beauty," refers to a state of maturity of a vital quality. It is the moment of completion which gives *generative power* to the object or the being. This refers either to its own seed (puberty) or to its particular quality (functional accomplishment), or again, to its own energy (increase in vitality and continuity). This diversity accounts for the different uses of *nefer:* perfection, goodness, beauty, virility, etc.

[3]A. Erman and H. Ranke, *La civilisation égyptienne,* p. 89.

This poem, stripped of its emphasis, could indeed very well give to understand what the people have a right to expect from their sovereign: The king knows all, hears all, sees all, and thus is capable of foreseeing all things and making the country prosper, an idea beautifully expressed by the gift of the breath of life.

But elsewhere particulars are given, affirmations which no longer permit us to take these words as common flattery. One such example is a text concerning Ramses III which in itself sums up the tradition of the king's divine origin, while at the same time evoking the mystery of origin described in the pyramids.

In this text it is said of User-Maat-Re-meri-Amon, "the power of Ra's consciousness attracting Amon, Ramses III":

> The son of Amon-Ra, enthroned in his heart, whom he loves more than anything and who is with him;
> He is the resplendent image of Master of the universe and a creation of the *Neters* of Heliopolis....
> His divine father has created him in order to increase his splendor.
> He is the immaculate egg, the sparkling seed raised by the two goddesses of great magic.
> Amon himself has crowned him on his throne in Heliopolis of Upper Egypt [Erman].
> He has chosen him as shepherd of Egypt and defender of men.
> He is Horus who protects [?] his father; the elder son of the god "Bull of his mother";
> Ra has begotten him in order to create a brilliant posterity on earth, for the salvation of men and as his living image.[4]

This text first summarizes the act of conception and shows the king procreated by Ra, the solar principle. It is therefore not the human king who is meant. Although the physical father of the king serves as intermediary to the cosmic power, in this child—just as with the Christic conception—there resides the divine and the human, and the paternal king can be placed in parallel with Joseph, the nourishing father.

The comparison between the divine conception of each one of these royal principles accentuates the precept underlying all of these Pharaonic texts: *"This is the man who will reign but who is to be overlooked in favor of the cosmic teaching."*

The divine conception of the King (theogamy) is the object of extensive descriptions, for example at Deir el-Bahari for Hatshepsut, and at the temple of Luxor for Amenophis III.

---

[4]Ibid., p. 90.

In the text of Ramses III cited herein, there occurs a rare epithet designating the king as *perfect egg*. This egg is suggestive of the world-egg, in the Hermopolitan phase of the myth, laid by a goose on a primordial hillock. The egg plays a very important symbolic role in Hermetic texts. It is the image of the entire Hermetic opus, as the shell represents the corporeal salt, the white being the mercury which can be coagulated by the sulphur effect of the egg-yolk. It is indeed the action of the *animate* solar yellow which will form the chick by means of the egg white's substance.

Another qualification is to be noted: The king is here called *shepherd* of his flock, as will be the Lord Christ. Is not Light the highest perfection as it attracts and leads the lost? And is it not said here that the king was engendered for the salvation of men?

The universal character of the cosmic teaching transmitted through these texts is confirmed by the words in this instance which speak of the king's birth and then of his coronation.

Crown and Coronation

The crown is more than an emblem, it replaces what is the human king's thinking, his destiny, personal character and, in the case of the Pharaoh, substitutes a *Neter*. In the bas-reliefs, the gift of the crown is always conferred by a *Neter;* the function which this *Neter* represents will be transmitted by the crown. This coronation announces a different state, a state of pure intuition: expressed is the innate knowledge of the *Neter,* the cosmic function which is the anthropocomos in man. This might explain why the king never carries out any act whatever, be it civil proceedings or a temple matter, without asserting that it is the *Neter* itself which is his inspiration or realizes the work. With respect to her obelisks, for instance, Hatshepsut certifies to have done nothing but what was dictated by Amon. She has executed her monuments through and for Amon.

The intention of suppressing the personal will is confirmed in the figurations of the king by the insistence with which the skullcap is encircled by a separating mark of one sort or another: a diadem, a joint in the stone blocks, or even by the inlay of a piece brought from another temple. As far as physiology is concerned, the part of the brain thus separated represents the seat of the will and of individualistic thinking, and is quite independent from glands and vital centers.

"See *Le Temple de l'Homme,* I, p. 639, "Le diadème," and III, Chap. VII, "La calotte cranienne."

The true understanding of the symbolic replacement of skullcap by crown must be found in a transformation which produces a new thinking being; it is indeed only after purification and coronation that the king has the right to officiate in the temple.

The true meaning of the *royal diadem* lies in this figurative separation of a part of the cranium. In ancient Egypt, the royal diadem is designated by *mh*, which is also the word for the cubit of measure. The circular line of the diadem is indeed the very measure of the royal cubit; for each man, it shows the measure of his own cubit.

Thus Pharaoh is not only the son of Ra—perfect and divine being—but he also measures the world; numerous consequences arise from the few points raised here.

It is certain that the coronation does not take place at any moment whatsoever, according to the convenience of profane considerations. Its date is always situated so as to conform astrologically with the characteristic features this king will represent in generating his particular phase of Pharaonic Egypt. Birth and coronation are certainly situated on an identical radius which intersects the spirals representing temporal becoming.

Enthronement is the accession of the king to his actual power. This power symbolizes the phase of the work which corresponds to the King. Thus Amen-hotep is not identical to Thoth-mes, and Ra-mes-s represents a passage of the lunar to the solar. Amen-hotep is the *hotep* of *Amon,* in other words, his sublimation or spiritualization. This is explained in the style of this king's bas-reliefs which are carved superficially with a relief of barely two millimeters.

As "birth of the Sun," Ramses draws from matter the Horian soul which remains hidden therein. Throughout this dynasty, his bas-reliefs are carved progressively deeper into the stone.

The King as Priest and the Priest as King

The great procession of Min, a detailed representation of which can be found in the funerary temple of Ramses III at Medinet-Habu, took place in the first month of the harvest season *shmu* on the day of the new moon. It is very likely that this ceremony coincided with the anniversary date of this sovereign's coronation, which was celebrated on the twenty-sixth day of that same month. This ceremony brings to mind certain gestures which are part of the enthronement ritual.[6]

[6]H. Gauthier, *Les fêtes du dieu Min* (Cairo, 1931), pp. 64-75. The celebration of the coronation of Ramses II took place on the 26th of *Pachons* and lasted approximately twenty days.

The ceremony of the *coming forth of Min* proceeds in five episodes.

The king leaves his palace and "makes his appearance," comparable to the rising sun. His Majesty Ramses III is carried on a palanquin toward the abode of his father *Min Ka-Mut-f,* the "Bull of his mother," to witness his "accomplishment." Wearing the blue *khepersh* helmet, the king is seated on a throne flanked by two lions and protected by two *Maats.* The throne is carried on two litters by twelve princes, their heads adorned with feathers. The inscription calls them *royal sons and great noblemen (seru).* The royal palanquin is preceded by personages in robes of state wearing two ostrich plumes on their heads and who are described as follows: *"known" of the king, his Majesty's followers, the royal sons, the great noblemen [seru] and all the dignitaries.*[7]

Fig. 46. *Appearance of the King.*
Detail of the first episode of the festival of "Min's Coming Forth."
Bas-relief, Medinet-habu, Twentieth Dynasty.

Speculation is rife as to the meaning of the title *"known of the king,"* an expression that goes back to the Ancient Empire: If these personages are only members of the court, as the classic translation would have it, it is difficult to understand why they should have precedence over the princes of royal blood who are mentioned in third

[7]Ibid., pp. 115-116.

place only. By their title, however, which can also be interpreted to mean *"those of royal knowledge,"* their place should be in first rank.[8]

The meaning behind these epithets can be reached with more precision through alternative translations. "Known of the king" could be rendered as *"those who know the royal path,"* by which is meant the direct path through Horus. The royal children must be understood in the light of tradition as *"the children of science,"* meaning those who participate in the esoteric knowledge. This would account for their subordinate position in the figuration.

Following the royal offerings comes the solemn procession called *"the coming forth of Min."* During this ceremony, the statue of the *Neter* is carried on a shield. With two feathers on his head and with seals and mummy-swaths around his neck, a *white bull* precedes the statue while the reader-priest declaims *the danced hymn of Min,* and the *black*

Fig. 47. *Min's Coming Forth.*
Detail of the second episode. Bas-relief, Medinet-habu, Twentieth Dynasty.

man of Punt extols this Neter. Egyptologists are at a loss to justify the presence of a black man from Punt among the important personalities of this ceremony. But geographical and historical explanations can be of no value on this subject. What is needed is an understanding of the

---

[8]"The etymology of this expression *rkh-w-nsw-t* (known of the king) is as yet uncertain. The Pyramid Texts apply this title to the four sons of *Horus* in so far as they are considered to be the grandsons of *Osiris.*" H. Gauthier, op. cit., p. 115.

characteristics of Min who was a *black bull* before becoming symbolized by a *white bull.*

Next shown are the statues of the beatified kings of Upper and
Lower Egypt which will become the object of the reigning king's cult.
Once the statue of Min is set down upon a temporary altar formed of
steps, the king releases four birds bearing the names of the four sons of
Horus. The hieroglyph of the stairway which designates Min's altar
should be considered as the functional determinative of this image: It is
the *ascension* whose character is underlined by the feathers on the head
of Min's white bull, and by the flight of the birds.

In the presence of the royal ancestral statues and of the white bull, a
priest offers the king a freshly cut sheaf of spelt as well as a sickle of black
copper inlaid with gold. As certain members of the clergy recite the
formulas seven times while circling the king, the latter makes the
gesture of cutting the sheaf with his sickle, *raises it to his nose,* and
deposits it in front of Min in further allusion to a fluidification, or
aeration. Once the ceremony is over, the statue is returned to its naos,
and the king performs the libation and incense-offering according to the
rules of the daily cult.

The ceremony of the flight of birds, here represented on the
occasion of Min's "coming forth," is part of the ritual of the royal
coronation and of its renewal (the Sed festival). After the purifications,
the latter mainly comprises the attribution of the crowns of the South
and of the North by Seth and Horus, and then the unification of the Two-
Lands under the feet of the king (Fig. 48). The name of the Pharaoh is
then written on the fruits of the Persea tree by Thoth, and lastly, four
birds are released toward the four directions in order to announce (?) the
royal accession to the respective divinities of the four cardinal points.
This rite is sometimes accompanied by the "archery" scene where Seth
and then Horus successively hold the king's shoulders so as to direct the
arrows to the four points of the horizon.[9]

In principle, an abridged version of the coronation ritual is
repeated each day before the "ritual of the divine daily cult," for it is
always *the royal principle which acts as priest* in the temple bas-reliefs.
This royal principle is the Horian power which animates all life. The
man is here no longer of any importance: Of value is the significance of
this royal principle only and *everything this puissance is able to
perform.* This is what analysis of the cult shows us so generously.

---

[9]This scene is represented in Karnak in the Sed festival edifice of Thothmes III. To the rites here described
must be added that of the "procession around the walls" and the "course of Apis" which can be traced back to the
first dynasties.

A text on the walls enclosing the temple of Edfu relates the existence of a testament of Ra. He is said to be "the first King of Egypt," bequeathing to the son of Osiris and Isis—the king—all the land of the South and the North and all the qualities reserved for Ra as creator.

It is true that if there is a myth which teaches the theogony, a myth which becomes the theological basis on which the temple and the empire are founded, and if on the other hand a fusion is made between the human king who reigns and the principles of this myth, then one or the other will be open to question.

The indefinable character of unity concealed in Ra, acting through Hap (the Bull) during a particular time, and then through Amon (the Ram) during another time, this abstract character would not suit the reigning king were it truly that king to which the cited texts refer. It is equally evident in the account of the battle of Kadesh that it could not possibly be the reigning king who is involved: This warrior single-handedly slays thousands of enemies and destroys thousands of combat chariots![10] It is meaningless to attempt to speak of this royal aspect in ancient Egypt without correctly situating the king and his actions. It is equally unproductive to approach these writings in a historical frame of mind and to neglect what they really are: a constant reminder of the secret of sacred science, the *Opus Magnum* of which the Franciscan says in his text: "Let us commence, then, in the name of God, the Great Work, so called because nothing on earth surpasses it. . . ."

Her, known in his Latinized form of *Horus,* specifically signifies "face"; *Horus is the face, the sensorially perceptible appearance of the invisible Ra.* The appearance of this face is a realization through the *Oeuvre,* the Work of cosmic genesis. From the beginning, Horus is held *prisoner,* held earthbound by his brother Seth. He is the divine Light carried along by what has become sensorially perceptible through *Tum,* the primordial hillock which issued from *Nun,* the domain of celestial archangels. This occurs through the irrational act which is the beginning of becoming, the renowned secret. All texts of all times, in one form or other, repeat exactly the same thing.

Pharaonic myth shows Seth and Horus as enemies; the one and the other, Plato's "same" and "other," the fundamental scission of what Lao-tse calls *Tao ko Tao,* "what is and is not," being and nonbeing, all these in one single state which becomes accessible only through the initial scission: *fa chang tao,* where the ideogram *fa* is double and opposed. The end of the completed genesis, the ultimate realization, is the union in *friendship* rather than in enmity, of Seth and Horus; they

---

[10]See Chapter 5, "Symbolique and Symbol."

will become what is affirmed by the Emerald Tablet: "... and its force or puissance is entire if it be converted into Earth... it is the strong Strength of all strength." As the texts specify, this means that all must become a living and fixed Fire, beyond the reach of any destructive fire. By "Fire" is meant the spiritual puissance which gives life to all things, just as the tender warmth of ordinary fire commonly sustains life.

The final union of the elements which were originally opposed is what Hermetism calls "the Stone," the "thing" which acts as ground for the universal edifice: this is the King par excellence, it is the son of Ra who is like Ra, the son of Heaven, generally speaking. *In this sole-singular King, the two crowns are unified*, the silvery-white crown of the South (Seth), and the golden red crown of the North (Horus). This is the King to which the "dithyrambic" texts refer; the human king is but the symbol, the image, the recall, the evocation of the real divine King, *the true King by the grace of God.*

Horus as appearance—the color of Ra—in the beginning must be delivered from his corporeal prison, as the soul of the mortal being must likewise be saved. In the end, he will be the divine specification of the perfect Being. Horus, therefore, is related to all the phases of genesis until man, and then from man to glorious resurrection. The *universal Horus* is in all that lives. The divine Logos is in all being, and when Saint Francis preaches to the fishes and the birds, he speaks in the name of such truth.

The Pharaonic temple anthropomorphizes principles and functions without humanizing them. The spiritual conception of Amon-Ra, the pure and perfect birth of the royal infant under the auspices of celestial forces, his baptism and his naming, all this is told in the "theogamy" chamber of the temple of Luxor. This is a reality unsituated in time. The father, Amon-Ra, is shown in place of Thothmes IV, the terrestrial father through whom he acts. The mother in this spiritual conception is *Mut-m-uia* (*Mut* in the barque): *Mut*, femininity conceiving "in the barque" which floats upon the hours of the day.

> This is what is said by the royal spouse, the royal mother Mut-m-uia in the presence of the majesty of this august *Neter*, Amon....Twice great are thy souls! Thy union with me is a beautiful thing; Thy divine dew is in all my members as prince of Thebes [*heq uas*]....

Amon takes up the queen's words and announces that the future king, the child, will be *Amon-hotep heq-uas,* the symbol of a historic

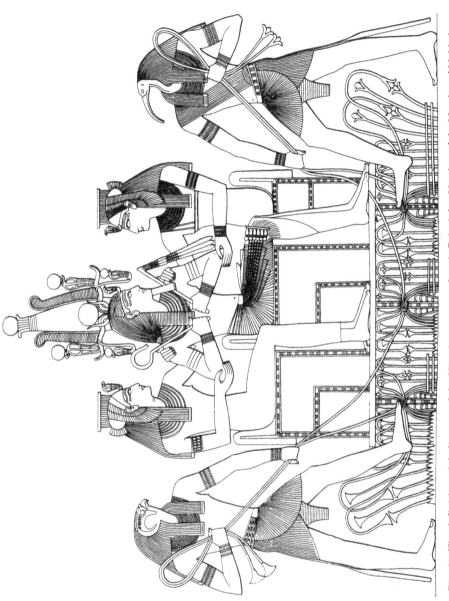

Fig. 48. The definitive triple ligature of the King between two female Principles. Uatchet of the North and Nekhebet of the South, who assist in holding the *beq* scepter (the ferment) and the *nekhakha* (spiritual) scepter. The triple throne is poised on a triple *sma* sign; the ligatures are carried out by Horus (the papyrus of the North) and by Thoth (the bulrush of the South). Image of Trismegistos. Bas-relief, Temple of Abydos, Nineteenth Dynasty.

phase in the Pharaonic *opus:* the *hotep* of *Amon* as leaven of the rising flux.

The child having been thus conceived, its perfection is announced by Khnemu, the divine potter from Elephantine, who will "fashion the child and give it forms more beautiful than that of all the *Neters.*" This promise is illustrated by Khnemu's action: He confers the proportions of an adult on the future king as well as on his *Ka.*

This child is brought into the world with the assistance of celestial principles. Next, it is nourished with the milk of the "heavenly cow," the "milk" which allows all beings to live.

—*Theogony* and *Theology,* the doctrine of metaphysical powers and of the becoming of being, its maintenance and return to its source;

—*Astronomy,* the science of cosmic harmony and celestial influences;

—*Medicine,* the relations of the living body with cosmic influx and its relationship with metaphysical powers.

. . . These three faculties are but one single science. It aims not only at the experimental revelation of what is taught by the three disciplines but also at the realization of the perfect being who is the aim of existence: the King of the tangible world by the grace of God.

This King's government is identical with his own self-definition; the laws of his becoming are the laws which govern visible life and life in the *Dwat,* the world of transformations, for those human beings still fettered by the mortal body.

The Pharaoh and his government are the image of this reality, they are its tangible symbols.

The Sed Festival

There exists a concept, obvious to the sages of all times, the meaning and very possibility of which are totally beyond the understanding of rationalistic thinking: the concept of *qualitative exaltation.*

This notion does not concern the elimination of impurities in order to retain the pure, unadulterated quality; instead, exaltation refers to a kind of spiritualization of the thing's characterizing quality. It is possible to bring simple chemical bodies, such as gold and silver, to states of purity that are absolute for all practical purposes. They are then perfectly *themselves,* but *only* themselves and nothing more, nothing beyond their own quality, characterized by a variety of typical aspects such as density, atomic weight, color, malleability, etc. This silver and this gold are incapable of transmitting their quality to another metal: they have nothing to give without losing something of themselves; they are not a "leaven," as is the *heq,* one of the king's scepters in the shape of a hook.

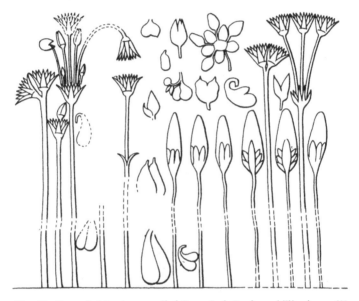

Fig. 49. *Bas-relief in the so-called Botanical Garden of Thothmes III.* Detail of the west wall, Karnak.

Strictly speaking, the action of fermentation concerns transmutation in its corporeal aspect.

Belief in this possibility implies a radical reversal of the materialistic foundation of rational science. It must be understood that these are not the atomic "transmutations" of our catch-as-catch-can atomists who destroy one edifice in order to erect another out of the salvaged materials.

The principle of true transmutation is totally different. It demands a qualitative exaltation of the *thing* and is based on the following fact: In a milieu assumed to be a substance without body, that is, a nameless energy (unless we choose to call it "spirit"), a styptic force comes to concretize this substance in order to define it spatially, to form a body.

The only possibility of exalting the quality of this *thing*, therefore, is to exalt the concretizing force which it carries but which at first had brought it only to its present characteristic state. This exaltation has no common measure with a multiplication as in the instance of one wheat kernel yielding a stalk of thirty to sixty new grains. Such multiplication is characteristic of all seed, and is nothing but regeneration, a faculty of vegetation. There is a kinship between the effect of a ferment and that of leaven in bread, but even more so with the phenomenon of gene mutation. The principle of qualitative exaltation can be illustrated by the transition of the sweetbriar to the rose. This intention of modifying the ferment of the seed explains the instances of "teratological proliferation" in plants represented on the walls of the so-called botanical garden in the Sed-festival temple of Thothmes III in Karnak.

Fig. 50. *An Instance of Proliferation.*
After terminating in one flower, "this inflorescence beyond the secondary stems develops a bud which produces leaves, hence a viviparity, that is, a new plant." Excerpt from Museum of Paris Bulletin.

Classical Egyptology has hitherto considered these cases of abnormal proliferation (Figs. 49-51) the "fantasy representations" of artists (see Wreszinski, *Atlas* II, Pls. 26-33).

Yet a report from the Paris Museum of Natural History describes two cases of proliferation as observed in 1878 in the Museum greenhouse aquarium (Figs. 50-52):

Fig. 51. *Bas-relief in the so-called Botanical Garden.*
Detail of the west wall.

> ...Without illustration until now in the genus *Nymphaea*, this fact shows
> once again how characteristics are formed, and proves the spontaneity of their
> appearance. It must be said, however, that this spontaneity is not surprising, as it
> is manifested everywhere in everything. Furthermore, were it better interpreted,
> it could explain a number of facts...in reality it reflects the well-known
> definitive maxim: "Let there be matter," of which it is a manifestation.

From the sculptured water lilies in the "botanical garden" of the
Sed-festival temple, we see that the ancients were not only acquainted
with this phenomenon of teratological proliferation, but also knew its
causes, as the latter contribute to the character of *qualitative exaltation*
represented by the Sed festival.

These carvings further confirm our affirmation that in ancient
Egypt, nothing is to be attributed to chance or fantasy; the deeper
motivation for every anomaly must be sought, and such motivations
might very well escape our rational mentality.

In this hall, the following text is to be found:

> ...all the strange plants, all the flowers which are in the divine earth
> [found by] his majesty when his majesty had gone to Upper Retenu in order to

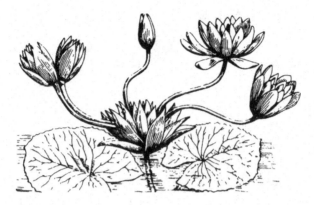

Fig. 52. *A Case of Proliferation observed at the Museum.*
Five secondary stems, two of which are *fused together,* develop
from a seemingly normal flower and each stem terminates in a bud
or a flower.

subdue all countries according to the order of his father Amon who placed
them beneath his sandals, from [this day on] until myriads of years.

His majesty thus said: "I swear, on my life, by the love of Ra, by the grace of
Amon, all these things happened in truth. No lie have I written [here]. The
"souls" of my majesty have made them be born and become in order to glorify his
"nourishments." My majesty has achieved this through love, in order to place
them in the presence of my father Amon, in this great temple of Akh-menu for
ever and ever."

Along with Wreszinski, naturalists agree that the plants and
animals represented in the "botanical garden" are typically African.
This contradicts the text asserting their provenance from the "Divine
Land" and from "Upper Retenu" which translates as "Syria," where the
king had gone presumably to subjugate "all the countries." Taken
literally, such a text would make no sense whatsoever.

"Divine Land" and "Upper Retenu" must therefore be understood
as an allusion to the Eastern and solar character of the milieu capable of
gestating these "strange plants."

The poetic and mystical character of the king's words, moreover,
prompts a search for deeper significance.

In order to approach the esoterism of the problem, the symbolique
of the lotus must be recalled, equally valid for both India and Egypt. It is
seen that the lotus has its roots in the earth, grows in and by means of
water, that its leaves are nourished by air and its flower by the sun's fire.
Thus the lotus symbolizes the four elements: *earth, water, air,* and *fire.*

The lotus flower represents the final product, not only regenerated but *exalted,* as the carvings show; from it springs anew a leaf (air), a bud (coagulation), and one or several new flowers. The first flower constitutes a new earth, a solar earth, capable of an exaltation represented by the leaves, the buds, and the flowers that spring from it.

Philosophically, such an exaltation finds its culmination in the absolute; practically, as soon as the concretizing force can no longer be detained in a bodily form, it returns to its spiritual source. This is the true meaning of an exaltation of the mortal toward the immortal.

The King is that *force,* that ferment. The Sed festival, a ceremony whose significance continues to puzzle Egyptologists, specifies the gesture of qualitative exaltation of the King (Life, Health, Strength).

Sed means "tail," the prolongation of the spinal column toward the ground, the renewal of the life that animates the column of Fire, for *"the Earth is its nurse."*

A number of symbols attest to the signification of this Sed festival; two of these suffice to remove all doubt as to its particular meaning. One of these symbols is formed by two thrones set back to back in a special pavilion. The King is seated on these thrones, his two fists placed one on top of the other and holding the scepters. On one of the thrones, he is wearing a white robe only; on the other, a red robe.

Fig. 53. To the left, a "picket column" in the festival hall of Thothmes III delimited by two bell-shaped pillars.
To the right, hieroglyph of the Sed festival pavillion.

The other image, more subtle, is architectural: the columns of Thothmes III's "festival hall" in this Sed-festival temple have the shape of the "cutout" delineated by columns with capitals in the form of full-blown papyrus plants. The symbol brings to mind the concretization of spirit or the "void" delimited by living and vegetating matter. These columns are in the image of the pickets in the Sed-festival pavilion.

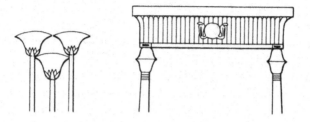

Fig. 54. Left, fragment of bas-relief, Karnak.
Right, upper section of a naos drawn on papyrus.

Like Osiris, the King must die in order to be renewed in a more perfect state. He must pass once again through the phases of the white crown and the red crown, for only the return of the concrete thing to the primordial state can offer it a heightening of the concretizing force.

The mystery of the Sed-festival, the celebrating of regeneration, entails the ceremony of rebirth: a return to the womb for a new gestation in order to be reborn in a higher state.

Symbolically, the King must pass through an animal skin, the *tikenu,* always associated with the mystery of Osirian renewal.

Alexandre Moret recalls scenes in Vedic ritual that are very similar to Sed-festival rites, and concerning which there exists explicit commentary:

> *The celebrant who offers the sacrifice is to be reborn to another existence.*
> He is to be divinzed by being made to die to earth and to be reborn in heaven.

"Then the *dîksâ* intervenes. The *dîksâ* is a set of preliminary ceremonies serving to deify the human creature. . . . A special structure is erected for the celebrant who is performing *dîksâ;* a black antelope skin is put on him: *the building is the womb, the black antelope skin is the chorion; the garment is the amnion; the belt is the umbilical cord: he who performs* dîksâ *is an embryo."*[11]

This ceremony is the "passion play" of Pharaonic Egypt, a symbol now taken for no more than a tale. The deeper sense of the ritual, which concerns every human being, is no longer understood.

The King, per *aâ,* the great House (of the *Neter*), or Pharaoh, is the living image of incarnation and of return to the source of the divine Word; it is an ever-present fact which the King's persona

---

[11]A. Moret, op. cit., p. 84.

makes tangible to the people. Such is the only true and great meaning of royalty as an idea.

Achieved through this symbol is the superimposition of several essential moments: a genesis of the Empire in which the symbol of the King evolves as the phases change; then the *principle* of a genesis where the King represents an epitome of the entire history, colored by what he symbolizes at his particular moment. Once again, this is the image of the large world where the becoming, where the genesis of a solar system contains each genesis of the beings that inhabit it, in the image of the All.

TABLE I
CHRONOLOGICAL TABLE OF THE PRINCIPAL PHILOSOPHICAL SCHOOLS

IONIAN SCHOOLS		ATHENIAN SCHOOLS				ATOMIST SCHOOL		ITALIC SCHOOLS			
School of Miletos		Philosophers		Various Schools				Eleatic School		Pythagorean School	
Thales	637-547	Solon	638-559					Xenophanes	fl.530	Pythagoras	fl. 540-510
Anaximander	611-546								620-520	Akmeon of Croton[1]	580-496
Anaximenes	598-528			*Sophists*				Parmenides	514-?	Hippasos[2]	500-?
Herakleitos	544-480			Protagoras	488-419	Leucippos	480-?	Zeno	490-?	Philolaus	460-400
Anaxagoras	500-428			Gorgias	487-380	Democritus	460	Melissos	460	Empedocles[3]	450-?
		Socrates	468-400					Empedocles	450-?	Archytas	400-?
		Plato	430-347	*Skeptics*							
		Aristotle	384-322	Pyrrho	384-?					*Neo-Pythagoreans*	
				Stoics		Epicuros	342-270			Apollonios of Tyana	1st c.
				Zeno	362-260					Nicomachos of Gerasa	1st c.
				Cleanthes	?-225					Theon of Smyrna	2nd c.
				Latin Philosophy		Lucretius	95-53				
				Cicero	106-?						
				Seneca	1st c.						
				Epictetus	1st c.						
				Marcus Aurelius	121-180						
					etc.						

NOTE: Most of the dates given here are still disputed and must therefore be considered as approximate.

[1] Alcmeon of Croton, disciple of Pythagoras, physician, and first Italic physiologist, would be the oldest witness of the Pythagorean School.

[2] Hippasos of Metaponte, a Pythagorean, was supposedly ousted from the School for having divulged certain teachings. He is sometimes also considered as being of the School of Ephesos.

[3] Empedocles cannot be classified as being either a Pythagorean or an Eleatic exclusively, having made a kind of philosophical synthesis of these two schools and of the Ionian School, to which he added a personal philosophy.

CHRONOLOGICAL RELATIONSHIPS

	ARCHEOLOGICAL CLASSIFICATION	EGYPTIAN SITES	DATES C 14	MESOPOTAMIA	APPROX. YEARS
PALEOLITHIC	Chellean	Arabian and Libyan deserts	B.C.		B.C. 100,000 50,000
	Acheulean Levalloisian	Arabian and Libyan deserts. Oases.			
	Mousterian	Rock shelters (elephants)	15,000 to 8,000		
	Aurignacian				
	Magdalenian	Rock shelters (ostrich, giraffes, gazelles)			
NEOLITHIC		Merimde-Beni-Salame Tasa			
		Fayum A[1]	4441 ± 180		
		Fayum A	4145 ± 250		
CHALCOLITHIC (Pre-Dynastic)	Badarian and Amratian Gerzean	Naqada I[2]	3794 ± 300	Al-Ubaid	5,000
		Naqada I	3669 ± 280	Susa I	to
		Naqada I[3]	3627 ± 300	Uruk	3,500
		Naqada II[2]	3070 ± 290	Jemdet-Nasr	to
		Naqada III	2770 ± 300	Susa II	2,800
First Dynasty	King Den	Sakkara (Hemaka)[4]	3367 ± 300 2923 ± 250	Byblos[5]	

NOTE: The chronological relations between Egypt and Mesopotamia are established by Scharf and Delaporte. See Massoulard, *Prehistoire et protohistoire d'Egypte.*
[1] Dated according to grains of corn and barley found in a well.
[2] Dated according to human hair found in a cemetery.
[3] Dated according to human skin originating from a tomb.
[4] Dated according to a splinter of wood originating from a roof beam of Hemaka's tomb.
[5] Dated from a piece of wood coming from the house of an ancient city and believed to be contemporaneous with Hemaka's wood.
In conclusion according to C 14, the Pre-Dynastic (Gerzean) would be contemporary with the Dynastic.

TABLE 3
CHRONOLOGICAL RELATIONSHIPS

EGYPT		C 14	Wilson Gregg Braidwood	Drioton	Meyer	Borchardt
		B.C.	B.C.	B.C.	B.C.	B.C.
First Dynasty	*King Den. Hemaka*	2923 ± 250	3150	3200	3315	4186
Second Dynasty	*Zoser*[1]	1830 ± 650	2750	3000	3105	3938
			2275	2778	2895	3642
Fourth Dynasty	*Snefru*[2]	2852 ± 210	2625	2723	2840	3432
Twelfth Dynasty	*Sesostris III*[3]	1671 ± 180	1800	1850	1850	

[1] The date given by Radiocarbon is less by about 1000 years to that adopted by the majority of chronologists. Three tests have given: 1749, 2041, and 2884. Average = 1830 + 650. Average = 1830 + 650 B.C.

[2] Four tests gave: 2236, 2771, 2867, 3598. Average = 2852 + 210 B.C.

[3] The exact date is known plus or minus four years, the date given by Radiocarbon misses the mark by 180 years.

It seems that the farther back one goes in time, the greater the inexactitude of C 14, and that as a general rule, the number marked + is to be added.

Appendix I

Excerpts From Greek Philosophers

1. Ionian Philosophy: The Schools of Miletos and Ephesos

Thales of Miletos	(c. 630-546 B.C.)
Anaximander of Miletos	(611-546)
Anaximenes of Miletos	(598-528)
Herakleitos of Ephesos	(544-480)
Anaxagoras of Clazomenae	(500-428)

Thales of Miletos is cited by both Diodoros of Sicily (I.96) and Clement of Alexandria *(Strom.)* as among those Greek philosophers and sages who received instruction in Egypt. One is inclined to believe, however, that Thales either learned very little from the Egyptian priests, or else transmits but a smattering of their teaching. For besides the theorem that bears his name, some merely fragmentary data of Egyptian origin, technical in nature, are attributed to him. These include:

—knowledge of the Pharaonic vague year of 365 days, but not of the Sirian year of 365¼ days.

—knowledge of the nonuniformity of the sun's annual circuit and the determination of the equinoxes and solstices;

—several dates of star risings relative to a much more southern climate than that of Miletos, hence obviously borrowed from the Egyptian star guides;

—prediction of a total eclipse of the sun in 610 B.C. which made him famous although he was not considered capable of explaining it. Given that no Greek contemporary had sufficient knowledge of astronomy for calculating eclipses in advance and that tradition places Thales in contact with Egyptian priests, one is compelled to admit that he must have derived from the latter his rudimentary knowledge of astronomy. The prediction of eclipses, which was common in Chaldea at that time, presupposes knowledge of luni-solar cycles. This knowledge was not introduced into Greece until about 400 B.C. by *Eudoxos of Cnidos* who was also instructed in Egypt; he apparently acquired a much more complete knowledge of astronomy in that country.

As for *Ionian philosophy*, no direct document survived; what was later stated very much resembled all the incoherent writings about the Hermetic art. It seems that these Ionian philosophers, having certain notions about this science either through tradition or through actual knowledge, gave oral instruction and were no better understood than were the master Hermetists of our West understood by a rational science.

We will discuss this no further here for lack of serious grounds; in basing ourselves on Theophrastos, the most trustworthy of doxographers, it is easy to come to a somewhat ridiculous conclusion. In his own words:

> Of all those who admit to a single moving principle, and whom Aristotle properly calls physicists, some consider it as limited: thus *Thales*, son of Examyes, a man of Miletos, and Hippon, *said that water is the underlying principle of all things.*
>
> *Anaximander*, son of Praxiades of Miletos, who was the disciple and successor of Thales, *said that the Indefinite is the principle* and the element of existing things; it was he, moreover, who was the first to introduce this term of "principles."
>
> *Anaximenes*, son of Eurystratos of Miletos, a companion of Anaximander, like his master maintains that the substratum is one and infinite, but instead of leaving it undefined, as does Anaximander, *he defines it in identifying it as air.*
>
> *Hippasos of Metapontion* and *Herakleitos of Ephesos* also said there is a single principle, moving and limited, but they took this to be *Fire,* whence they say all things emerge or return through condensation and rarefication; *thus fire would be the only underlying principle....*
>
> Theophrastos, Simplicios in *Physics, 6a and 6b.*[1]

Thus Thales poses *Water,* Anaximander the *Indefinite,* Anaximenes *Air,* and Herakleitos *Fire,* as the principle of all things. Here we have an ensemble, Chaos and the four elements, but what is to be made of it?

---

[1] P. Tannery, *Mémoires pour servir à l'histoire de la science hellène* (Paris, 1930), 2nd ed., pp. 79, 118, 169, 195.

Of those who say that the principles are infinite in number, some suppose them to be simple and homogeneous; the others, composed, heterogeneous, contrary, and characterized by what predominates. *Anaxagoras*, son of Hegesiboulos, of Clazomenae, after having followed the philosophy of Anaximenes, was the first to reform opinion regarding the principles and to complete them by the cause which was lacking. On one hand, he posited an infinity of material principles: Indeed, all the homoeomeries (e.g., water, fire, or gold) are nonengendered and imperishable; they seem to come into being and perish as a natural consequence of simple compositions and decompositions, a portion of everything in everything, and each characterized by what predominates in it. Thus whatever seems like gold would contain gold to a large extent, but all the other principles would also coexist therein.

Theophrastos, fr. 4, Simplicios in *Physics*, 6b[2]

Among the principles enunciated by his predecessors—*Water, the Infinite, Air,* and *Fire*—only *Earth* was lacking in order to complete the series of four elements, but here we find it attributed to Anaxagoras:

Anaxagoras of Clazomenae, who through succession belonged to the school of Thales, *added earth as a second element to water*, in order that the union of dry and humid produce by temperament the concordance of opposed natures. The origin of this opinion also goes back to Homer, who provided Anaxagoras with the seed of his idea. . . .

Herakleitos, *Allégories homériques*, 22.[3]

One receives the impression of a very serious teaching related by uncomprehending commentators.

2. Xenophanes of Colophon

Theophrastos says that *Xenophanes of Colophon*, the teacher of Parmenides, *supposed that the first principle was one, or considered all being as one,* neither finite nor infinite, neither in motion nor at rest. Theophrastos agrees that the mention of this opinion belongs rather to another inquiry than that into nature, because, according to Xenophanes, this universal one is God.

He shows that he is one because he is the most powerful of all; because if there were several beings, says he, it would be necessary for the puissance to be equally divided among them; but God is what is the

[2]Ibid., p. 305
[3]Ibid., p. 308.

most excellent and, in his power, he is superior to all. He is unbegotten because what is born must be born either from like or from unlike; but like, he says, cannot play this role in relation to like, for there is no more reason for one rather than the other to be engendered or to engender. On the other hand, if Being were born of the unlike, it would be born of that which is not. Thus does he prove nongeneration and eternity.

The One is neither infinite nor limited because on the one hand, infinity is non-Being, since it has neither beginning nor middle nor end; yet on the other hand, it is the objects in plurality which limit themselves reciprocally.

He likewise does away with movement and rest: for the unmoving is non-Being, which never becomes anything else and which nothing else ever becomes. Movement, to the contrary, pertains to plurality, for then there is a changing of one into the other. And when he says that *Being remains always in the same state, moving not at all,* it must be understood that he does not mean rest as opposed to movement, but that stable state which knows neither movement nor rest.

Nicolas of Damascus, in his treatise *On the Gods,* mentions him as having asserted that the first principle is infinite and immobile. According to Alexander, he said that it was *finite and spherical in form.* But it has been clearly seen how he proves noninfinity and nonlimitation; *limitation and the spherical form are indicated when he says that Being is alike* on all sides: again, when he says that *it sees all over, thinks all over, and hears all over* (Theophrastos, fr. 5, Simplicios in *Physics,* 5b; Diels, 50, 13-26).[3]

3. Fragments of Parmenides

Toward Truth

Come now, I will tell thee—and harken to my words—the only two ways of quest that are open to the intelligence. The first, that Being is and that non-Being is not, is the way of certitude, for truth is its companion. The other, that Being is not and that non-Being must needs be—that, I tell thee, is a path which must never seduce thee.

For you can never come to know that which is not; you can neither

[3]See P. Tannery, op. cit., p. 144, tr. after Burnet.

grasp it nor utter it, for that which it is possible to think is identical with that which can *be.* . . .

It is necessary to think and to say that Being is; for there is Being and there is no non-Being; behold what I bid thee to proclaim. I hold thee back from this way of inquiry upon which mortals knowing naught wander astray; perplexity leads their wandering minds therein so that they are borne along like men deaf and blind, stupid and uncritical. They believe that Being and non-Being are the same and not the same; and their path always leads them back to the same point of departure. . . .

For you will never prove that that-which-is-not exists; therefore restrain thy thought from this route of inquiry; let not habit force thee to cast thy wandering eye, resounding ear, or thy tongue upon this beaten path; judge by the reasoning of the irrefutable condemnation which I herewith pronounce.

One way only is left to be spoken of: that Being is; on this path are numerous signs that what-is is ungenerated and imperishable, universal, unique, unmoving, and without end. Nor was it ever, nor shall it be; it *is,* now, all of it, at once, one, continuous. For what kind of origin would you seek for it? Whence and in what way could it have been derived? Out of that which is not? I will not allow thee to say it or think it, for it is neither sayable nor thinkable that Being does not exist. What necessity could have impelled it to arise later, rather than earlier? Therefore it must either altogether be or be not at all. Nor will the force of reason permit that out of what-is-not, something should come to be born. Wherefore Justice never loosens her fetters and permits anything to come into being or to perish, but holds it fast.

Judgment thereupon depends on this: It is or it is not; but it has been decided that we are to set aside the one way as unthinkable and nameless, devoid of truth, and take the other path, that Being is real. But how, then, can that-which-is come to be in the future? How could it come into being? If it came into being, it *is* not, and no more so if it is going to be at some future time. *Thus is coming-into-being extinguished and death unheard of.* Nor is it divisible, since it is all alike; no more of it is in one place than in another, to hinder it from cleaving together continuously, nor less of it; *everything is full of Being, hence eveything is continuous, and what-is clings to what-is.* But it is unmoving within the bonds of mighty fetters, without beginning and without end, since genesis and perishing have been driven afar, banished by the certitude of truth. It remains the same, abiding in the same state and subsisting by itself; thus it remains unvaryingly; for powerful necessity keeps it fettered and restrained in the bonds of its limits. Wherefore it is not permitted to what is *to be unlimited;* for it is in need of nothing and were it otherwise, it would stand in need of everything. . . .

Look in thy mind's eye at things afar as if they were at hand. That which is cannot be separated from that-which-is; it is not scattered throughout the world, nor does it come together. . . .

It is the same thing that can be thought and for the sake of which the thought exists; for you will not find thought without what-is, in relation to which it is uttered; there is not, and never shall be, anything else besides what-is; fate has chained it so as to be *universal and unmoving;* its name is All[that it is]; wherefore all these things are but names which mortals have given, believing them to be true—coming into being and passing away, Being and non-Being, change of place and alteration of color.

But, *since it is perfect* within an extreme limit, it resembles *the mass of a well-rounded sphere,* equally distant from its center in all directions. For it cannot be greater or smaller in one place than in another; for there is no non-Being that can hinder it from reaching out equally; nor is there anything that can be more here and less there than what-is, since it is an inviolate whole, without exception.

Thus, equal on all sides, *it is uniformly contained within limits. Here I end my trustworthy discourse and thought concerning truth.*[4]

4. Life of Pythagoras[5]

Three biographies of Pythagoras are extant:

1. The oldest constitutes part of the famous work by *Diogenes Laertios* (second century A.D.), in which the author cites witnesses justifying the facts he relates: for example, Xenophanes, a contemporary of Pythagoras, then Herakleitos, Aristotle, Aristoxenos, and Dicaearchos.

2. *Apollonios of Tyana,* the neo-Pythagorian of the first century A.D. Fascinated by the marvelous, he intersperses many neo-Platonic ideas with Pythagorean philosophy. His *Life of Pythagoras,* of which Porphyry and Iamblichos availed themselves, is replete with

[4]See Paul Tannery, op. cit., and John Burnet, et al.
[5]Summary after A. Ed. Chaignet, op. cit., pp. 23-94.

unbelievable stories which place one on guard against his assertions and oblige the modern critic carefully to discern which parts of his narration can be considered as reliable.

3. *Porphyry* (233-303), a student of Longinus in Athens, of Plotinos in Rome, is the author of a *Life of Pythagoras*. He bases himself on Aristoxenos and Dicaearchos, in addition to Nicomachos of Gerasa, Moderatos of Gades, and Apollonios of Tyana, the last three being too late to produce direct evidence either on the life or on the philosophy of the ancient school.

After eliminating the phantasmagoria, the essential facts which emerge from these biographies are the following:

Pythagoras was a native of Samos, the son of Mamarchos (or Mnesarchos), an engraver of signet rings or a wealthy merchant, or perhaps both.

The birth date of Pythagoras is disputed: 608, according to Fréret, 580-576 according to Chaignet, and the duration of his life could have been 80 or 90 years according to most of the authors, or 99, 100, 104, or even 117 years, according to others.

One of Pythagoras' childhood teachers was *Hermodamas* (or Leodamas), son of Creophyle of Samos, leader or mythical ancestor of a brotherhood of rhapsodists and Homeridae which probably included Homer himself. Pythagoras must have attended the discourses of Pherecydes (a contemporary of Thales), who is said to have held forth on the immortality and the transmigration of souls. Subsequently, he was apparently a student of Anaximander in Miletos, and later of Epimenides in Crete, where he is said to have been initiated into the mysteries of the Dactyls and where he supposedly descended into Jupiter's sanctum. He is also said to have gone to Sparta in order to familiarize himself with the institutions of Lycurgos in Delos, Syros, and Lesbos. Very likely he was initiated into the Orphic and other mysteries. In short, there is not a single celebrated philosopher of his time with whom he was not in contact, not one initiation into the mysteries of the principal sanctuaries that is not accorded him.

Cicero and *Valerius* show Pythagoras in Egypt and in Persia, *Strabo* and *Justinian* in Egypt and in Babylon, *Diogenes* and *Porphyry* in Egypt, in Chaldea, and in Persia, as does *Clement of Alexandria*. Isocrates maintains that Pythagoras became a disciple of Egyptian priests and from them brought back all the philosophy he taught the Greeks. Diodoros of Sicily (I.98) affirms that the Egyptian priests relate that Orpheus, Musaeus, Homer, Lycurgos, Solon, and others came to be instructed by them, as well as Pythagoras, Plato, Eudoxos, Democritos, and Oenopides of Chios. . . . They reflect the influences of their sojourn and affirm that all those men must have borrowed their doctrines and their sciences from the Egyptian temples. . . .

Plutarch likewise traces all the Pythagorean symbols back to an Egyptian origin and with Diodoros repeats that all the Greek sages—Solon, Thales, Lycurgos, Pythagoras, and Eudoxos—had visited Egypt and been in contact with the priests (*Isis and Osiris,* 10). Plutarch even mentions the name of the priest in Heliopolis, Oenuphis, who probably instructed Pythagoras, as well as that of his master in Persia, Zaratas.

According to *Porphyry,* Polycrates, tyrant of Samos, gave Pythagoras a letter of introduction to King Amasis (a fact confirmed by Diogenes Laertios, VIII.3). Iamblichos adds that Pythagoras probably remained in Memphis and Thebes for twenty-two years, but received instruction from the priests only after having patiently submitted to a long period of examination. Finally, made a prisoner by Cambyses, Pythagoras supposedly spent twelve years in Babylon, where he doubtless became familiar with the Magian religion, returning to Samos at the age of fifty-five. It is there that he would have founded his first school, the Hemicycle, and led a secluded and meditative life with his disciples.

We do not know the precise reasons for Pythagoras' exodus to Croton, almost contemporaneous with that of Xenophanes' to Elea.

If one may question such assertions as that of Apollonios, who adds that Pythagoras would have understood the Druids in Gaul and the Brahmans in India, there remains one certain fact on which all the authors agree, namely, the voyage to Egypt besides the very probable one to Babylonia. Thus (according to Porphyry and Iamblichos, it was in Egypt that Pythagoras learned to master *geometry* and *astronomy,* while the Phoenecians and the Chaldeans taught him *astrology, astronomy, the science of numbers,* and the Magi taught him the magistery of the cult and its observances.

When Pythagoras arrived in Croton, that city was already flourishing. Inhabited chiefly by Achaeans originating from the Peloponnesos who had come to colonize the savage populations of southern Italy, this city was governed by the Senate of One Thousand.

The role played by Pythagoras in Croton is uncertain. The biographies tell us that his discourse enraptured the crowds. The Senate, which was immediately won over by him, even invited him to address the youth whom he steered toward moderation, turning them away from their ruinous pleasures. " '*He doesn't teach,'* they said, *'he cures souls.'* Pythagoras taught that the entire world exists only through harmony, and is nothing but harmony. God himself, the primary One, constitutes supreme harmony, harmony of unity and of plurality, of dissonances, differences, and complements. Order is the essence of all things; hence, it is the essence of the State. A city where there is no order represents nothing but shapeless social chaos, a blind vortex swept away by violence...."

The application of these theories to politics necessarily clashed with the intense concept of democratic liberty in passionate public debates which frequently degenerated into violent disturbances and stained the free cities with blood.

But the people of Croton, intoxicated and exalted by the attitudes toward order and harmony preached by Pythagoras, finally agreed to accept a government increasingly conducive to the aristocracy. Personal sentiments, restrained for a period of almost forty years, suddenly started to recover their authority and the reaction began.

Cyron, who had been denied entry into the Order because of his stormy, undisciplined, and imperious character, became the implacable enemy of the Pythagoreans. He stirred up the people, reminding them that he had been deprived by Pythagoras of the right to judge and to decide. The words of Homer who represents the Prince as a shepherd of his people, comparing the latter to lowly flocks, were taken as an image of the situation. Persuaded by Cyron's inflammatory speech, and faced with the injustice done him, the democratic party deemed that the Pythagoreans were not even entitled to a trial. It was thus they set fire to the house where forty members of the brotherhood had gathered to deliberate. Two disciples (Archippes and Lysis) are mentioned as having managed to escape from the Croton fire and taking refuge in Tarentum and at Thebes in Greece. Other members of the Order (which numbered in the hundreds) were exiled to Greece where they disseminated the Master's doctrine.

As for Pythagoras himself, the most probable version is that he took refuge in Metapontion, where Cicero visited the house in which he died, sometime between the years 500-496 B.C.

"Man and the State ought to be what the world itself actually is, a harmony, a visible reflection of supreme harmony...."[6] Notwithstanding this magnificent ideal which prompted the Pythagoreans, the revolt in Croton was the consequence of Pythagoras' failure to heed the precept forbidding every disciple of sacred science to establish a school and to engage in politics.

[6] A. Ed. Chaignet, op. cit., I. pp. 97-98.

The Pythagorean and the Orphic doctrines have often been equated, their resemblance in certain respects being such that it is difficult to distinguish between them. But isn't there only one single gnosis? One single truth?

There is every reason to believe that Pythagoras attempted to devise a doctrine based on a philosophy of truth, divested of vain superstition and free of the humanization of the Greek myth, and that he went to the fountainhead for the bases of his teaching. From the little we know of his philosophy, it is not at all surprising to find it shares a common origin with Orphic and other mysteries. Is it not known that *Orpheus* and *Pythagoras* went to Egypt? Doesn't the former, a mythical personage, symbolize the entirety of a doctrine of harmony?

If, on the other hand, as Archytas lets us infer, Pythagoras had the dream of a State directed by a perfect, just, and moderate prince, but had recognized that this form of government was incompatible with the Greek character, it is probable that Pythagoras attempted to establish a *theocratic government* conducted by a Pythagorean Order. This Order would be composed of incorruptible and carefully selected men who, even while remaining outside of it, were capable of realizing a State thus reflecting its ideal of harmony. In this attempt, Pythagoras was very likely inspired by the social organization that he had had occasion to observe in Egypt.

In order to complete these notes, let us cite the only personages whom tradition puts into direct relation, either with Pythagoras himself or with his disciples.[7]

According to legend, *Hippasos of Metapontion,* probably a direct disciple, was excluded from the school during the Master's lifetime for having revealed the doctrine of the irrational (i.e., that some geometrical quantities cannot be expressed in terms of whole numbers) and for having publicly boasted that he had added the dodecahedron to the number of regular solids enumerated by Pythagoras. These two instances are intimately linked. It was to punish him for having divulged the notion of irrational numbers that the gods must have caused him to perish in a shipwreck. But prior to that incident, it is likely that he had also become politically involved, siding against the Pythagoreans, and by distorting the import, had no doubt revealed symbolism reserved for the initiated. He became the leader of a sect known under the name of *Acousmatic* in which the

[7]After P. Tannery, op. cit., pp. 206 et seq.

Mathematicians, the true heirs of the Pythagorean science, acknowledged only an imperfect understanding of their doctrine.

Alcmeon of Croton is the oldest witness mentioned as a disciple of
Pythagoras, but he seems to have been particularly concerned with
medicine and his "opinions" on this subject are known only through
very late anthologists.

Parmenides, of the Eleatic school, at times seems to have
borrowed some ideas from Pythagorean theories in the realm of
"physics" but without citing his sources.

Neither can *Empedokles* be considered for his opinion
concerning the Pythagorean doctrine, since according to Theophrastos himself, the theories of the Agrigentin are connected with
Parmenides of Elea and the Pythagoreans. With him, moreover, we
again encounter the notion of the elements of Ionian philosophy, but
with the addition of two principles, Love and Strife, which modern
critics translate as "attraction and repulsion":

> *Empedokles of Agrigentum:* He posits the four material elements, fire, air,
> water, and earth, as eternal, while admitting that the combination and
> separation thereof causes the quantity to vary more or less; also to impart
> motion to these, he has two principles, properly so called: Love and Strife; for
> the elements are subject to an alternate movement, combination through Love,
> separation through Strife; thus, according to him, there are six principles, for in
> one passage he attributes to Love and Strife an efficient power, in another he
> ranks them with the four elements.
>
> Theophrastos, fr. 3, Simplicios in *Physics*, 25, 14; Diels, 204[8]

5. Citations of Zeno of Elea

Aristotle quotes and comments several times upon Zeno of Elea,
in order to contradict not his doctrine but rather his form. He
reproaches him, for example, for not having more precisely defined
the meaning he accords to the term *"One"* and to the term *"being."*
Hence he does not criticize Zeno's arguments "except those
concerning motion which had acquired great renown as paradoxes and
concerning which misunderstanding is so easy."[9]

The most precise texts are those due to *Simplicios* in his
compilation of books on physics, in which he bases himself on
Eudemos and *Alexander of Aphrodisias, disciples of Aristotle.*

The most famous arguments are meant to contradict the so-called

[8]See P. Tannery, op. cit., pp. 330-331.
[9]Ibid., p. 260.

naturalist Ionian philosophy because it bases itself on physical facts and on Pythagorean philosophy which asserts, on the one hand, divine Unity, and on the other, plurality and complementaries.

Hence Zeno's arguments are directed *against plurality* and *against motion*.

Alexander of Aphrodisias thus defines Zeno's position:

> Plurality is a sum of units, thus it is necessary to know what unity would be in existing things; according to the adversary, it is the point; but the point is nothing; hence there is no plurality.

"Zeno thus denies that unity is a point which is nothing. Unity, for him, as for Parmenides, is the totality of things; the divisions introduced therein do not take away its real continuity nor its character of unity; this character must not be ascribed to a supposed indivisible element of the bodies."[10]

Arguments Against Plurality[11]

A. In his writing, which includes several *epichiremata* (syllogisms), Zeno shows with each one of them that he who affirms plurality will come to affirm contradictories.

In one of these syllogisms he shows, for example, that if there is plurality, things will be both large and small, so large as to be of infinite size, and so small as to have no size at all. For this, he shows that that which has neither size nor thickness nor volume, is nothing.

If, indeed, he says, it were added to another thing, it would not make the latter any larger at all; for nothing can become larger by the addition of anything without magnitude; and thus the augmentation will be null. Then, to the contrary, deduct, and the other thing will be no smaller, just as it did not increase by addition; therefore, augmentation and diminution are null.

Zeno speaks thus without denying unity, *but he denies the size of any one element of infinite plurality,* for below any size considered, there will always be another *because of division ad infinitum;* having proved this, he shows that the size is null, because each element of plurality is one and identical to itself. . . .

Simplicios in *Physics,* 30a, Diels, 174, Fr. 2.

B. After having demonstrated that "if what is had no size, it would not even be," Zeno adds;

[10]Ibid., p. 261.
[11]Ibid., pp. 262-265.

If it is, each thing must have a certain size and a certain thickness, and each part of it must be at a certain distance from each other part.

The same may be said of what surpasses it (of the part of this thing that surpasses it in smallness, in the dichotomous division). The latter will also have a certain magnitude and will itself be surpassed in smallness by another.

What is said here one time can be repeated indefinitely, for no such part of it will be the last, nor will any one part ever be unrelated to another. *Thus, if plurality exists, things must be both small and large; so small as to have no size at all, so large as to be infinite.*

Diels, 174, fr. 1.

C. *If plurality exists,* things must be just as many as they are, and neither more nor less. And if they are just as many as they are, *they will be finite.* But *if there is plurality, things will be infinite,* because there will always be other things between the units, and yet others between those others. And thus the things that are are infinite.

Diels, 175, fr. 3.

The Four Arguments Against Motion

Zeno's arguments (*logoi*) regarding motion, which cause such difficulty to those who try to solve them, are four in number: the first asserts that there is no motion because a moving body must first reach the halfway stage before it reaches its goal. The second, known as the Achilles argument, amounts to this, that the fastest runner will never overtake the slowest, because the pursuer must first reach the point whence the pursued started out, so that the slower runner will always remain in front.

Third is that the arrow in flight is at rest. This results from the assumption that time is composed of moments. Without this premise, the conclusion will not follow.

Aristotle, *Physics,* VI, 9.

I. Plurality in the continuum is infinitely divisible.

1. *Dichotomy.* You cannot reach the end of the stadium. You cannot traverse an infinite number of points in a finite time. Before you reach the far end you must first reach the halfway point; before you reach the halfway point you must reach the point halfway to it; and so on *ad infinitum;* so that there are an infinite number of points in any given space, and you cannot reach an infinite number of them one after another in a finite timespan.

Aristotle, *Physics,* VI, 9, 239b 11.

2. *Achilles*. Achilles can never overtake the tortoise. He must first reach the place from which the tortoise started out. During that time, the tortoise will have moved on to another place. By the time Achilles reaches that second place, it will have moved on again. He will steadily come closer to the tortoise but will never overtake it.

Aristotle, *Physics*, VI, 9, 239b 14.

II. Plurality in the continuum means that the latter has a finite number of parts which therefore are indivisible.

3. *The Arrow*. The flying arrow is at rest. For if each thing that occupies a space equal to itself is at rest, and what flies occupies always and at any given moment a space equal to itself, it cannot move.

Aristotle, *Physics*, VI, 9, 239 b 30 and 25.

4. *The Stadium*. The fourth argument concerns rows of bodies (material points, the indivisible, the limited), each row being composed of an equal number of bodies of equal size passing each other in a stadium, parallel to each other, proceeding with equal velocity in opposite directions, one row coming from the extreme end of the stadium and the other from the middle point. From this, Zeno thinks he can conclude that half a given time is equal to double that time. This is a paralogism in that he postulates that a body occupies an equal time in passing with equal speed a body that is in motion and a body of equal size that is at rest.

Aristotle, *Physics*, VI, 9, 239b-240a.[12]

The Argument Against Space

Another essential argument of Zeno's exposé concerns space. He attempts to demonstrate that space, like time, inasmuch as a composite, is no more real than plurality itself:

> If space is something, it must be in something, and what is in something is in space. Thus space too will be in space, and so on *ad infinitum;* that is why *there is no space.*

Aristotle, *Physics*, A I, 209a and 210b.

As to the argument concerning the flying arrow, which is only possible, as Aristotle says, if one accepts the premise that time is a sum of instants, it would be valid for an arrow in an absolutely empty universe, or within relativity, for an arrow in relation to itself. But Zeno says that there is no multiplicity!

[12]Abel Rey, *La jeunesse de la science grecque* (Paris, 1933), pp. 167-169.

Appendix II

Excerpts from Laplace and Berthelot

I. Laplace (1749-1827)

When Laplace presented Napoleon with a copy of his *Exposition du système du monde (Exposition of the World System)*, the Emperor, who was fond of posing embarrassing questions, received it with the remark:

"Monsieur Laplace, they tell me you have written this large book on the system of the universe, and have never even once mentioned its Creator."

Laplace answered bluntly:

"I had no need of such an hypothesis."

Napoleon, greatly amused, told this reply to Lagrange, who exclaimed:

"Ah! That's a beautiful hypothesis; it explains a great many things."

Since the publication of his discoveries on the world system and on light, the great geometer [Newton], given to speculations of another kind, sought to find through what motives the author of Nature gave to the solar system the constitution of which we have spoken. After having exposed, in the scholium at the end of the book of *Principles,* the peculiar phenomenon of the movement of planets and satellites in the same direction, almost in the same plane and in almost circular orbits, he adds: *"All these very regular movements have no mechanical cause, since the comets move in all parts of the sky and in very eccentric orbits.... This admirable arrangement of the sun, the planets, and the comets could only be the work of an intelligent and all-*

powerful being." At the end of his *Optics,* he again presents the same thought in which he would be even more confirmed if he had known what we have demonstrated, that is, that the conditions of the arrangement of the planets and the satellites are precisely those which assure stability. *"A blind destiny,"* he says, *"could never make the planets to move in this manner, save for some hardly noticeable irregularities that could stem from the action of planets and comets upon one another, irregularities which will probably increase after a long period of time, until at last this system need be ordered anew by its author."*

Leibniz, in his quarrel with Newton concerning the invention of Infinitesimal Calculus, strongly criticized the intervention of the divinity in order to put the solar system in order. *"It is,"* he says, *"to hold very narrow ideas concerning the wisdom and power of God."* Newton replied with an equally heated criticism of Leibniz's preestablished Harmony which he qualified as a perpetual miracle. Posterity has not accepted these vain hypotheses, but it has rendered complete justice to the mathematical works of these two great geniuses. . . .

(Excerpts from Laplace, *Exposition du système du monde,* Book V, chap. VI.)

2. Berthelot (1827-1907)

Today's world is devoid of mysteries: the rational approach claims to elucidate and understand everything; it endeavors to give everything a positive and logical explanation, and extends its fatal determinism even into the moral sphere. I do not know whether the imperative deductions of scientific rationality will one day clearly grasp this divine prescience which once stirred up so much discussion and which one never succeeded in reconciling with the no less imperative consciousness of human liberty. At all events the entire material universe is claimed by science and no one openly dares to oppose this claim. The concept of the miracle and of the supernatural has vanished like a shadowy mirage, an antiquated prejudice.

This has not always been so: This purely rational conception appeared only with the Greeks; it was brought into general knowledge only among European peoples, and only since the eighteenth century. Even in our time, many enlightened minds are still involved in the grip of spiritism and animal magnetism.

At the dawn of civilization, all knowledge appropriated a religious and mystical form. Every action was attributed to the gods, identified with the stars, with the great celestial and terrestrial phenomena, with all the natural forces. Hence no one dared to pursue a political, military, medical, or industrial undertaking without recourse to the sacred formulas intended to conciliate the good will of the mysterious powers which governed the universe. Deliberate and rational proceedings came only later, always strictly subordinated.

However, those who were accomplishing the work itself were not slow to notice that the latter came about chiefly through the efficient employment of reason and of human activity. In turn reason introduced surreptitiously, so to speak, its precise rules for the practical execution of the procedures involved, while awaiting the day when it would succeed in dominating everything. Thenceforth a new period, half rational and half mystical, which preceded the birth of pure science. Later on came the flourishing of the intermediary sciences, if one may speak of them as such: astrology, alchemy, the ancient medicine involving the virtues of stones and talismans, sciences which today strike us as chimerical and quackish. Their appearance, however, marked a tremendous progress at a certain point, marking an era in the history of the human mind. They constituted a necessary transition, from the ancient state of minds engaged in magic and in theurgic practices to the contemporary, absolutely positive spirit which, even in our own day, seems too rigorous for many of our contemporaries.

The evolution which took place in this respect, from the Orientals to the Greeks and to us, was not uniform and parallel in all orders. If pure science rapidly came to the fore in mathematics, its reign was more delayed in astronomy, where astrology subsisted parallelly down to modern times. Above all, progress has been slower in chemistry, where alchemy, a mixed science, preserved its marvelous hopes down to the end of the last century.

The study of these equivocal sciences, intermediaries between the positive knowledge of things and their mystic interpretation, presents a matter of great importance for the philosopher. It equally interests those scholars desirous of understanding the origin and the connection between ideas and words they continually employ.

(Excerpts from Berthelot, *Les origines de l'alchimie*, Paris, 1885.)

Appendix III

From the Infinite to the Transfinite

The infinite *largeness* of the universe, or the infinite *smallness*, the constant exceeding of all totals of largeness or of the smallest subdivisions our brain can grasp—these are questions that disturb layman and scientist alike.

Neither does the infinite of time, calculated in geological periods, find beginning or end for human intelligence.

To these two infinites of space and time, mathematicians add another:

Here we have a third kind of infinite, and it introduces the subject of our study. It is qualified by an attribution that could be found surprising: the *limited* infinite, the least intuitive of the three, a logical infinite, occasion for many a paradox, the most renowned of which becomes for us the essential argument of the transfinite doctrine. Is it surprising that the limit of an infinite deserves the name and plays the role of a *transfinite,* in other words, *beyond the infinite?* Let us recall the specious reasoning of Zeno of Elea.

(The story of Achilles and the tortoise, which ended with the conclusion that "the infinite succession of all integers, inconceivable for the mind, is without doubt equally unrealizable in nature.")

Does modern physics lead us away from this conception of an incompatibility between the infinite and Nature? On the contrary, it brings us back to it. The question today among a number of the most prominent theoretical physicists is whether movement may not be effected by a discontinous succession of discrete positions. The impression of continuity is said to be an illusion which our eyes lack the perspicacity to dispel by means of observation. Moreover, relativity leads astronomers and physicists to think of the *universe as finite. Continuity as well as the infinite would be fictions created by our minds and refuted by reality.*

(Example of Laplace.)

It would be a curious enterprise for an atheist to collect and then submit to deduction and analysis, all expressions, all aspects humanly conceivable which it would be necessary to attribute to God as soon as his existence is established in principle.

Nature offers the spectacle of astronomical immensity populated, though with uneven frequency, by molecules of unimaginably minute dimensions. Our philosopher therefore would note that the enumeration designated by the universe has recourse to integers whose largeness confounds us. And yet this Nature seems finite in the gigantic as well as in exiguity. Thus his conclusions would be:

The spirit of God unfolds in the innumerable, yet never escapes from the finite.

In vain does human imagination attempt to storm the innumerable. It soon exhausts itself. To escape this challenge, it has created the infinite and continuity.

The modes by which the work of God has been accomplished are the discontinuous and the finite. Continuum and infinite are the refuge of our intelligence which is incapable of scrutinizing the subtleties of Nature and to conceive the numberless accumulation of elementary objects....

(Development of the transfinite which brings the mind to rest.)

But the transfinite has raised problems before which the logic formerly used by mathematicians has proved powerless.

Whatever the increasing succession of transfinite numbers, characterized in one way or another, it is always possible (at least admittedly, though wrongly so) to conceive a transfinite number immediately following all others. The set of transfinite numbers would therefore be such that this set would itself remain as it was when a foreign element is added to it. It is not surprising that such a conception should have resulted in inextricable logical difficulties.... Since the lengthy discussions pursued for a century and a half concerning infinitely small quantities, never had mathematical logic weathered a crisis comparable to the one which the transfinite put it through.

This irresolution, this disarray of reasoning in the science considered to be the surest of disciplines because of its essentially purely deductive character, shows us in the quick the fragility of our strongest certitudes. Or rather the relativity of our logic, the impossibility of affirming that any demonstration controlled and validated by this logic will be free of error, and of grave error at that; this ineluctable and organic failing of our most rigorous thinking can motivate a prejudicial suspicion that extends to all our knowledge.

With its purely human origin, this infinite is the stumbling block of reason, though the latter had counted on finding it a convenient and submissive servant. Irrational numbers, commonly known as "incommensurables," that is to say the continuum obtained by applying to rational numbers (fractions) the idea of an infinite sequence of alterations of diminishingly perceptible amplitude; the infinitely small quantities introduced with differential and integral calculus by Leibniz and Newton; infinite convergent series; and more recently the transfinite—these diverse forms, under which the infinite has repeatedly made different incursions into mathematics, have all left the logic of their time in a state of toal disarray, this same logic which the geometers in their day held to be an infallible mechanism for the production of unerring truths.

And every time, mostly by a process of blind groping, logic has been obliged to search laboriously and painfully for the complementary rules that were lacking. Not by splendid *a priori* views, but at the school of failures and successes analyzed one and the other as to their causes, has logic modestly and humbly learned the rules of correct reasoning in this order of questions which were so new for it.

In mathematics as elsewhere, rationality is periodically invigorated by plunging into the empirical in order to acquire the strength it cannot muster itself.

Even within those mathematical disciplines which seem to be its sanctuary of certitude, science no longer appears to us as the immovable structure built on rock and of materials that defy eternity, an edifice constantly amplified by new yet always definitive strata and appendages. Science is a vessel on the high seas. The wave that carries it is not petrified. It undulates and propagates itself, yielding its place to the wave that follows. But, and this is essential, the ship floats and progresses in the desired direction, rejecting in its wake the waste of obsolete or counterfeit knowledge while taking on new acquisitions. And we renounce the ingenious and frivolous dream of ever reaching the shores of one sole original causality.

Fallen from the pedestal upon which we thought ourselves to

have raised it above the universe, science now integrates itself in this universe in order to espouse its aspects of instability and perpetual evolution. Its ossified armature is its most sterile part. Its most perishable elements are perhaps the most fertile. Every day, science finds itself betrayed by the principles that had seemed to be the most secure, and it is obliged to ask the sovereign oracle of Sibylline nature for the revelation of new guides in which it can place its trust. Science seeks its light in the darkness looming before it and no longer in the clarity it has outgrown.

Arnaud Denjoy,
Professor of the Sorbonne,
Member of the Academy of Sciences
(Excerpts from: *L'Innéité du Transfini* in F. Le Lionnais,
Les grands courants de la pensée mathématique (Paris,
1958), pp. 188-195.)

Appendix IV

Clement of Alexandria and Egypt

1

> *In short, by the word Philosophy, I do not mean the Stoic, Platonic, Epicurean, or Aristotelian doctrine, but whatever has been well said by each of these sects, which teach righteousness and justice, along with a science pervaded by piety.... Truth is one, falsehood has a thousand bypaths. Just as the Bacchantes tore asunder the limbs of Pentheus and scattered them, so the sects both of barbarian and Hellenic philosophy have done with truth, and each vaunts as the whole truth the portion which has fallen to its lot.... They have torn off a fragment of the eternal truth, not from the mythology of Bacchus but from the theology of the ever-living Word. And he who brings together the separate fragments and makes them one, will without peril of error, be assured, contemplate the perfect Word, the Truth.*
>
> *Stromata*, Book I, chap. VII, 37, and chap. XIII, 57.

"This is what Clement of Alexandria attempts to reunite and to reconstitute. Truth being a harmony composed of different tones, he gathers the dispersed notes from all sides, convinced that all the philosophers knew it and that there was not a single one who possessed it entirely. In order to do this, he questions antiquity, and to the extent that his investigatory means allow him to so do, he seeks for the origin of things, their evolution and the laws to which they conformed, in order to liberate the rays of truth emanating therefrom. And here, be he dealing with pagan religions, their gods and their cults, or considering science, art or morals, or dealing with some matter of chronology or history and studying the most ancient epochs, he keeps encountering Egypt like a universal nurse, somehow, of human intelligence. When the nations of Europe were barely beginning to emerge from barbarism, Egypt had already undergone numerous vicissitudes and traversed several successive periods of grandeur and of decadence."[1]

Clement of Alexandria elucidates what the Greeks owe to Egypt, and he cites Thales of Miletos, Homer, Pythagoras, and then Plato, who received instruction in the Egyptian temples, Plato who qualifies these "barbarians" with the title of "race of philosophers."

Eudoxos of Cnidos and many others attained glory for themselves after having wandered for many years in the valley of the Nile and making themselves disciples of those whom they found living there.

2

Wherefore, in accordance with the method of concealment, the truly sacred Word, truly divine and most necessary for us, deposited in the shrine of truth, was by the Egyptians indicated by what were called among them adyta, and among the Hebrews by the veil. Only the consecrated—that is, those devoted to God, circumcised in the desire of the passions for the sake of love for that which is alone divine—were allowed access to the sanctuary. For Plato also thought it not lawful for "the impure to touch the pure." Whence the prophecies and oracles are spoken in enigmas, and the mysteries are not exhibited incontinently to all and sundry, but only after certain purifications and previous instructions....

Stromata, Book V, chap IV, 19-20.

All then, in a word, who have spoken of divine things, both barbarians and Greeks, have veiled the first principles of things. They make the truth be known only in enigmas, and symbols, and allegories, and metaphors, and such like tropes.[2]

3

"There is another reason explaining the words cited by Clement of Alexandria: in addition to the Egyptians' facility in representing ideas by symbols and the consequent necessity of a special initiation for their understanding, there is the importance which they attached, as did all antiquity moreover, to the symbol itself. It was not just an image, sign of a moral, philosophical, or religious idea in the form of an allegory such as the lily can serve for innocence or the dog for fidelity, or like other real or supposed relations between the object and the

---

[1] A. Deiber, *Clément d'Alexandrie et l'Egypte* (Cairo, 1904), p. 5.
[2] Ibid., line 21 et seq. Tr. after Wilson.

thing signified. As we well know, hieroglyphic writing is full of these comparisons. The ancients went even further: They attributed a magic significance to it. They saw therein a potent, efficacious, active cause whose nature was to accomplish or to destroy the thing it represented.

"To portray a divine emblem was to involve the divinities in one's own cause through a convenient and appropriate cult because it was believed that nothing was more pleasing to the gods. It was supposed that the god was summoned through his image. When the Pharaoh wore the symbols of his victory, he was rendered victorious because the power of Amon which dwelt in his breastplate penetrated and communicated its force to him."[3]

[3]A. Deiber, op. cit., p. 35.

Appendix V

Catalogue of Egyptian Books According to Clement of Alexandria

"Two books containing hymns honoring the gods and regulations for the king's life, placed in the hands of the Chanter.

"Four books dealing with the stars, one regarding moving stars, the other about the conjunction of the sun and moon, the other two respecting their risings, confided to the Astronomer whose symbols are a clock and a palm branch.

"Eight books dealing with knowledge of what are called hieroglyphics and including cosmography, geography, the positions of the sun and moon, the phases of the five planets, the chorography of Egypt, the charting of the Nile and its phenomena, a description of the equipment of the temples and of the places consecrated to them and information regarding the measures of all that is used in the sacred rites. These books are entrusted to the care of the Scribe. His head is decorated with feathers and in his hand he holds everything necessary for writing: inkwell, palette, and the reed with which they write.

"Two books on the art of teaching and the art of marking young sacrificial victims are entrusted to the Stolist or keeper of sacred vestments.

"Ten books which relate to the cult of the gods and precepts of worship, that is, to the sacrifice of first-fruits, hymns, prayers, ceremonies, and festival days.

"Ten books called 'hieratic' containing everything concerning the laws and the gods, the administration of the State and of the city, and the whole of the training of the priests. It is the Prophet who takes care of them and knows what is in them.

"These six-and-thirty works contain the entire philosophy of the Egyptians," concludes Clement, who adds:

"Six volumes dealing with medical subjects, treating of the structure of the body and its diseases, of the organs and of remedies and also about the eyes and lastly, knowledge concerning the female organs.

Such, to speak briefly, is the science of the Egyptians."

It is possible to verify the statements of Clement of Alexandria regarding the existence of veritable libraries. One of the chambers in the Temple of Edfu, bearing the name of Chamber of Writings, has a list of works carved on one of its walls:

"Numerous chests containing books with large rolls of parchment."

1. Book of what is in the temple.
2. Book of domains [?].
3. Book of all the writings of works in wood.
4. Book of the direction of the temple.
5. Book of the guardians of the temple.
6. Rules regarding the disposition of walls... [the plans].
7. Book of the royal guard in its house.
8. Chapter of opposing what leads to evil.
9. [Book] of knowing the return to their stations of the Sun and the Moon.
10. Book which regulates the return of the stars.
11. Detailed account of all places and the knowledge of what is in them.
12. All the reckonings of the rising of His Majesty Horus in the retinue of thy house in thy festivals. [Risings of the sun?]

This first catalogue, if it indicates notable differences with that of Clement of Alexandria, in its last four listings apparently mentions the four books dealing with stars which were cited by that philosopher.

The ancient Egyptians' knowledge of astronomy is confirmed by most of the classic authors (see *Diodoros of Sicily* I, 81) and the royal tombs offer many examples of astronomical ceilings and veritable lists of "star-risings," for example that of Seti I, Ramses IV, Ramses VI, Ramses IX, as well as the Ramesseum. The lists of the decans of which no mention is made in the "catalogues," are represented at Abydos in the tomb of Ramses VI and in numerous other monuments.

The second catalogue mentions twenty-two works, most of which are qualified as "magical" because the titles indicate "protection," be it of the divine barque, a city, a house, a year, etc., as well as the Horoscope of the hour, the *Royal Book,* the *Book of Incantations,* the

Book of Functionaries, the *Book of Divine Offerings,* the *Book of all the Mysteries* (or recipes) *of the Laboratory,* and a *Book on the Hunting of a Wild Beast.*

In all these works cited at Edfu, no mention is made of the medical and surgical texts of which several copies are extant. Thus these are not lists of real inventories but a very general indication of the works kept in the *House of Books.* Moreover, there are known to exist several mathematical papyri, some of numerous hymns and papyri concerning the daily cult which very likely are included in the thirty-four or thirty-six "rubrics" mentioned by Clement of Alexandria or in the temple of Edfu.

The royal hypogea of Thebes reveal the existence of the renowned Books-Concerning-What-Is-in-the-Netherworld (the *Dwat)* which have already been mentioned.

There is nothing excessive, then, in these enumerations. They can even be reproached for being too cursory and as for those of the temples, for being strictly limited to works concerning the particular site of the cult, because an analogous list at Dendera reveals the existence of different works.

In any case, "all these Books or this collection of Books was known to the Greeks under the name of *Hermetic Books,* because having assimilated the Egyptian *Thoth* with *Hermes,* they considered him, according to the ancient tradition along the banks of the Nile, to be the author of these Books."[1]

---

[1] A. Deiber, op. cit., p. 72.

Appendix VI

The Egyptians' Knowledge of Astronomy

Now with regard to mere human matters, the accounts which the Egyptians gave and in which they all agreed, were the following: According to them, the Egyptians were the first to discover the solar year, and to portion out its course into twelve parts both the space of time and the seasons which they delimit. It was observation of the course of the stars which led them to adopt this division... It is also the Egyptians who first brought into use the names of the twelve gods, which the Greeks adopted from them.

Herodotos, op. cit., II, 4.

The Egyptians, taking advantage of the favorable conditions, appropriated to themselves the knowledge of astronomy, which they were the first to study... the Chaldeans of Babylon, being colonists from Egypt, enjoy the fame which they have for their astronomy because they learned that science from the priests of Egypt.

The disposition of the stars as well as their movements have always been the subject of careful observation among the Egyptians... they have preserved to this day the records concerning each of these stars over an incredible number of years, this study having been zealously preserved among them from ancient times.

Diodoros of Sicily, op. cit., V, 57, and I, 81.

"I have heard," states Simplicios, "that the Egyptians possessed written observations of the stars embracing no less than sixty-three myriads of years." That would make 630,000 years which is obviously very exaggerated. But Plato, as well, said that the great purity of the sky over Egypt allowed the Egyptians to observe the stars *"for ten thousand years or so to speak, for an infinite time."*[1]

---

[1] E. M. Antoniadi, *L'Astronomie égyptienne* (Paris, 1934), pp. 3-4.

Whatever be the exaggerations, there still remains a tradition of the highest antiquity for Egyptian astronomy and the existence of "star tables" which served the Greeks in their own works.

No doubt can be cast on the word of Aristotle who, after discussing the spherical shape of stars, their order and their movements, explains the following phenomenon which he himself observed:

> For we have seen the moon, half-full, pass beneath the planet Mars, which vanished on its shadow side and came forth by the bright and shining part. Similar accounts of other stars are given by the Egyptians and Babylonians, whose observations have been kept for very many years past, and from whom much of our evidence about particular stars is derived.
>
> Aristotle, *De Caelo*, II, 12, 292a, tr. Ross.

(Kepler calculated that the phenomenon described by Aristotle took place on 4 April 357 B.C. It was a matter of demonstrating that if the moon hid Mars it was because the former is nearer to us.)

Lastly, Manetho was an admirer of Egyptian science:

"Know that we would be universal scientists if it were given us to inhabit the sacred land of Egypt."

Appendix VII

The Monuments and Astronomy

I. The Pyramids

The partially astronomical character of the pyramids is established by the following facts:

1. They are almost exactly, and intentionally, on the 30th parallel of the latitude North.

2. They are marvelously oriented on the cardinal points, which was pointed out by de Chazelles in 1694.

3. Their inclined passageways were, with their closing, colossal meridian instruments, by far the largest ever constructed.[1]

The Pyramid of Cheops

The astronomer Nouet determined the position, of the great pyramid to be 29°59'48" of latitude North. Piazzi Smith, 29°58'51", which corresponds very satisfactory to the estimate of apparent latitude of 30°, uncorrected for astronomic refraction.

The meridian line traced in order to orient the plan of the pyramid has a deviation of 4'30" toward the West, according to Piazzi Smith, and of only 3'43" according to Flinders Petrie.

According to Borchardt's maps, the median north-south line is deviated 4' westward, and the perpendicular east-west median is deviated only 2'.

"This wonderful fact allowed Proctor to remark that the orientation of the monument 'is much closer to exactitude than the best observations of Tycho with the renowned Uranibourg quadrant.' "[2]

---

[1] Antoniadi, op. cit., p. 119.
[2] Ibid., p. 121.

"Precision of Construction. The base is remarkably horizontal: The greatest difference does not reach 0 m 021....

"The precision of the four angles of the base is absolutely marvelous; the average variation of a right angle is of the order of 12" according to Petrie, and the perfection of the stone joints, which are almost invisible, excite the admiration of all travelers, from Herodotos to our day.

"...The facing was still intact in 1340, but in 1395 its removal was actively taking place...."[3]

Antoniadi offers thirty observations by different authors concerning the properties of the pyramid, proportion of *pi*, etc., and at the end he states: "The perimeter of the base of the pyramid formed a half-minute of the degree proper to Egypt" (Jomard)....

"As for paragraph 30, if it is not a coincidence, it would prove that the Egyptians possessed a knowledge of astronomy not generally attributed to them."[4]

(The perimeter is indeed exactly 921.45 meters according to Borchardt, or one-half of 1,842.9 meters which is exactly the value of an arc-minute at 0° latitude.)

"Intuitively discovered by Jomard, the unexpected fact that the perimeter of the base of Cheops' monument equaled a half-minute of a terrestrial degree seems to indicate that the Egyptians had measured the earth with the greatest success."[5]

Proctor studied the method with which the Egyptians had been able to determine their position on the 30th parallel with such precision: operating by means of the gnomon's shadow, the latter would be bathed in soft semidarkness. Operating by means of the Pole Star, "they would have observed the upper and lower culmination at the meridian, of the Pole Star and the average of the two altitudes obtained would have given them the approximate size of the pole above the horizon, equal to the approximate latitude of the site."

"If the Egyptians did not know the astronomic refraction, Proctor is of the opinion that they would have been mistaken in their estimation of the 30° latitude as being 1,028 meters to the north with the first method (that of the sun) and 2,077 m. to the south with the second. The center of the pyramid being located some 2,130 m. to the south of the 30th parallel, the English astronomer concluded that the

[3]Ibid., pp. 123-124.
[4]Ibid., p. 142.
[5]Ibid., p. 142.

Egyptians had especially utilized the Pole Star method. At 30° the refraction is 1'40"."

"One must applaud the magnificent results obtained by the priests in their effort to find the latitude of 30° with observations made by the naked eye."[6]

Antoniadi observes that the approximation of the angle 1 to 2 of the descending passageway with a length of 105 m. is remarkable, and he mentions the diverse opinions of authors who have seen in this passageway the greatest meridian instrument in the world, thanks to which the ancients would have been able to see the passage of the circumpolar stars and observe the exact moment of their passing.

2. The Zodiacs of Dendera

The temple of Dendera, consecrated to Hathor, possesses two zodiacs: One, rectangular in shape, is carved in the ceiling of the hypostyle hall; the other, which is circular, occupies the ceiling of a chapel constructed on the temple roof.

The circular zodiac is presented as the projection of that part of the celestial vault visible from Dendera's latitude, as seen from below. The pole for that time is located in the center of the disk, in one of the paws of the jackal, itself corresponding to our Little Bear (Ursa Minor). The thigh of Taurus represents our Great Bear, and the female hippopotamus represents Draco.

The signs of the zodiac are arranged on an eccentric circle having as its center the ecliptic pole situated in the udder of the hippopotamus. In the interior of this circle we find the principal boreal signs and the five planets: *Jupiter* near Cancer, *Mercury* above Virgo's Spica, *Saturn* close to Libra, *Mars* above Capricorn, and *Venus* near Pisces: In accordance with contemporary astrology, these are the sites of planetary *exaltation*. The rectangular zodiac presents another arrangement: *Venus* precedes Taurus, *Mercury* precedes Gemini, *Saturn* is between Capricorn and Aquarius, and finally, *Jupiter* and *Mars* precede Aries and Pisces. These are the sites where the planet is *dominant* but with the inversion of *Mars* and *Jupiter* in relation to contemporary astrological attribution.

Beyond the zodiacal circle, the austral signs are found, among which *Orion* represented by *Osiris*, *Hydra* represented by a serpent upon which *Leo* reclines, *Centaurus* corresponding to a bull-headed personage holding a hoe, etc. Lastly, on the periphery of the disk, we

[6]Ibid., p. 144.

find the thirty-six decans. All the figures face east-south-west, following the apparent course of the star-spangled heavens.

Jean-Baptiste Biot, after having located a certain number of
constellations that could be superimposed upon the images of this
zodiac, verified that *Sirius* was mentioned twice: once by the full-blown
papyrus stem supporting a falcon, situated in the temple's axis, aligned
with the constellation Gemini; a second time between the horns of the
cow of Isis, her symbol, in alignment with the stars of Cancer. This
astronomer calculated that in the year 716 + 165 years, the *direct rising*
of Sirius corresponded exactly to the papyrus stem situated in the
temple's axis:

> ...all special, singular circumstances, as we shall presently see, were
> linked to the relations that then existed between the orientation of this building,
> its latitude, and the absolute position of Sirius in the sky.

It is indeed certain that between the epoch estimated by Biot and
the date of Dendera's construction, the direct rising of Sirius took place
on an alignment situated between Castor and Pollux, precisely as
indicated by the zodiac, and as it is possible empirically to verify on a
celestial sphere. It remained to seek the signification of the second
configuration of Sirius, and it is there that the importance of
orientation intervenes: The *general axis* of the temple is at
approximately 18° east of true north, an axis corresponding, as has
been said, to the position of *Sirius* in the heavens. Furthermore, the
star *Sirius* situated between the cow's horns, is found in the true north-
south axis, marking the *colure of the solstices*. As Biot points out, it is
indeed in alignment with one of the stars of Cancer that "the *solstice
was found at that time and with which Sirius was rising.*"

> According to a multitude of literary documents, we know that the ancient
> astronomers made frequent use of simultaneous risings to indicate the points of
> the ecliptic to which they especially wished to draw the attention... According
> to the singular precision with which we here find the emblem of Sirius placed on
> our monument *near the solstice*, it would appear that the astronomers who
> drew that celestial tableau knew with uncommon skill how to make use of that
> procedure.

In other terms, *Sirius* is marked once in relation to its rising at the
time of the summer solstice, which was then in Cancer, and once in its
real position in the sky of "fixed" stars.

> That is to say "exactly, or almost," in the horizontal direction, according to
> which the south and north walls of the temple were turned. One can therefore

with the greatest facility find Sirius at its rising, and observe it at that moment
by aligning oneself on the horizontal direction of its transversal walls....

The temple of Esna, likewise possessing a rectangular zodiac, *is
oriented in such a way that it forms a complementary angle with the
axis of the temple of Dendera,* which leads Biot to conclude:

> Accordingly, if one were convinced that the two temples had really existed
> during the remote epoch represented by the circular zodiac; if one were to
> suppose, further, that the Egyptian priests had been sufficiently instructed to
> profit from the advantages offered by the directions of those buildings, one
> would imagine that they would have been able, even in the course of a few years,
> to recognize that the rising and setting points of the different stars were
> changing place on the horizon and after a certain period of time, were no longer
> at the same terrestrial alignment. They would thus have been able to verify the
> general and progressive displacement of the celestial sphere relative to the
> meridian line, that is to say, the most apparent effect of the *precession of the
> equinoxes.*[7]

The texts concerning the foundation of the temples affirm that
the ritual of "stretching the cord" (ascertaining the four angles of the
temple) is carried out after sighting the circumpolar stars, hence
defining a precise orientation at a given date, which happens to
support Biot's hypothesis concerning the importance of the temple's
orientation from the astronomical point of view, and which makes it
impossible to believe that the ancients would not have known how "to
profit from the advantages offered by the directions of those
buildings."

Moreover, the fact that *Sirius* is represented twice, at 18°
intervals, thus marking *two precise moments* in relation to the starry
sky, confirms Biot's assertions, perhaps not for the precise date which
he assigns to the zodiac, but for a more extended period, just as other
anomalies of the zodiac make one think.

In a general way, the observations of this astronomer are valid for
all the Egyptian temples whose orientations consequently demand
very scrupulous examination in order to arrive at their meaning.

The ancient Egyptians' knowledge of the phenomenon of the
equinoctial precession has often been disputed. Yet modification of the
calendar of festivals relative to the *seasons* (hence to the solstices and
the equinoxes) in relation to the calendar of the Sirian year, which

[7] J.-B. Biot, *Recherches sur plusieurs points de l'astronomie égyptienne,*

remained permanent, constitutes an incontestable proof thereof. At this point, in order to avoid confusion, we must recall two fundamental notions:

—During the entire historical period of Pharaonic Egypt, *the heliacal rising of Sirius, which marked New Year's Day, always took place when the sun was in the constellation Leo.*

—On the other hand, the *summer solstice* occurred coincidentally with the heliacal rising of *Sirius* around the year 3400 B.C., at the very time when the vernal point (spring equinox) was in *Taurus*. But between the epoch of the pyramids and that of the foundation of the Dendera temple, *the summer solstice had slowly retrograded toward the stars of Cancer,* where it was to be found during the entire period of Amon's domination, that is, to the very end of the New Empire, while the vernal point (the spring equinox) was in *Aries*.

Another important matter is further indicated by the Dendera zodiac lending support to their acquaintance with the equinoctial precession in conformity with the changing of the cults:

1. *The perpendicular to the temple's axis* marks the colure of the equinoxes for the beginning of the *Piscian era,* the date of the Dendera temple's construction.

2. *The true east-west line traverses Aries,* marking the equinoctial colure on the date of the apogee of the Amonian domination.

3. *A third line indicated by the hieroglyphs* of East and West drawn on the exterior of the disk, marks the equinoctial colure passing between *Taurus* and *Gemini,* indicating the date of *the foundation of the empire and of the calendar.*[8]

Can the assertion of Proclos Diadochos still be doubted?

> Let those who, believing in observations, cause the stars to move around the poles of the zodiac by one degree in one hundred years toward the east, as Ptolemy and Hipparchos did before him, know...that the Egyptians had already taught Plato about the movement of the fixed stars. Because they utilized previous observations which the Chaldeans had already made long before them with the same result, having again been instructed by the gods prior to the observations. And they did not speak just a single time, but many times...of the advance of the fixed stars.
>
> Commentaries on the *Timaeus,* IV.

---

[8]See *Le Temple de l'Homme,* I, p. 711, *"Zodiaque et précession des équinoxes."*

Appendix VIII

The Establishment of the Calendar

The establishment of the calendar must ultimately be traced back to one of the coincidental dates between the vague year and the Sirian year, by about four years, to 1321, 2781, or 4241 B.C.

The closest approximate date is excluded because in the Pyramid Texts which commenced in the year 2800 or 2600, the five epagomenal days and Sothis are already mentioned as the "New Year."

Pyr. 965. *"Sothis is your beloved daughter who prepares yearly sustenance for you in this her name of "New Year."* (Pepi 189, M. 355, and N. 906.)

Pyr. 1961. *"To say: The prince* [?] *N. appeared as a great falcon on the inner horizon; he saw the preparation for the festival; and the preparation of the hearths when the gods are born, in the five epagomenal days which are before thee...."* (Pepi II Nefer-ka-Ra 754.)

References to Orion, to Sothis, are numerous, and the general effect of the texts reveals a profound knowledge of the heavens, expressed in an archaic style, that is to say dating from the beginnings of the empire, which makes it almost impossible to adopt the date of 2781 B.C. for the foundation of the calendar, in which case it could only have been established in the year 4241 B.C.

On behalf of this thesis, Meyer points out that for this period and for the entire beginning of the empire, the coincidence between the beginning of the flood season and the beginning of the Sothic cycle was perfect:

In the year 4241 B.C., the "flood season" *(akhet)* occurred from July 19 to November 15 according to the *Julian* calendar or from June 15 to October 12 by the *Gregorian* calendar.

"In the beginning of June the river slowly begins to rise; between the 15th and the 20th of July it swells impetuously; toward the end of September, the waters regularly remain at the same level for 20 to 30 days, reaching their maximum during the first half of October."[1]

Between mid-June and mid-October, the flood reaches its crest, which in effect corresponds to the Gregorian dates of the year 4241. One cycle later, the seasons are retarded by about eleven days.

The Coptic calendar of today, which appears to have conserved several old traditions, has continued to observe the following Nile festivals:

"*Night of the Drop*" (when a drop from heaven, the tear of Isis, falls into the river and causes it to rise) (June 18th, Gregorian)
"*Beginning of the swelling of the Nile*" (25 June Gregorian)
"*Proclamation of the Nile's flooding*" (3rd July Gregorian)[2]

From this continuation of an ancient tradition which perpetuates the festival of the *Night of the Drop* marking the onset of the flood, one may infer a traditional date corresponding to 18 June *Gregorian,* and it is thus easy to see which of the dates marking the foundation of the Sothic calendar comes nearest to it:

Night of the Drop of the Coptic calendar . . . . 18 June Gregorian
New Year's Day: beginning flood season in 4241 . . . . 15 June Gregorian
New Year's Day: beginning flood season in 2781 . . . . 26 June Gregorian

At the beginning of the second Sothic period, the New Year then fell on a day when the Nile, in accordance with tradition, had already been rising for some time, whereas in the year 4241, on the contrary, New Year's Day fell on 15 June Gregorian, only three days earlier than the date on which the *Night of the Drop* is still celebrated.

After studying the different seasons and their displacement of 21 days in the course of two periods, Meyer concludes:

We can therefore affirm in all confidence that the Egyptian calendar was created to reflect that condition of the seasons which is presented to us in the year 4241 B.C.[3]

The majority of Egyptologists have accordingly accepted the date of the calendar's establishment as being in the year 4241 B.C.; however,

[1]Ed. Meyer, op. cit., p. 52.

[2]Ibid., p. 53.

[3]Ibid., p. 55.

for the last quarter of a century the question has been disputed anew because it is evident that the establishment of this calendar implies long preliminary astronomical observations. Furthermore, assuming that the rising of Sirius does not take place on the same date in all points of Egypt, that the date of "the first of the year" corresponds precisely to the heliacal rising of Sirius for Heliopolis, and that one knows from the texts that this rising had been announced as many as twenty-two days in advance for each temple, Meyer concludes that the calendar was established in the year 4241, at Heliopolis, at the moment of the unification of the country which would then go back before Menes.

This theory of the solar calendar is unquestionably very ingenious but it rests on several postulates which all Egyptologists do not accept: the existence, among the Egyptians of the fifth millennium, of rather widespread knowledge of astronomy; existence at the same time, of a single kingdom having Heliopolis as its capital. Now these are but hypotheses.

Undoubtedly this is the reason why Otto Neugebauer rejected Meyer's theory. For him, the Egyptian calendar with its year of 365 days "is certainly not derived from astronomy.... A year established in accordance with the position of the sun would not have been divided into three seasons, as we find it at all times in the Egyptian calendar, but rather into four or two seasons. The names of the seasons clearly demonstrate their relationship with the Nile.... The simplest supposition is that the Egyptian year is purely agrarian. The flood, the growth of plants, the harvest, constitute the principal divisions thereof and the onset of the flood marks the beginning of it." On the other hand, Neugebauer makes the observation that the flood doesn't always make its first appearance on a fixed day. "The fluctuations are very important; even today they run over a period of six weeks and more, as statistics demonstrate. But, on taking the average over a series of years one soon verifies that the duration of the period is 365 days." Furthermore, "this figure of a year entirely determined by the Nile, fulfills its function at least during two or three centuries. With a 60-day movement for the beginning of the flood, it would take 60 × 4 = 240 years before the coming of a New Year's Day of a year of 365 days would fall beyond the possible limits of the flood. Even in that case, some time must have elapsed before it was possible to realize that the theoretical moment of the flood had nothing to do with the flood properly so called. And yet it could have happened that the observation of that fact led the Egyptians to investigate a phenomenon which would betoken the flood of the Nile, such as the heliacal rising of Sirius."[4]

One hesitates to accept Meyer's proof only because the ancients' knowledge of astronomy before Menes is disputed. But there is a willingness to accept Neugebauer's account which is entirely based on suppositions. Among others, he imagines that a certain number of years are sufficient to establish an average that makes it possible, following the recurrence of the Nile's flooding, to fix the duration of the year and to reconcile the New Year with a remarkable astronomical phenomenon such as the heliacal rising of Sirius....[5]

The variations in dates marking the beginning of the Nile's flooding are not at all regular, and to wish to deduce therefrom the establishment of a year of 365¼ days (the Sirian year) is a feat of skill which would dignify clairvoyance rather than ratiocination! As for wishing to place the onset of the flood in relation to the heliacal rising of Sirius, one would have to be able to observe this star in broad daylight since it is a matter of the heliacal rising, because during several months before and after that date, Sirius is no longer visible at night.

We are astounded by this obstinacy on the part of certain Egyptologists in their desire, at any cost and thanks to such an absurdity as this, to belittle the knowledge of the ancient Egyptians. Now it is evident and proved that the heliacal rising of Sirius must be calculated since it is impossible to observe it, and the texts confirm that, indeed, this date was calculated and announced in advance to all the temples in Egypt.

Let us again interpolate to the above that this coincidence of the period of 365¼ days for the heliacal rising of Sirius is an entirely exceptional celestial phenomenon, and that knowledge thereof can result only from long centuries of observations.

This reality, which is confirmed by the texts, for some incomprehensible reason displeases Egyptologists....

---

[5]The hypothesis of Neugebauer who imagines a duration of 240 years was needed in order to establish a year of exactly 365 days, only after the periodic recurrence of the Nile's flooding, which he admits may vary by as many as 60 days, this hypothesis is valid only if one *already knows* that the duration of the year is 365 days!

On the other hand, why seek such complications when it is perfectly well established that the ancients measured the twelve hours of the day by means of the gnomon (or sun dial) and the twelve hours of the night with the water clock (clepsydra) and observations of star risings? Observation of the length of the solar shadow in the course of a single year alone, is sufficient to establish the length of time that elapses between the shortest shadow (summer solstice) and the longest shadow (winter solstice). The periodic return of the shortest shadow determines *the year of 365 days,* a duration which can be rigorously determined and verified in the course of very few years.

[4]E. Massoulard, op. cit., p. 73.

Appendix IX

Alternation in Developmental Growth

The study of the formation of continents, of geological eras and of the appearance of life on the globe has led to ascertaining *the law of alternation* which governs the broad movements of the earth.

Although it is still fairly difficult to estimate the duration of the periods between each phase, the to and fro movements of the seas upon the continents has been considered as a phenomenon analogous to the great seasonal tides, albeit obeying a very slow rhythm. This kind of pulsation of the earth in its entirety, the cadence and cause of which is being researched in our day, must necessarily influence the entire evolution of life, just as in turn the development of life constantly influences the surface of the globe. This is explained by H. and G. Termier in their definition of the *"geochemical role of life"*:

> As the comparison of chronological results seems unfavorable to stratigraphic paleontology, it would be in order to rehabilitate the role of life in the elaboration of the geological clock. First we take notice that the succession of phenomena which we shall call the Drama, representing the lithosphere's structural evolution as a unit, can in a certain sense be considered as repeating itself in a fairly regular way in the course of time, without being a rigorously cyclical phenomenon, however, as there is no clear-cut return to the point of departure. To the contrary, the organic evolution grafted on this ceaseless travail of the earth's crust is absolutely irreversible and plays the role of a force which forbids us to set back the hands of our geological clock. The behavior of the Biosphere is thus, in a certain measure, in opposition to the behavior of the Lithosphere. Although this mode of being of life is particularly obvious as far as organic structures are concerned, it must not be forgotten that it begins to appear in the geochemical evolution of sediments and rocks....[1]

---

[1] H. and G. Termier, *Formation des continents et progression de la vie* (Paris, 1954), p. 12.

The authors conclude their interesting study with the following summary:

> Epitomizing in a few words the history of the earth's crust according to what is known of it today, it can be said that the great geological phenomena obey regular laws, most of them forming a sequence which we have called *dramas*.
>
> The activity of life has become grafted on a background of recurring physicochemical processes. Under cover of the relative movements of earth and sea which began at a fairly precise moment of the history of the globe, life has fashioned matter: It has developed for its own account, unrolling the irreversible chain of organic evolution.
>
> Lastly, evolution crossed an undeniable discontinuity in passing to man capable of thought.[2]

As general conclusion: One phase of development prepares another more complete one. Backtracking is impossible, only rests can occur, or else decompositions of what has become.

As there exists a geological stratigraphy, there exists a stratigraphy in the biosphere ordered by cosmic ambiance; the ultimate term of the vital phenomenon, globally speaking, is for us the human. It is specifically separated from the other vital phases, though the latter are nevertheless indispensable to its creation, that is to say, to its corporeal apparition.

[2]Ibid., "Conclusion."

BIBLIOGRAPHY

[Andreae, Valentin.] *Chymische Hochzeit Christian Rosenkreutz.* Strasburg, 1456. In *Verlägung Lazari Zetzners,* anno MDCXVI.

Antoniadi, E. M. *L'Astronomie égyptienne.* Paris, 1934.

Armstrong, E. A. *La vie amoureuse des oiseaux.* Paris: Albin Michel, 1952.

Berthelot, M. *Les origines de l'alchimie,* Paris, 1885.

Biot, J-B. *Recherche sur plusieurs points de l'astronomie égyptienne.* Extrait des mémoires de l'Institut Royal de France, Académie des Inscriptions et Belles-Lettres. Imprimerie royale, Paris, 1846.

Borchardt, L. *Pyramide de Sah-ou-Rê.* Leipzig: J.-C. Hinrishsvsche Buchhandlung, 1910.

Boule, M., and Vallois, H. *Les hommes fossiles.* Paris: Masson, 1921.

Breasted, James Henry. *Ancient Records of Egypt.* Chicago: University of Chicago Press, 1905.

Brien, P., and Dalq, A., *Traité de Zoologie.* Paris: Masson, 1954.

Budge, Sir E. A. Wallis. *A History of Egypt.* Oxford, 1902.

Chiagnet, A. Ed. *Pythagore et la philosophie pythagoricienne.* Paris, 1873.

Clement of Alexandria in T. and T. Clark, *Ante-Nicene Christian Library,* Edinburgh, 1867. Tr. William Wilson.

Cohen, M. R., and Drabkin, J. E., *A Source Book in Greek Science.* New York: McGraw-Hill, 1948.

Deiber, A. *Clément d'Alexandrie et l'Egypte.* Cairo: I.F.A.O., 1904.

Diels, H. *Die Fragmente der Vorsokratiker.* Berlin, 1922.

Diodoros of Sicily. *Library of History.* London: Loeb Classical Library, 1933. Tr. C. H. Oldfather.

Diogenes Laertios. *Lives of Eminent Philosophers.* London: Wm. Heinemann, 1935. Tr. R. D. Hicks.

Emery, Walter B. *Great Tombs of the First Dynasty.* Cairo: Government Press, 1949.

Erman, A. *Die Agyptische Religion.* Berlin, 1904. Cited in text as *La religion égyptienne* (*A Handbook of Egyptian Religion,* London: Archibald Constable, 1907).

Erman, A., and Grapow, H. *Wörterbuch der ägyptischen Sprache.* Leipzig, 1926-55.

Erman, A., and Ranke, H. *La civilisation égyptienne.* Paris: Payot, 1952.

Fabre, Jean-Henri. *Souvenirs entomologiques.* Paris: Delagrave, 1879.

Festugière, R. P. (O.P.). *La révélation d'Hermès Trismégiste.* Paris, 1944.

Flammarion. *Annuaire astronomique et météorologique.* Paris, 1953.

Fouillée, A. *Histoire de la philosophie.* Paris: Delagrave, 1924.

Gauthier, H. *Les fêtes du dieu Min.* Cairo, 1931.

——————.*Dictionnaire des noms géographiques contenus dans les textes hiéroglyphiques.* Cairo, 1925-31.

Herodotos. *History.* London, 1880. Tr. George Rawlinson.

Holmberg, Major Sandman. *The God Ptah.* Lund, 1946.

Hortulain. *Commentaires* in *Bibliothèque des philosophes alchymiques ou hermétiques.* Paris, 1756.

Jéquier, Gustave. *Le livre de ce qu'il y a dans l'Hadès.* Paris, 1894.

Laplace, Pierre Simon. *Exposition du système du monde.* Paris, 1796.

Lefebvre, G. *Romans et contes égyptiens de l'époque pharaonique.* Maisonneuve, Paris. 1949.

——————. *Grammaire de l'égyptien classique.* Cairo, 1955.

——————. *Essai sur la médecine égyptienne de l'époque pharaonique.* Paris: Presses Universitaires de France, 1956.

Le Lionnais, F. *Les grands courants de la pensée mathématique.* Paris, 1958.

Lexa, Ph. Dr. François. *La magie dans l'Egypte antique.* Paris: Paul Geuthner, 1925.

Libby, Willard. *Radiocarbon Dating.* Chicago: University of Chicago Press, 1955.

Lucretius. *On the Nature of Things.* London: Henry Bohn, 1851. Tr. John S. Watson.

Mabilleau, L. *Histoire de la philosophie atomistique.* Paris: Alcan, 1895.

Marcus Aurelius. *The Meditations.* London, 1862. Tr. George Long.

Maspero, Prof. G. *Histoire ancienne des peuples de l'Orient classique* (*The Passing of the Empires,* New York: Appelton, 1900, tr. M.C. McClure).

Massoulard, Dr. E. *Préhistoire et protohistoire d'Egypte.* Paris: Institut d'Ethnologie, 1949.

Meyer, E. *Chronologie égyptienne*. Tr. Moret. Annales du Musée Guimet, Paris, 1912.

Michel, Paul-Henri. *De Pythagore à Euclide*. Paris: Belles Lettres, 1950.

Mihaud, G. *Origines de la science grecque*. Paris, 1893.

Moret, Alexandre. *Du caractère religieux de la royauté pharaonique*. E. Leroux, ed. Paris, 1902.

——————. *Mystères égyptiens*. Paris: Armand Colin, 1913.

——————. *Le Nil et la civilisation égyptienne*. Paris, 1926 (*The Nile and Egyptian Civilization*, New York: Knopf, 1927, tr. M. R. Dobie).

Osborn, Henry Fairfield. *The Origin and Evolution of Life*. New York: Scribner, 1918.

Perrier, Rémy. *Zoologie*. Paris: Masson, 1929.

Petrie, Sir W. M. Flinders. *The Royal Tombs of the Earliest Dynasties*. London, 1900.

——————, and Quibell, J. E. *Naqada and Ballas*. London, 1896.

Piankoff, Alexandre, and Drioton, E. *Le livre du jour et le livre de la nuit*. Cairo, 1942.

——————. "La déscente aux enfers dans les textes égyptiens." *Bulletin de la Société d'Archeologie Copte*, VII (1941).

Piveteau, J. *Traité de Paleontologie*. Paris: Masson, 1957.

Pliny. *Natural History*. London: Loeb Classical Library, 1962. Tr. D. E. Eichholz.

Plutarch. *Moralia*. London: Loeb Classical Library, 1936. Tr. Frank Cole Babbitt.

Quatrefages, A. de. *Hommes fossiles et hommes sauvages*. Paris, 1884.

Rey, Abel. *La jeunesse de la science grecque*. Paris: Renaissance du Livre, 1933.

Geheime Figuren der Rosenkreutzer, aus dem 16ten und 17ten Jahrhundert. Altona, 1785.

Rostand, Jean. *Les Chromosomes*. Paris: Hachette, 1928.

Sageret, Jules. *Le système du monde*. Paris: Felix Alcan, 1913.

Schwaller de Lubicz, Isha. *La Lumière du Chemin*. Paris: La Colombe, 1960.

——————. *Her-Bak, Egyptian Initiate*, New York: Inner Traditions, 1978.

Schwaller de Lubicz, R. A. *Le Temple de l'Homme*. 3 vols. Paris: Caractères, 1957.

Sethe, Kurt. *Die altaegyptischen Pyramidentexte*. Leipzig, 1908-22.

Tannery, Paul. *Mémoires pour servir à l'histoire de la science hellène*. Paris, 1930.

——————— . *La géométrie grecque.* Paris: Gauthier-Villars, 1887.

Termier, H. and G. *Formation des continents et progression de la vie.* Paris: Masson, 1954.

Thibon, Gustave. Preface to Gilbert Tournier's *Babel ou le vertige technique.* Paris: Artheme Fayard, 1959.

Vandier, Jacques. *Manuel d'archéologie égyptienne.* Paris: Picard, 1952-58.

Weill, Raymond. *Recueil de travaux,* **XXIX.** Imprimerie de l'Institut Français d'Archéologie Orientale, Cairo.

Zahan. *Société d'initiation Bambara.* Paris-La Haye: Mouton, 1960.

Zaki y Saad. *Fouilles de Hélouan* in *La Revue du Caire,* 1954.

Zeller, Eduard. *A History of Greek Philosophy.* London: Longmans, Green and Co., 1881. Tr. S. F. Alleyne. *(Die Philosophie der Griechen,* Leipzig, 1856.) Cited in text as *La philosophie des grecs.*

Translation References

Budge, Sir E. A. Wallis. *The Egyptian Book of the Dead.* London, 1895.

Burnet, John. *Early Greek Philosophy.* London: Adam and Chas. Black, 1892.

Faulkner, R. O. *The Ancient Egyptian Pyramid Texts.* Oxford, 1969.

Piankoff, Alexandre. *Le "coeur" dans les textes égyptiens.* Paris: Paul Geuthner, 1930.

INDEX

BOOKS OF RELATED INTEREST

The Temple of Man
by R. A. Schwaller de Lubicz

The Temples of Karnak
by R. A. Schwaller de Lubicz

The Temple in Man
Sacred Architecture and the Perfect Man
by R. A. Schwaller de Lubicz

The Egyptian Miracle
An Introduction to the Wisdom of the Temple
by R. A. Schwaller de Lubicz

Esoterism and Symbol
by R. A. Schwaller de Lubicz

Esoteric Egypt
The Sacred Science of the Land of Khem
by J. S. Gordon

Point of Origin
Gobekli Tepe and the Spiritual Matrix
for the World's Cosmologies
by Laird Scranton

Awakening Higher Consciousness
Guidance from Ancient Egypt and Sumer
by Lloyd M. Dickie and Paul R. Boudreau

Inner Traditions • Bear & Company
P.O. Box 388
Rochester, VT 05767
1-800-246-8648
www.InnerTraditions.com

Or contact your local bookseller